INSCRIPTIONS
OF
PAGAN, PINYA AND AVA.

INSCRIPTIONS
OF
PAGAN, PINYA AND AVA.

Translation, with Notes

EMANUEL FORCHHAMMER,
TAW SEIN KO

GYAN

Published by

Gyan Publishing House
5, Ansari Road
Daryaganj, New Delhi-110002
Phone: 011-47034999, 9811692060
E-mail: books@gyanbooks.com

Distribution Network
gyanbooks.com
India, USA, Canada, UK, Australia, France

ISBN : 978-81-212-2530-4 (HB)
First Published, 1899

2nd Impression 2021

Printed at: Gyan Press, Delhi.

Inscriptions of Pagan, Pinya and Ava
Author: Emanuel Forchhammer, Taw Sein Ko

INSCRIPTIONS

OF

PAGAN, PINYA AND AVA.

TRANSLATION, WITH NOTES.

RANGOON:

PRINTED BY THE SUPERINTENDENT, GOVERNMENT PRINTING, BURMA.

1899.

INTRODUCTION.

THE inscriptions translated in the present volume were collected by the late Dr. Forchhammer, Government Archæologist, since 1886, at Pagan, Pinya and Ava, the ancient capitals of Burma. They were edited by Mr. Taw Sein Ko, who for some time acted as assistant to the learned Archæologist. Five of the inscriptions being in Talaing have not yet been deciphered for want of competent assistance. The volume was made over in 1892 to Mr. Taw Sein Ko for translation during his term of leave in England, but unfortunately nothing was done owing to ill-health and other duties, and at his suggestion I took up the translation last year.

The oldest inscription in the present collection bears date 446 B.E., corresponding with A.D. 1084. The language of this and several other inscriptions of the same and the following century is considerably archaic and palæographical peculiarities are numerous. There is sufficient material in this collection to trace the evolution of the Burmese alphabet from the eleventh century down to the present time. For instance, ဘုရား the Burmese word for Buddha, passed through fifteen distinct stages during the period named before attaining its present form, thus:

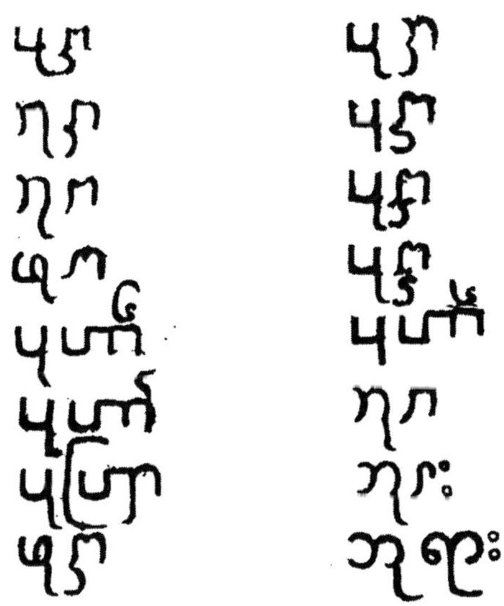

The present form has been in vogue ever since Bodawpaya's reign (1781—1819 A.D.), a reign noted for literary culture.

The alphabet itself is of Indian origin. Mr. Taw Sein Ko, in his Notes on the Kalyani Inscriptions, page 13 (*c*), says that "Inscriptions of the eleventh and twelfth centuries have been found at "Pagan whose palæographical development is clearly traceable to "the Indo-Pâli alphabet of Kanishka (*vide* Cunningham's *Corpus "Inscriptionum Indicarum*, Plate XXVII), and not to the South "Indian alphabet of the Eastern Chalukya dynasty of Kalinga (*vide* "Burnell's *Elements of South Indian Palæography*, Plate IV), from "which the Talaing alphabet was undoubtedly derived."

Many of these inscriptions are the outcome of the impetus given to religion and letters by Anawrata's conquest of Thatôn in the eleventh century. Anawrata took with him captive to Pagan the Talaing King Manuha and family, and a large number of his subjects and dedicated them all as pagoda slaves. Several of these slaves are mentioned by name in the inscriptions, and there used to be whole villages of them in the Pagan district as some of the place names there clearly testify. These people being originally Talaings and captured enemies, it is easy to understand why they are universally looked down upon throughout Burma. They feel keenly the social ostracism and contrive by every means in their power to conceal their origin and descent. They have accordingly committed such acts of vandalism as the demolishing of many of the smaller shrines to which they were dedicated, and broken down, obliterated or removed several lithic inscriptions.

Most of the inscriptions are religious: they contain grants of land and slaves to pagodas, caves and monasteries. The boundaries of the grants are, in the majority of cases, imperfectly defined, and many of them have since reverted to the State. Some of the inscriptions which are of historical value have been utilized in the compilation of the different Mahayazawins, the latest compilation, namely, the Hmannan, compiled in Bagyidaw's reign (1819—1837), specially referring to three of those in the present collection. This Mahayazawin is generally accepted as the most authentic history of Burma, and it bears evidence of learned and careful editorship. But there is still room for much improvement, and it would be well if the Archæological Department could undertake the publication of an edition revised in the light of the present and several later collections of inscriptions. Queen Pwa Saw's inscription, erected at the monastery built by her in Thawati quarter, Pagan, and inscriptions Nos. 15 and 16 found at the Shwezigôn Pagoda, Pagan, the Tetnwègyaung and other inscriptions erected in Bodawpaya's reign (1781—1819), have also been used as models of high literary style.

BURMA SECRETARIAT:
30th January 1899.

TUN NYEIN.

INSCRIPTIONS

OF

PAGAN, PINYA, AND AVA.

TRANSLATION, WITH NOTES.

INSCRIPTIONS OF PAGAN.

I.—Found at the Shwezigôn Pagoda.

[Inscriptions numbered (1) to (7) have not been deciphered. They are in Talaing.]

The first 44 lines of Inscription No. (8) are in Talaing-Burmese and have not been deciphered.

Line 45 to end (five lines): "On Monday the 11th of the month of Tabaung 611 Sakkarâj (1249 A.D.), I dedicate Nga Pyi, his younger brothers Thin Gyan and another, and Thupubyit Nga Nyo, to the Sigôn* Pagoda."

NO. (9).—OBVERSE.

Locality.—South-east corner of inner wall of pagoda.

Date.—751 Sakkarâj (1389 A.D.).

Substance of inscription.—Bestowal of rewards upon the builders of and dedication of lands to monastery.

BEING apprehensive of . . . . , this (monastery) with the three-tiered porch was built on the full-moon day of Kasôn 751 Sakkarâj . . . . It was painted white within. . . . . The builders were bounteously supplied with provisions and were rewarded abundantly for their labour . . . . To the west of the Shwezigôn Pagoda† . . . . The monastery was adorned with several white flags and banners. Kunalankâ,‡ the architect, was rewarded

* This word in itself means a pagoda or stupa enshrining some sacred relic; hence Shwezigôn signifies golden pagoda.

† The Hmannan Yazawin and Cetîvamsa agree in saying that this pagoda was built by Anawrata in 1059 A.D. to enshrine a tooth, the frontal bone and collar bone of Gautama Buddha.

‡ Guṇâlaṅkâra. The name evidently of an Indian architect.

with a . . . ., a female slave, a salver with lid and stand, a cow and two pieces of turban cloth; and Tahe Thuyan,* the wood-carver, received . . . . pieces of white cloth, a salver and stand, a cow and a goat. For the maintenance of the presiding monk of the monastery during the 5,000 years of the Religion, a golden bowl weighing 622 ticals, 30 pieces of silver, ... a handsome pony, and, with the consent of His Majesty Sîritribhava-ṇâdipavarapaṇḍitadhammarâjâ,† 30 *pès* of *mayin*‡ land situated at Magyigan were dedicated to the monastery. (The carpenters were rewarded with) 10 ticals of silver and three goats each. Two clerks demarcated the land, whose boundaries are as follows:—

East—A large tamarind tree and a *nat* temple.§

South—A large *hnanbè* tree.

West—Land belonging to Nga Taung We and Thin Tôn.

North—Kantetwet land.

The boundaries were marked with stone pillars. The clerks who demarcated the land were rewarded with five ticals of silver, a large brass tray and a quantity of liquor. To the *Mahâthera* (ပထိ) of Mindôn were given the lands of that village, 33 ticals of silver, a salver with stand and a tray with cover. Nga Thôn Thin, the village headman, received a large brass tray and a large bowl. Five ticals of silver were given to the four carpenters Chit Hla Kè Pa, Nga Pauk Hla Pa, Chit Ya U Pa, and Ein Hla Ya Pa . . . . (The headman and carpenters were also given) a tray and stand. A large bullock and 13 jars of liquor were given to the villagers, their headman and the four carpenters; and the headman and carpenters received suits of clothes besides. A large number of people partook of the feast.

"For this my good deed may I, on the advent of Metteyya,‖ become an excellent *Rahan*, freed from concupiscence and all carnal ties . . . . may I be enabled to make offerings with a mind as clear and calm as the sky at dawn; may I be possessed

* ထဟေသုရှ်။

† King Narapatisithu.

‡ A species of early paddy cultivated on alluvial lands, along river banks and in silted-up lakes.

§ These temples or sheds are still commonly met with in the districts under large trees and in grave-yards; and they show that Buddhism has not yet entirely superseded the ancient *nat* or devil worship. Periodical *nat* festivals are still held by all classes all over the province, especially among the Talaings, and in cases of sickness and pestilence the *nats* are invoked and propitiated by weird dances accompanied with offerings in the shape of rice, cocoanuts, plantains and other eatables. Liquor is freely imbibed by the spirit mediums at these festivals.

‖ The coming Buddha.

of great power and might, majesty and glory, beauty and birth; may I also be possessed of such vigorous health as would enable me to minister to the wants of Metteyya, thereby securing to me the means of salvation. Prior to the advent of Metteyya, and while being tossed about in the sea of transmigration, may I be free from all lusts of the flesh and evil desires, and be able to observe the laws of asceticism . . . ." [The continuation on the reverse has not been deciphered because the letters have been nearly obliterated.]

No. (10).

Locality.—North-east corner of Shwezigôn Pagoda platform; within the inner wall.

Date.—643 Sakkarâj (1281 A.D.).

Founder.—Queen Asaw.*

Substance of inscription.—Dedication of lands and slaves to pagoda.

Reverence to the Blessed, Holy and Enlightened One!

ON Monday the 7th waxing of Tagu 643 Sakkarâj, Queen Asaw offered 100 *pès* † of rice-land called Môktabetswe and 10 bullocks to the monks, headed by her spiritual Mentor, the Acalo *Mahâthera*, who was also preceptor of the king. The *Mahâthera* enjoyed the produce of the land for eight years and died. Before his death he was presented with 200 *pès* also of irrigated rice-land south of the Shwezigôn Pagoda and known as Chinthemaya, together with a broom, three bowls, one lion-shaped stand and one *lota*. Five pagoda slaves, namely, Nga Pôn She, Nga Sat Ti, Nga Pôn Daung, Nga Shan and Yami Gyi, were directed to look after the pagoda. "Out of the produce of the 100 *pès* of land let a daily offering of three *pyis* ‡ of rice, three lamps and three quids of *pan* (betel leaf) be made to the Buddha. Let my nephews Pyinnyanyanathiyi (Paññâñâṇasiri) and Pyinnyayathi (Paññârâsi) represent me in making constant offerings, and let the five pagoda slaves do their bidding. Let my two nephews also collect the produce of the rice-lands."

---

* This queen was a commoner, who was raised to the throne for her beauty and intelligence by King Narathihapade (1255—1286 A.D.). She was the chief queen also of the next king Kyawzwa.

† One *pè* = 1·75 acres.

‡ *Pyi* = $\frac{1}{16}$ basket. This offering is a remnant of *nat* worship. The notion of endowing objects of worship with material appetites is clearly one of the traces of Animism, and is foreign to Buddhism, which did not recognize idolatry during the early centuries of its existence. Its receptivity, however, and its readiness to adopt the forms of worship and the superstitions of its converts, is notable. In Burma and Siam most Buddhists are also *nat* worshippers and firm believers in witchcraft and other primitive superstitions. In China and Japan the Buddhist converts are adherents of Confucianism, Taoism and Shintoism also.

In ratification of the deed of dedication, water was poured on the ground by the queen's mother, and the queen's two nephews were formally declared to be her representatives. Instructions were also left with Tannatpi, head pagoda slave of the Culâmani Pagoda, and with Thinmatamanneik. "Let my three slaves Thinwaramagônna, Ôktamanyanagônna and Yakalanyin safeguard the interests of my benefactions. May he who injures my pagoda, lands, or slaves be burnt at the bottom of the nethermost hell,* and may he be precluded from adoring the successive Buddhas to come. But whoever appreciates my good deed, may he share equally with me the merit that has accrued to me. Let (this inscription) be placed in the old Sigôn monastery."

The royal preceptor poured water on the ground in ratification of the deed.

No. (11).—Obverse.

Locality.—North-east corner of the Shwezigôn Pagoda platform; within the inner wall.

Date.—546 Sakkarâj (1184 A.D.).

Founder.—King Narapatisithu.

Substance of inscription.—Dedication of lands and slaves to the Shwezigôn Pagoda.

Adoration to Omniscience!

When King Narapatisithu, bearer of the title Sîritribhavanâtityapavarapaṇḍitadhammarâjâdhirâjâ, lord of 39 white elephants and an army of 17,645 soldiers, the acknowledged suzerain of all chiefs, the mighty and powerful ruler of the territory bounded on the *west* by Patikaya,† on the *south* by Kwetkyi, on the *east* by Sapipati,‡ and on the *north* by Kadunawgyi and the tract where fire burns on water, made a progress up the river, the royal barge stopped of its own accord at Kôkkan-Paunglaung and the king's helmet fell off. The king then demanded an interpretation of the omen, and Shwe In Dauk informed him that lands should be dedicated to the pagoda of the locality. Accordingly, on Thursday the 3rd waxing of Tazaungmôn 546 Sakkarâj, a piece of land having the following boundaries was dedicated: *south* by Tada-u, *north* by Sittawa, *south-east* by the *sauk* tree to which the royal barge was moored, *north-east* by a *tindipara* tree, *south-west* by a fishery, and *north-west* by the place where the royal helmet fell off. The land measured 50 *pès*, and the produce thereof was to be utilized in providing daily

---

* *Avîci*—literally (suffering) without intermission.

† Chittagong.

‡ Panthay territory.

rice-offerings and lights at the pagoda. Five slaves, five lamps, and five copper *lotas* were also offered to the pagoda.

"May all creatures inhabiting every region, from the uppermost heaven to the nethermost hell, share with me the merit accruing from this my good deed. During the course of 5,000 years* prescribed for the continuance of the Religion, if any of the kings, ministers, nobles or freeborn persons safeguard the interests of this my good deed, may they share equally with me the merit accruing therefrom; and further, may they enjoy long life and increased might and power. But during the same period, if any of the kings, ministers, nobles or freeborn persons destroy or injure the effects of my good deed, may they be precluded from the enjoyment of long life and happiness, and of increased might and power; and further, may all their undertakings be doomed to failure; may they be subjected to the eight forms of punishment; and may they, on their death, suffer in the four hells. In the *kalpas* to come may they fail to adore the Buddhas, and may they be precluded from the attainment of salvation under the guidance of any of the Buddhas. And finally, may they be doomed to suffer as charred pillars in that hell which is assigned to confirmed and hopeless heretics."

REVERSE.

Date.—743 Sakkarâj (1381 A.D.).

Founder.—Wathe Thugyi and wife.

Substance of inscription.—Dedication of lands, toddy-palms and slaves to the Shwezigôn Pagoda.

Adoration to Omniscience!

IN the year of the Religion 1925, corresponding with 743 Sakkarâj, the thugyi of Wathe † conceived a feeling of reverence to the Shwezigôn Pagoda, and of fear in respect of the sufferings of *samsaro*; and in order that he might be relieved from such sufferings, he dedicated the following to the pagoda: Nga Kin Maung, a male slave, to represent himself, Ein Byu, a female slave, to represent his wife; a bullock, a cow, a piece of land at Alègan called Palaungo, another called Kano at Sape, a third at Einsisin called Mahagôn, a fourth at Chauktaung called Kalangan, together with the toddy-palm trees growing thereon.

* This popular limitation has recently been controverted by Mr. Taw Sein Ko in his Notes on the Kalyânî Inscriptions [*vide* note (19), pages 16 and 17].

† The date of this inscription corresponds with the 13th year of Minkyizwasawkè's reign (1368—1400 A.D.). It is recorded that several thugyis were then appointed by the king to "eat" various towns and villages; and the Wathe Thugyi was evidently one of these and not a mere revenue collector like the present day thugyis.

"Representatives of my wife and of myself have thus been appointed to minister to the pagoda. For performing this good deed with my wife, I pray that the king, ministers and nobles may always hold me in high esteem. May the prime minister and his wife and other ministers and nobles share with me my merit. May my parents by whom I was begotten, my uncle and my other relatives who are in Government service or otherwise, also share with me my merit. By virtue of the merit accruing from this gift, may I in my future existences be not deformed, blind, leprous, crafty or wicked, or be born as a bondsman; and, in my present existence, may I not fall into a condition of poverty or wickedness. And when I pass away, may I be born as a Veshya or Brahmin devoted to the Three Gems. Further, on again passing away, may I be born as a superior human being able to succour all others, both human and celestial, from the sufferings of *samsaro.* May those who destroy my good work suffer in the *avîci* hell, and even if they are again born as human beings, may they always be destitute of food and raiment. On the other hand, may those who safeguard my dedication equally share with me the merit accruing therefrom."

No. (12).

Locality.—At the southern porch of the Thate-Môkku Pagoda.
Date.—595 Sakkarâj (1233 A.D.).
Substance of inscription.—Apparently dedication of lands and slaves to some pagoda or monastery.

[A few words only in lines 1—8 have been deciphered. They indicate that certain lands and slaves were dedicated to some pagoda or monastery on Thursday the 5th waxing of Tabaung 595 Sakkarâj.]

No. (13A.).

Locality.—At the western porch of the Thate-Môkku Pagoda.
Date.—559 Sakkarâj (1197 A.D.).
Founder.—Seya Thate.
Substance of inscription.—Apparently dedication of lands and slaves to some pagoda or monastery.

Adoration to the Buddha, Dhamma and the Samgha!

ON Thursday the 7th waxing Pyatho 559 Sakkarâj, the year called Sayhata Samvacchora, Ceyya Seṭṭhi and . . . .
[Enumeration of the names of slaves dedicated.]

[No. (13B.) and No. (13C.) are a continuation of No. (13A.) and contain a list of the slaves and lands dedicated.]

No. (14).

Locality.—North-east corner of the Shwezigôn Pagoda; within the inner wall.

Date.—718—21 Sakkarâj (1346—59 A.D.).

Founder.—Nurse Mathâragasa.

Substance of inscription.—Dedication of a village, rice-lands and toddy-palms to some pagoda apparently.

On Thursday the 7th waxing Tazaungmôn 718 Sakkarâj, the year of Krataik, Mathâragasa, Nurse of Queen Saw,* was staying at Môkletti, attending on King Kyawzwa, the lord of white elephants, and his Queen Saw, when she, in the presence of the royal ministers Thamantabyit, Takkhanâ and Chinbo, presented their majesties with 100 fine mats and solicited a boon. Their majesties were accordingly pleased to dedicate the Thaman village with a view to enable the building (?) to last during the 5,000 years of the Religion. The revenue of the Thaman village amounts to 350 ticals of silver . . . . The dedicated palm groves are bounded on the *north* by two mango trees, on the *south* by Taungzin, on the *east* by the . . . . Aungyaung stream, and on the *west* by Thiyamyein . . . .

"May the merit accruing from this my good deed be shared by their majesties the king and queen and by their royal fathers. May those who safeguard the interests of my dedication equally share with me my merit. May all beings, including men and *nats*, inhabiting every region extending from the highest heaven to the lowest hell, likewise participate in this merit. May those who injure my gift be excluded from the privilege of adoring any of the Buddhas in the worlds to come; may they suffer in the four states of punishment; and if they are ever reborn as men, may they be destitute of happiness, power and long life."

* This is not the consort of Narathihapade and Kyawzwa, but the Chief Queen Sawônma of Kyawzwangè of Pinya. She was the youngest granddaughter of Kyawzwa of Pagan and was also known by the name of Ônmadandi. She continued to occupy the position of chief queen during the reigns of the two successive kings Narathu and Uzanabyaung, brothers of her first husband, as well as in the reign of the next king Thadominbya. On the return of this last king from a military expedition to Sagu, he was stricken down at Swègyo, in Pagan, with an attack of small-pox. He then sent for Nga Nu, a minister, and strictly enjoined him with his dying breath to put her to death, saying that he could not entertain the idea of her becoming the wife of another when he had passed away. Nga Nu accordingly took the queen in a boat up the river with the intention of fulfilling his master's behest; but, in an unguarded moment, he disclosed his errand, and the queen appealing to his manly sympathy, succeeded in prevailing upon him to land with her at Ava and install himself as Governor. The couple subsequently moved to Sagaing, but they were not long left in peace. Soon after the accession of Minkyizwasawkè to the throne on the death of Thadominbya an expedition was sent against Nga Nu. The expedition was headed by Nga Mauk, a minister known by the title of Yazathingyan and elder brother of Nga Nu, who had the promise of the king that, if he were successful, he would be rewarded with the hand of Sawônma. Nga Mauk captured his brother by stratagem, but secretly sent the captive away. He brought Sawônma to the capital and the king kept his word. Sawônma was thus the wife of four kings and two ministers, enjoying extraordinary long life and prosperity.

On the 5th waning of Nadaw 721 Sakkarâj, Pinngwe Ein Lat, Nga Hnôk and wife, and Sa Mè U were purchased and dedicated to the (pagoda). For the purpose of making a daily rice offering . . . . . .

No. (15).—Obverse.

Locality.—In a cave at the north-east corner of the Shwezigôn Pagoda platform; within the inner wall.

Date.—727 Sakkarâj (1365 A.D.).

Founder.—King Thadominbya.

Substance of inscription.—Dedication of lands and cultivators to the Shwezigôn.

On Tuesday the 5th waning of Nwèda* of the Tharawun (Saravanna) year 727 Sakkarâj, King Thadominbya,† who adores the Three Gems and is a zealous promoter of the interests of the Religion, proceeded down the river to Sagu.‡ When he arrived at Pagan, the king made the following offering to the Shwezigôn in order that the Religion might flourish during its prescribed period of 5,000 years: namely, the State paddy-land in Myingôndaing known by the name of Pyinnaukkya-Puletthaik. "It is to be worked by the undermentioned cultivators in the proportion indicated: Nga Kan Tu, 3 *pès*; Nga Pya Daung, 3; Nga Pya Daung Myit, 1; Nga Shun, 5; Nga Shun Daung, . . .; Mônthayan, 4; Nga Naung Ngè, 5; Yiru Milya,§ 5; Nga Pôn, 5; Nga Naing Ngan, . . .; Nga Myaung, 5; Innet Ngè, 1; Nga Lu Gyi, 5; Nga Nyo, 1; Ein Taya, 5; Nga Taba, 1; Nga Pyan, 5; Nga Kywè, 5; Thugyi Thara, 1; Nga Kyan Ya, 2; Nga Tauk To, 4; Nga Pyi, 2; Nga Wet To, 3; Nga U Yaung, 5; Nga Tha Yaung, 5; Nga Sôn Lettaw, 15; Nga Aung Byi, 5; Nga Pwa, 1; Nga Aung Pyi Byit, 1; Nga Myi, 5; grand total 100 *pès*. This rice-land has not fallen into my possession because I was elected king by public suffrage, but was secured by right of conquest in the interests of the Religion; and this land I do hereby dedicate. In virtue of this my good deed, may I, during my present existence, overcome all my enemies and be enabled to promote the interests of the Religion."

---

* The obsolete equivalents of the months of—

Wazo		Nwèda.
Wagaung		Nanka.
Tawthalin	are	Thitsin.
Thadingyut		Thandu.
Tazaungmôn		Tharada.

† Founded Ava in 1364 A.D.

‡ The expedition was organized with the object of suppressing the rebellion of Theinkathu, Myoza of Sagu.

§ Evidently a native of India.

REVERSE.

"And when I pass away to other forms of existence, may I become the ruler* of the four islands and be able to foster the continued existence of the Religion; and when I have once attained a position of power and prosperity, may I never fall from my high estate. May all beings inhabiting every region, from the highest heaven to the lowest hell, participate in the merit enjoyed by me. Hereafter, during the 5,000 years of the Religion, if any kings, ministers, nobles, or freeborn persons safeguard the interests of my endowment, may they share equally with me the merit enjoyed by me through the performance of this good deed; and moreover, may they live long and prosper. On the other hand, during the 5,000 years of the Religion, if any kings, ministers, nobles, or freeborn persons injure or destroy my endowment, may they be deprived of long life, happiness and prosperity, and may they meet with failure in every undertaking; and further, may they suffer the eight kinds of punishment and undergo torture in the four kinds of hell; and may they be deprived of the privilege of adoring any of the Buddhas in the worlds to come. Finally, may they suffer as burnt pillars in the hell assigned to confirmed heretics who are beyond the pale of salvation."

"Out of the produce of 20 *pès* of the land let the pagoda slaves make daily offerings of rice, and let the produce of the remaining 80 *pès* be utilized in repairing the pagoda, whenever repairs are necessary; and if there are no repairs to be executed, let the produce be utilized in providing other offerings to the shrine."

No. (16).—OBVERSE.

Locality.—About 200 feet north of the staircase of the Shwezigôn Pagoda and outside the western face of the outer wall.

Date.—737 Sakkarâj (1375 A.D.)

Founder.—Pagan *Myosa.*

Substance of inscription.—Erection of pagoda and dedication of rice-lands and toddy-palms to it.

ON Wednesday the 5th waxing of Kasôn of the Cissa year 737 Sakkâraj, corresponding with the year of the Religion 1919, the Thettawshe† minister and his wife, being apprehensive of the dangers of *samsaro* and desiring to do honour to the Religion during its allotted period of 5,000 years, constructed the western wall of the

* Chakravatin.

† One who is exempt from capital punishment. In this case it is the Pagan *Myosa*, Prime Minister of Minkyizwasawkè, King of Ava.

Shwezigôn Pagoda, a lofty and massive *kalagyaung* pagoda with pyramidal tiers, and also the *Yadanazedi* (Ratanâcetiya). For the maintenance of the pagoda and the monks, Paganmin Thettawshe availed himself of the occasion of the visit of their majesties the king and queen to the pagoda to apply for a piece of land, and His Majesty was pleased to grant the application and to ratify it by pouring water on the ground. The land is called Taukat, and it is situated in the Kukan (Pakan) circle between Myinwin and Lèlya. Its boundaries are—*north*, the Natein hills; *east*, a toddy-palm grove; *south*, the river; and *west*, the Kyaukauk palm-grove and a stone pillar now erected. Another piece of land is likewise dedicated. It is a piece of forest land situated to the south-east of Singyo. Its boundaries are—*east*, a stone pillar east of the Sinlin canal; *south*, the Teingyaung river; *west*, a stone pillar west of Nga Kyè Chaing; *north-west*, Taungzin Thapin Wutlèpa; *north*, Ngapwet-Ngapyet forest. The witnesses to the dedication are—His Majesty's son Prince Sinbyuthakin, His Majesty's son-in-law Uzanâ, Pinlé Anawrata, Min Theingapade, and Mahathaman, a secretary. Upon the secretaries and freeborn persons who demarcated the boundaries of the land suitable gifts were bestowed. An elephant was given to Ingatheinga; a silver bowl weighing 20 ticals to the Tetthe Thugyi; to Nga Kin Hla Thin and his son a pair of buffaloes, a pair of bullocks, and 12 pieces of white cloth; to the Kyunnwa *athis*,* a pair of buffaloes, a pair of bullocks, two pieces of black cloth, and five pieces of white cloth of good quality; to Nga Ni Ngè a brass tray, a piece of head cloth, and a bullock; to Nga Taung Bu a brass tray and a piece of head cloth; to the Sinbyuyin Prince 100 ticals of silver; to the Thinthi Thugyi a silver bowl and a bullock; to the Kyunnwa Thugyi a gold necklace and a buffalo; to Tetkana, the clerk, 30 ticals of silver, one buffalo, and two cows; and to the three men Aung Tha, Aung Thabi Sin and Pônmasin-Pônmathein, 25 ticals of silver, 50 baskets of paddy, and 7 pieces of loin cloth. "As a result of this my good deed, may I always be charitably inclined towards Buddha, his law and monkhood in whatever station I may be placed in life, and may I always be imbued with zeal in the observance of the *pañcasîla*†. May those who approve of this my offering share its merits with me."

Twenty-five bundles of gold-leaf were used in gilding the ornamental *ti*‡-rest; 100 glass balls for the *ti*, and 90 bundles of gold-leaf for the pagoda itself. The following expenditure was further incurred, namely, 30 ticals of silver for tiles, 35 for stones, 30 for

---

* Private individuals as opposed to service men or conscripts.

† Five commandments (lit. virtues).

‡ Umbrella, or cone which surmounts the top of a pagoda.

mortar, 10 for jaggery cement, 35 for masons' wages; four bullocks for timber; 100 baskets of paddy, one bullock and two pieces of cloth for carpenters' wages; 100 baskets of paddy, seven pieces of cloth, two turbans, and two bullocks for the carvers; one bullock for solder;* 30 ticals of silver for the bricklayers; two pieces of cloth for the blacksmith;

REVERSE.

thirty ticals of silver and 10 pieces of cloth for the carpenters; 25 ticals of silver and two pieces of cloth for a marble statue† of the king; 300 ticals for distribution among cripples. One thousand suits of yellow robes, 500 bullocks, 1,000 goats, 5,000 baskets of paddy, and 60 pieces of cloth were offered for the consecration ceremonies of the monastery. An elephant was given to Thingayaza, 300 ticals of silver to the painters, and 400 viss of blackwood varnish, 450 viss of prepared vermilion, 400 viss of resin, 1,500 viss of crude vermilion, 10 ticals worth of lac, and four viss of solder were used in the construction of the monastery.

"The towns and villages granted me by the king are Pyagaung, Kuntaung, Pinthi, Yangôn, Myingôndaing, Myittha, Pyinmana, Sale, Pagan, Salin, Pakanngè, Taungdwin, Talôk, and Pagandôn. In the last town I constructed a gilt monastery and appurtenances. To the monastery at Sale I dedicated 1,000 *pès* of land known by the name of Mibayakawzwè, and to the monastery at Salin I dedicated 280 *pès* of land. The following are the offerings made by me from my youth up, namely, 7,000 bins of paddy, 1,000 suits of yellow robes, 1,000 alms-bowls, 1,000 kettles, 1,000 spittoons and filters, 100 *kateins*,‡ 2,000 bullocks, and 290 pagodas. By virtue of these my meritorious offerings, may I always be charitably inclined towards Buddha, his law and monkhood, in whatever position in life I may find myself, and may I always be imbued with zeal in the observance of the *pañcasīla*. May those who approve of my offerings share the merits with me. This is my grandchildren's and great-grandchildren's monastery."

No. (17).

[About half a dozen lines only, both on the obverse and reverse, are decipherable, the rest being indistinct, and nothing can be made

* Required for fixing the *ti* in its rest.

† Statuettes of kings, queens, and nobles in gold, silver, and marble are enshrined in many pagodas in company with any precious images or reputed relics of Gautama Buddha which the founders of the institutions may have had in their possession.

‡ Wickerwork cones on which are hung different articles required for use in monasteries, somewhat after the manner of English Christmas trees, and which are offered to monks on the first full-moon day after the Buddhist Lent (July—October).

out of them beyond the fact that the founder of the inscription was a monk called Yunmingyi Sayadaw and that it was erected in 754 Sakkarâj (1392 A.D.).]

No. (18).

Locality.—North-east corner of inner wall of pagoda.

Date.—757 Sakkarâj (1395 A.D.).

Founder.—Anandathu, Prime Minister.

Substance of inscription.—Dedication of pagoda, brick monastery, *thein*,* and *tasaung* and lands attached to them.

ON Wednesday the 4th waxing of Wazo 757 Sakkarâj, Anandathu, the Prime Minister of his most pious and most glorious majesty the King of Ava, the lord of the white elephant, being with his lady Saw Shwe Ein† anxious to avoid the miseries of *samsaro*, and to promote the cause of the Religion during its allotted period of 5,000 years, constructed and offered a three-winged brick monastery, an image cave 10 cubits in diameter and containing an image 3½ cubits high, and a four-storied *thein* * (sima). . . . . (19 lines).

No. (19).

[Almost every other line in this inscription has been obliterated, but there still remains sufficient to show that it was erected in 813 Sakkarâj (1451 A.D.) by Kaninawyata, a minister of King Narapati of Ava, and that certain paddy lands were dedicated to the Aungmyebôntha Pagoda, west of Nyaungu village, Pagan. The stone, which is far from entire, lies near the *thein* attached to the pagoda.]

No. (20).

Locality.—In the cave at the north-east corner of the pagoda wall.

Date.—1130 Sakkarâj (1767 A.D.). 1768?

Founder.—King Sinbyuyin of Ava.

Substance of inscription.—Dedication of a *ti* or umbrella for the pagoda and of *wuttagan* lands mentioned in former inscriptions as being offered to the pagoda by previous kings.

---

* Place where Buddhist monks are ordained.

† Lesser Queen of Minkyizwasawkè. She was one of the sisters of Thadominbya, the founder of Ava.

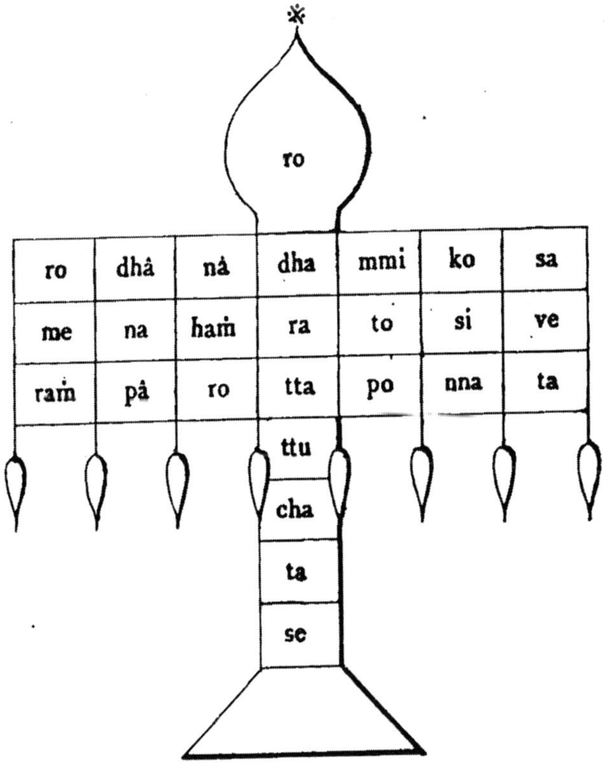

Reverence to the Blessed, Holy, and Enlightened One!

I ADORE at all times the Buddha, who has overcome the five enemies; who has passed through the three periods of night in

* This diagram represents a white umbrella, one of the emblems of royalty. The mode of reading of the text thereon is to proceed from *se*, the lowest letter, upwards to *ro*; then start from *dha*, the one next below the topmost, to the right, and again from the same starting-point to the left; and then do the same for the other two lines below. This method has to be followed when reading the inscriptions on the bells belonging to the Shwe Dagôn Pagoda at Rangoon. The text, when written out *in extenso*, runs as follows:—

Seta chattuttara dharo dhammiko sa dhanâ dhâro rato sive raham name taponnatataro pâram,

which being translated means:

I adore the excellent Buddha, who possesses the most excellent white umbrella; who observes the law; who is the promulgator and possessor of the doctrines of righteousness; who delights in the calm of Nirvâna; who is worthy of all adoration; and who has by virtue of meritorious deeds gained the other shore.

continuous succession; who has the wisdom to perceive, like the all-pervading celestial eye, the previous existences he has passed through. His most excellent majesty the Emperor, who is as resplendent in glory as the rising sun; who is the giver of excellent gifts and possessor of untold wealth; who is the over-lord of all the kings of the earth; who is replete with every virtue; who is the possessor of several ruby and other mines; and who is able to subdue every enemy, has delighted his numerous subjects by making an offering of a most excellent bejewelled *ti*, at the most auspicious moment, on Sunday the 6th waning of the moon of Nayôn 1130 Sakkarâj, corresponding with the year 2312 Anno Buddhæ.

As the *Thagyamin* * had so willed it, the graceful Shwezigôn Pagoda stands well within the firmament which is the highway of the winds. It was erected by the eminent Emperor Anawrata,† who, in consultation with the *Thagyamin*, conveyed the sacred tooth relic from the Isle of Lanka‡ and enshrined it within this sanctuary.

Having accumulated every virtue by the performance of the three kinds of meritorious deeds § throughout the 20 *asankkeyyas* ‖ and 100,000 *kalpas* ¶ of his series of existences, and having in his last existence enjoyed for over 29 years, within three magnificent palaces, the life of a king mightier and more glorious than the famous Mandatmin, ruler of the four continents of the world, our Buddha assumed, on the banks of the Anawma river, the yellow robes which were reserved for him from the beginning. After six years of rahanship,** the preceptor of the three kinds of superior beings, namely, *nats*, men and brahmas, approached the throne under the banyan tree from the north-east, and having seated himself thereon, attained Buddhahood. A great concourse of *nats* then came down to worship him. While thus seated with a highly contented and serene countenance, he was, as it were, anointed lord of the heavens and the earth, with *maggo* as his white umbrella; virtue as the walls of his city; good conscience as the moat; wisdom as the porches of the city gates; diligence as the ramparts and battlements; equanimity as the portals; vigilance as the gates; the *suttapitakam* as the streets; the *abhidhamma* as the crossings; the *vinaya* as the main roads; and the four kinds of *satipathâna* as the king's highway. Along the streets of this great city of Nirvâna are displayed everything pleasant and useful for the inhabit-

* King of *nats* or *devâs*, the Indra of Hindu mythology.
† 1017—1059 A.D.
‡ Ceylon.
§ (1) To become Buddha, (2) for relatives, (3) for the world.
‖ The numerical value of an *asankkeyya* is 1, followed by 140 ciphers.
¶ Worlds.
** Or probationary period of penance.

ants, namely, the virtues as various kinds of incense and flowers; the *sotâpatti* and other *phalam* as fruit; the different kinds of penances and contemplations as drugs for the healing of every ailment and for safe protection from all evil influences; and large quantities of valuable mixtures for the promotion of health and wealth, wisdom and beauty. The suzerain of every kingdom and principality in the whole universe, after having reigned in this fair city for 45 years, during which period he conveyed several converts to it, from Kundinnya* down to Thubatta, and having contemplated the 20,600,000 *jhâna*, himself abode permanently in Nirvâna. "Two "thousand, two hundred and ninety-five years after this event, or in "the year 1113 Sakkarâj, the ruler of the Talaing kingdom of Ramañ-"ñadesa, consisting of three states,† conquered Ava and deposed the "King Lokasarapucetidâyakâ. Misfortune thus befell the Burmese "empire and the Religion commenced to decline. But in accordance "with the oracle of the Buddha subsequently recorded by the *nats* "and *rishis*, I,‡ who had by the ceremony of water-pouring prayed "for strength to overcome every enemy in case I were predestined "to become an embryo Buddha, overthrew the Talaings and thus be-"came Defender of the Religion." At that time the Shwetaza Paya§ offered by King Narapatisithu indicated|| the place where the capital of the Burmese Empire should be. Accordingly the City of Ratanasingha¶ was built, and Alompra erected a magnificent golden palace there and occupied the throne for a long period and promoted the cause of the Religion with fervent zeal. Great good fortune attended his military expeditions, and the provinces conquered by him included Panmè, Mogaung, Mohnyin, Moda, Momeik, Theinni, Thibaw, Nyaungywe, Monè, Mobyè, Zimmè, Kyaingtôn, Kyaingyôn, Kyaingthein, Toungoo, Hanthawaddy, Martaban, Tavoy, Bassein, Myaungmya, Tilin, Kale, and portions of Siam and Cambodia. In all these states the king encouraged the propagation of the Religion and spent large sums of money and large quantities of jewels in erecting pagodas, images, monasteries, rest-houses and other religious edifices. The *sawbwas* and *myozas*** were allowed to retain their offices and their brothers and sons were admitted as courtiers.

* One of the first five *rishis* who heard the preaching of Gautama Buddha.

† Hanthawaddy, Martaban, and Bassein.

‡ Alompra (1753—60).

§ One of nine pieces of *saga* (champa) wood said to have been obtained by supernatural agency.

|| It is related that this image was one day found to have faced round towards the site of Shwebo, and that subsequently it would always persist in doing so in spite of repeated efforts to replace it in its former position.

¶ Shwebo.

** Shan chieftains.

The petty kings and rulers also were granted pieces of land and residences befitting their rank. It was thus that Alompra during the 10 years* of his reign promoted the interests of the state and the welfare of the country, and then departed for the abode of the *nats* in the same manner as the Mandat Setkyamin, who abrogated the heritage of the whole universe in favour of his son and heir, being desirous of prolonging his sojourn with the *Thagyamin* Devindra. Accordingly, on the 8th waning moon of Nayôn 1122 Sakkarâj, the eldest son,† and heir-apparent of Alompra, donor of the Mahabôntha monastery and the Kadwin Pagoda, ascended the throne and continued to foster the cause of the Religion and the interests of the people, after having suppressed rebellion and intrigue and adopted proper measures to preserve the integrity of the empire. After enjoying the pleasures of this earth for a length of time,‡ but not so long as to be weary of them, the king departed to the abode of the *nats*. He was succeeded by his younger brother,§ the donor of the Bônzantulut monastery, on Wednesday morning, the 4th waning Nadaw 1125 Sakkarâj, corresponding with Anno Buddhæ 2307. The emperor was replete with wisdom, and with every virtue and kingly attribute; was possessed of tact and foresight, and was very mighty. Within 17 days of his accession his most glorious majesty succeeded, where others failed, in conveying to the palace from Haripunça‖ the sacred hair and the four images called Brahisinga, Candaku, Brakyan, and Brasin. His life on the throne was as blissful as that of the *Thagyamin*, but having the interests of the Religion at heart, he was always making either new charitable offerings or renovating the old ones. As predicted by Gautama Buddha that Ratanapura¶ would one day become the centre of the Religion and the capital of many kings able to promote its cause, the emperor contemplated the removal of his capital there, and the guardian *nats* of the Religion indicated by explicit signs and legends their approval of the project. Accordingly, on Tuesday the 11th waxing of Tagu 1125 Sakkarâj, the building of the city was commenced** and was completed in a short time. The coronation ceremony took place on Wednesday the 4th waning of Nayôn 1126 Sakkarâj, when the *Thagyamin* and his *nats* came down and presented a full complement of exquisite and correctly formed conch shells neces-

* Actually only eight. The language of flattery would, however, include both the year of accession and that of death.

† Commonly known as Naungdawgyi or elder brother of Sinbyuyin.

‡ 19 years.

§ Sinbyuyin (1763—76 A.D.).

‖ Classical name for Zimmè.

¶ Ava.

** More correctly, rebuilt and fortified, for Ava was originally founded by Thadominbya in 1364 A.D.

sary for the occasion, and which is not given to every king or emperor to possess. On Wednesday the 14th waning of Nayôn 1126 Sakkarâj, the emperor ordered the erection of the Neikban-seiku * Pagoda, which stands on a piece of *bônminetthan* land south-west of Shwebo, and directed to be enshrined within it several sacred relics of Gautama Buddha contained in both plain and be-jewelled gold, silver, ruby, and amber caskets. The pagoda was designed to afford relief and shelter to the poor and the wayfarer. High were the festivals held and lavish were the charitable offerings made on its completion.

The whole of Candapurî† and Lanzin (Linzin) were conquered, and these states had to pay tribute in the shape of elephants, ponies, gold, silver, and precious stones, and the sons and daughters and other relatives of the chieftains had to come up and serve in the palace. On Sunday the 8th waning of Pyatho 1126 Sakkarâj, the emperor invaded Manipur. Hôn, the *sawbwa*, surrendered his state together with a tribute of elephants and ponies, and the emperor returned with over 30,000 Manipuri cavalry men and several sons and daughters of the *sawbwa*, whom he treated as prisoners of war and retained in his service.‡ On Tuesday the 7th waxing Wagaung 1127 Sakkarâj, the magnificent seven-storied golden palace, which is 120 cubits high, was commenced and completed in a very short time, like that of King Mahâpanâta, who invoked the aid of the *devâs* in his undertaking.§ Then on Thursday, the 11th waxing of Tagu 1127, which is the anniversary of the installation of King Duttabaung on the throne of Tharekittaya (Prome), the emperor ascended his throne. In Thadingyut 1128 Sakkarâj it was reported to the emperor that the petty chieftains on the northern borders of the empire had entered into an intrigue with the Chinese, and that an army of over a hundred thousand Chinamèn had come as far as Zethitseik, Bhamo township, with intent to occupy the tributary states of Maingmè, Sigwin, Hotha, Latha, Mona (Maing-na) and Sanda. The emperor accordingly sent out an army to meet the Chinese and succeeded in capturing all of them, together with their arms and ammunition. On Thursday the 10th waxing of Tagu 1128, the emperor sent an expedition to Siam under the leadership of his generals,|| annexed that country for the first time to the empire of Ava, and obtained tribute in the shape of elephants, ponies, gold, silver, and precious stones. Subsequently the famous

* Literally, starting-point to Nirvâna.

† Shan State of Mainglôn, or the Laos States.

‡ There are still many descendants of these Manipuris in and about Mandalay.

§ According to the legend, Mahâpanâta's palace was seen growing up out of the earth.

|| Myinwun Mingyi and Athiwungyi.

*pañcalohâ** gong, which Asoka had obtained from a Cingalese monk and placed in a cave at Thatôn with the prayer that it may be brought to light during the reign of some sovereign gifted with the ability to overcome every enemy and to promote the cause of the Religion, was discovered and was duly presented to the emperor. On Thursday the 5th waxing of Pyatho 1129 Sakkarâj, the emperor held his second coronation ceremony in emulation of Narapati and Thalunmindaya of Ava, Alaungsithu of Pagan, Asoka of Pâtaliputra, and other eminent kings and emperors of old, and he was presented for a second time with a full complement of genuine conch shells. When the Chinese army which encamped at Zethitseik in Bhamo township did not return, the Chinese emperor raised an army of over three hundred thousand men and, under the leadership of his ablest generals, ordered the invasion of Ava in three columns by three different routes, marching through Mowun, Kaungtôn, Maingmaw, Theinni, Kaingma, and Kyaingyôn. The army was furnished with war chariots, cannon, guns, rockets, bows, arrows, lances, and various other kinds of offensive weapons and munitions of war. On the 11th waxing of Pyatho 1129 Sakkarâj it reached the ears of the emperor that the Chinese army had arrived at Kaungtôn, Theinni, and Kyaingyôn.† Two armies were accordingly sent out under two ministers by different routes and the heretic Chinese were utterly routed and large quantities of their arms and ammunition were captured. Great festivals were subsequently held in celebration of the victory. At the most auspicious hour on Friday the 6th waxing Wagaung 1129 Sakkarâj, the capital was redemarcated with a view to extend its limits and its perimeter then measured 2,443 *tas*.‡ The building operations commenced on the 8th waning of Tabodwè 1129 Sakkarâj, and were completed on the 10th waxing Nayôn 1130 Sakkarâj, that is to say, in 106 days.

Our present universe is the only one out of a hundred thousand others which has the honour of being the birthplace of the Buddhas who are the guides to Nirvâna. There are in it four continents and 500 islands, and of these the *Jambudipa* is the starting-place to Nirvâna, and is therefore the chief continent. And in this continent the great empire of Ava is the greatest; because it is the richest in gold, silver, ruby, amber and other precious minerals; be-

* An alloy consisting of five varieties of metals.

† History relates that the Chinese came up to the village of *Bôkthetkèbyin*, which is only about 8 miles from the capital, and that Sinbyuyin had to resort to stratagem to overcome the enemy, that is to say, he despatched several detachments of troops by different routes to cut off the retreat of the Chinese and to waylay the supplies of provisions for them.

‡ One *ta* = 7 cubits or 10½ feet.

cause it comprises several tributary kingdoms,* namely Sunâparanta, Tampadipa, Kampoja, Yonaka, Haripuñca, Khemâvara, Khemâratha, Mahanagara, Zeyyavaddhana, Sirikhetta, Mahîsaka, Âlavî, Ayuddhaya, Tâmalitti and the country of the Seins; and lastly, because it is the chief centre of the Religion. As for the emperor, he is the suzerain of all the rulers of the earth, and the possessor of innumerable weapons of war, including the four monster cannon, each measuring 12 cubits in length, 9½ cubits in girth, with muzzles measuring 9 inches in diameter. The golden palace is situated at the centre of the great city of Ava, which stands on the Minwun hill at the confluence of the seven ? (6) great rivers, Samôn, Sanma, Panlaung, Zaya, Nayinzaka, and Irrawaddy. Within this magnificent palace sits enthroned the emperor, whose glory and splendour may be compared with that of the king of *devâs*, and who is continually attended by a host of queens and concubines and maids of honour. But the emperor never loses sight of the interests of the country and the Religion, and the welfare of himself and his descendants in this and all future existences. He has therefore repeatedly performed several meritorious deeds and has consequently increased in power and wisdom. Being actuated by a highly charitable disposition, the emperor has constructed several new pagodas, images, caves, and monasteries, and repaired many old ones, and has thus acquired much virtue; but he is still insatiable. He is always eagerly longing to add to his merits by accomplishing some new charitable deed. So the thousand-eyed *Thagyamin*, with the assistance of his *devâs*, afforded the emperor a fresh opportunity of indulging in his favourite pursuit by taking away, on Thursday the 6th waxing Kasôn 1130 Sakkarâj, the *ti*† of the Shwezigôn Pagoda, which was offered by Kyanzittha, grandfather of King Alaungsithu, in 432 Sakkarâj, the pagoda itself being built in 421 Sakkarâj by Anawrata, who enshrined within it the frontal bone relic and tooth relic. The emperor gladly availed himself of this opportunity, and, having employed a number of experts to compute the proper weights and dimensions of the different component parts of a new *ti*, offered his own valuable crown of refined gold, a quantity of gold plate, flowers and nuggets, gold dust, silver and precious stones, towards the making of the *ti*, while the queen dowager ‡ and other members of the royal family also, wishing to partake of the emperor's merits, contributed a large quantity of jewellery. Moreover, the ministers applied for and obtained permission to con-

* *Cf.* the classical names of these so-called kingdoms with those contained in the Po-udaung inscription, lines 40—45.

† It must have fallen down because of natural decay or an earthquake or a storm.

‡ Mahayaza Dewi, Alompra's queen.

tribute refined gold nuggets and silver bullion. The construction of the new *ti* was commenced on Saturday the 14th waning of Kasôn 1130 Sakkarâj on the reserved enclosure in front of the *hlutdaw*.

The *ti* is of iron, plated over first with copper and then with pure gold. The central iron rod is 13 cubits long, 13 *letthits* * in girth, and weighs 63·75 viss. The *ti* is composed of 11 tiers: the first is made of 36·71 viss of iron, 8·938 viss of copper, 2·5285 viss of gold, and is 10 cubits, 1 *maik* † and 4 *letthits* in circumference, and 2 *maiks* and 4 *letthits* broad; the second tier is made of 23·217 viss of iron, 6·703 viss of copper, and 2·237 viss of gold, and is 10 cubits in circumference and 2 *maiks* broad; the third tier is made of 15·368 viss of iron, 5·673 viss of copper, and 1·93 viss of gold, and is 9 cubits, 1 *maik* and 4 *letthits* in circumference, and 1 *maik* and 6 *letthits* in breadth; the fourth tier is made of 12·14 viss of iron, 4·498 viss of copper, and 1·236 viss of gold, and is 9 cubits in circumference, and 1 *maik* and 3 *letthits* in breadth; the fifth tier is made of 10·96 viss of iron, 3·686 viss of copper, and 1·182 viss of gold, and is 8 cubits and 9 *letthits* in circumference, and 1 *maik* and 2½ *letthits* in breadth; the sixth tier is made of 9·5 viss of iron, 3·351 viss of copper, and 1·211 viss of gold, and is 7 cubits and 15 *letthits* in circumference, and 1 *maik* and 1½ *letthits* in breadth; the seventh tier is made of 8·36 viss of iron, 2·982 viss of copper, and 1·51 viss of gold, and is 6 cubits and 18 *letthits* in circumference, and 1 *maik* 1½ *letthits* in breadth; the eighth tier is made of 7·51 viss of iron, 2·465 viss of copper, and 89⅓ ticals of gold, and is 5 cubits and 18 *letthits* in circumference, and 1 *maik* and 1 *letthit* in breadth; the ninth tier is made of 3·96 viss of iron, 1·918 viss of copper, and 68$\frac{1}{10}$ ticals of gold, and is 4 cubits and 9 *letthits* in circumference, and 1 *maik* and 1 *letthit* in breadth; the tenth tier is made of 3·76 viss of iron, 1·58 viss of copper, and 53⅖ ticals of gold, and is 4 cubits and 3 *letthits* in circumference and 1 *maik* in breadth; and the eleventh tier is made of 3·44 viss of iron, 1·352 viss of copper, and 49$\frac{9}{10}$ ticals of gold, and is 3 cubits and 18 *letthits* in circumference and 1 *maik* in breadth. The weight of the different metals used is altogether 134·854 viss of iron, 43·142 viss of copper, and 13·862 viss of gold. Forty-four miniature porches and 44 flags are attached to the *ti*. The *satthapu* ‡ is made of 5·38 viss of iron, 7·306 viss of copper, and 3·503 viss of gold. It is 3 cubits, 1 *maik* and 4 *letthits* in circumference and 5 cubits in height, and is studded over with 998 precious stones, including

* One *letthit* = ¾ inch.

† One *maik* = 8 *letthits*, or 6 inches.

‡ Metal cone forming the apex of the *ti*.

45 emeralds, 818 rubies, 65 diamonds, 34 sapphires, 6 cat's-eyes and two pearls. Moreover, to represent the sacred relics of Gautama Buddha 1,000 emeralds and 111 coral beads are placed within the cone. The *ti* rest is made of 1·7 viss of silver. The bells are 105 in number and are made of 44·174 viss of silver. The aggregate weight of gold used is 17·368 viss, and silver 64·618 viss. The aggregate number of precious stones is 2,109. The whole work was successfully accomplished on Saturday the 13th waxing Nayôn 1130 Sakkarâj. The emperor then invited every member of his imperial family, as well as the ministers and generals, to witness the ceremony of putting up the new *ti*, and in a golden barge adorned with three turretted canopies, one at the bow, one at the stern, and the third amidships, accompanied by a large fleet of gaily equipped boats, proceeded down the river on Monday, the full-moon of Nayôn 1130 Sakkarâj, and reached Nyaungu in four days. On the sixth waxing day of the same month, the day on which the usual yearly festival was held at the pagoda, the emperor, attended by the queen dowager, the queen, his three younger brothers,* the princes and princesses, performed the ceremony of offering the *ti* by pouring water out of a gold cup studded with rubies. The whole pagoda was then gilt and a large number of titled and other monks renowned for their learning and piety were invited and were lavishly supplied with food and raiment. The emperor then rededicated the following offerings made by his ancestors, namely, the sacred lands offered on Friday the 3rd waxing Nayôn 510 Sakkarâj by Alaungsithu; 50 *pès* of paddy land and two villages called Chiye and Thumyattha, comprising an area of 1,000 *pès*, and 30 *pès* of old fishery land, offered on Thursday the 13th waxing Tazaungmôn 545 by Narâpatisithu; the lands offered by Thadominzaw on Tuesday the 5th waning Wazo 727 Sakkarâj; the lands at Myingôndaing offered in 730 Sakkarâj, and 23 *pès* of land opposite Lamaing village offered in 757 Sakkarâj by Minkyizwasawkè; and the piece of land offered by Pagankyawzwamin and yielding a rental of 350 baskets of paddy. The emperor made these offerings in order that the Religion might flourish throughout its allotted period of 5,000 years.

"By virtue of these my meritorious deeds may I soon attain Buddhahood and so be enabled to confer the white umbrella of future bliss to men, devâs and brahmâs; may I in the present existence be endowed with power and ability to further the cause of the Religion and promote the interests of my family and my people. If in my future existences my lot should fall among devâs, may I

* Pindalèmin, Bodawpaya and Pakanmin.

always be their king, and if among men, may I be their sole emperor able to observe every kingly duty. May every devâ and every creature inhabiting this world, as well as my parents and other relatives, share my merits equally with me, and may they acclaim their glad approval of my benefactions. May those who have, be enabled to give freely, and thus promote the cause of the Religion. May all grow in wealth and power and enjoy peace and prosperity. May my imperial father and elder brother hear my prayers from their celestial abode and express their approval. May the guardian *nat* of the earth do the same."

, Our Buddha overcame every enemy before he departed to Nirvâna. Throughout his previous existences and during his life on this earth he acquired every virtue and performed every deed necessary for the benefit of the world. Before his attainment of Nirvâna, moreover, he ordained that his Religion shall flourish for full 5,000 years. In the year 2307 of the Religion, the illustrious Emperor Sinbyuyin, bearing the honoured title of Sirisudhammamahârâjâjanindâdhipati, ascended the throne of Ava. As conspicuous as the lunar orb in a clear sky, there stands in Pagan the famous and wonderful Shwezigôn Pagoda. It has for centuries withstood the rigours of the climate. In the year 2312 of the Religion, corresponding with the year 1130 Sakkarâj, the emperor in a happy moment asked himself what he should do to add to his own merit and to please the people. No sooner had he done so than the *ti* of the Shwezigôn Pagoda, without being affected in the least by wind or weather, bodily detached itself from its rest and slowly glided down to the earth. When this was brought to the notice of the emperor, he gladly welcomed the news and forthwith commanded the new bejewelled *ti* to be made and set up, and rededicated the sacred lands and pagoda slaves offered by the ancient kings. The setting up of the *ti* was accompanied with high festivals, and the water-pouring was performed by the emperor in person with great pomp and ceremony. May the pagoda and the new *ti* last long. In the year 2312 of the Religion * the emperor who set up this new *ti* removed his capital from Shwebo to Ava.

[Here follows the last line, which is undecipherable, being almost obliterated].

* This corresponds with 1130 Sakkarâj or 1768 A. D.

No. (21).

Locality.—North-east corner of inner wall of pagoda.

Date.—1147 Sakkarâj (1785 A.D.).

Founder.—Bodawpaya.*

Substance of inscription.—Re-dedication of a number of *wuttagan* lands.

MAY the Religion flourish throughout its period of 5,000 years, and may it be as resplendent in glory, as long-abiding and conspicuous as Mount Meru and the solar and lunar orbs. It is with this object in view that His Most Excellent Majesty has performed the meritorious deeds detailed below. Like King Nemi of old, one of the embryo Buddhas, His Majesty is descended from a race of kings who reigned over vast dominions, and who were thus able to further the cause of the Religion, His Majesty being a son of Alompra, the founder of a dynasty which is as notable in history as that of the primeval king Mahâ Thamada. His Majesty is, moreover, a brother of Naungdawgyi, the founder of Sagaing, who was as mighty as the king of lions in war, and also of Sinbyuyin, founder of Ava, who also succeeded in overpowering his enemies even as the Galôn † can when surrounded by other birds. His Majesty is the lord of an innumerable army and possessor of vast armaments and several white elephants. He is the donor of several pagodas and monasteries, and is celebrated for his well-merited title of Siripavaravijayânantayasatribhavanâdityâdhipatipaṇḍitamahâdhammarâjâdhirâjâ. Following the ancient traditions, His Majesty performed the coronation ceremony twice in Amarapura, the highly pleasant and impregnable city founded by him. Being blessed with a son and heir and everything requisite for present happiness, His Majesty could turn his attention to the welfare of the country and the people, and to the interests of the Religion ; and seeing that if the inscriptions recording the offerings made by the excellent kings of old were allowed to fall into decay and ruin, the original purpose of the donors would miscarry, commanded that the inscriptions should be collected and properly examined, and in order that the Religion might continue to flourish, and he himself attain Buddhahood ultimately, re-dedicated the offerings found mentioned therein.

After having been anointed king twice like King Devânampîyatissa ‡ in the great capital of Amarapura, His Majesty reigned in the golden palace as glorious and as blissful as the king of *devâs*, and like Asoka administered his vast dominions, including distant

* Founder of the first city of Amarapura.
† The Garuda, a fabulous bird.
‡ King of Ceylon and contemporary of Asoka.

Arakan, with equity and justice, despatched missionary monks to over 50 places, erected pagodas and caves enshrining several sacred relics in over 150 towns and villages, and brought over from Arakan the Mahâmuni image * which was set up in the time of our Lord Buddha. Having done so, His Majesty, being gifted with as much foresight as the thousand-eyed king of the *devâs*, proposed to re-dedicate the religious lands offered by his royal ancestors to enrich the Religion, knowing that they would otherwise be lost sight of in course of time and in order that he might obtain Buddhahood and that his descendants might continue to foster the cause of the Religion throughout its allotted period of 5,000 years. Accordingly His Majesty re-dedicated the land attached to the Zeyakôn† (Shwezigôn) pagoda. The boundaries of the land are: east, Bawdigôn; south, a banyan tree at Mingalatèdaw; west, Baludet landing-stage; north-west and north, the *thalweg* of the Irrawaddy for a distance of 700 *tas*.‡ Several disputes arose formerly in respect of the right to utilize the usufruct of the land. In the reign of the founder of Zeyapura or Sagaing (Naungdawgyi), the Governor of Pagan, sued for the recovery of the land from the pagoda slaves on the ground that the Zeyakôn pagoda was not the Shwezigôn. The case was decided by water ordeal on the 14th waxing of Tawthalin, 1124 Sakkarâj, and the governor lost the suit. Again, in the reign of Sinbyuyin, founder of Ratanâpūra or Ava, a similar dispute arose between the Governor of Pagan and the Thugyi of Nyaungu on the one side and the pagoda slaves on the other. The king referred the matter to the abbot of the Bônzantulut monasteries for decision, and the abbot, after having examined the records relating to the land, decided the dispute in favour of the pagoda slaves on the 13th waning of Kasôn, 1134 Sakkarâj. Accordingly His Majesty, the founder of Amarapura, hereby confirms the above decisions and re-dedicates the land, which is fully 700 *kalele tas*§ square, by pouring water out of a golden kettle on the morning of Thursday, the 9th waning of Thadingyut, 1147 Sakkarâj, in order that the pagoda slaves might continue to utilize the usufruct of the land in

---

* This huge brazen idol, which is now in Mandalay, was conveyed over the Western Yoma mountains, not, however, in bulk, but in convenient pieces, in 1784 A.D. It was, according to Burmese history, originally cast by Sandathuriya, 29th King of Arakan, during Gautama Buddha's visit there.

† Originally Thègôn, a sandbank. Tradition relates that Anawrata, the hero-king of Pagan, obtained by right of conquest a tooth-relic and a frontal bone relic of Gautama from Prome, and on his return to the capital, placed them on a white elephant and set it free with a "wish" that it might indicate the place where the sacred relics should be enshrined. The elephant wandered to the site of the pagoda, which was then merely a sandbank and stood there with its precious burden until those who followed in its wake arrived.

‡ A *ta* = 7 cubits.

§ A bow measuring 4 cubits or 2 yards in length.

making the daily offering of rice and lights and in maintaining the pagoda in good repair.

No. (22).

Locality.—South-east corner of inner wall of pagoda.

Date.—1205 Sakkarâj (1843 A.D.).

Founder.—King Tharrawaddy.*

Substance of inscription.—Demarcation of the land attached to the pagoda.

In accordance with a royal order issued on the 2nd waxing of Tazaungmôn, 1205 Sakkarâj, to the effect that the land attached to the Shwezigôn pagoda, which is according to the inscription 700 *ka!ele tas* square, should be demarcated with boundary pillars in order that the disputes regarding it might for ever be set at rest, eight pillars were erected along the boundaries, and the fact is hereby recorded. A distance of 700 *tas* was measured from the central porch of the eastern wall of the pagoda to a point 45 *tas* north-west of the Shitmyethna pagoda, and a pillar was set up there on Thursday, the 3rd waning Tazaungmôn, 1205 Sakkarâj. Then the same distance was measured from the western wall westward to a sandbank, but this spot being found unsuitable for the erection of a pillar, another spot 250 *tas* south of it and 44 *tas* north-west of the Shwegu pagoda was selected and a pillar was set up thereon on Sunday, the 6th waning of Tazaungmôn, 1205 Sakkarâj. At the same distance from the southern wall and at a spot 50 *tas* north-west of the Tazingu pagoda a pillar was set up on Monday, the 7th waning Tazaungmôn, 1205 Sakkarâj. Next, a distance of 758 *tas*, one cubit and four *letthits* was measured from the central pillar facing the southern wall westward to a point 25 *tas* west of the masonry steps of the Kinminga monastery ruins, this point being situated at the same distance from the sandbank facing the western wall, and a boundary pillar was set up there on Saturday, the 11th waxing Nadaw, 1205 Sakkarâj. Again the same distance was measured from the central southern pillar eastward and from the eastern central pillar southward to a point 50 *tas* south of the Zedihla pagoda built by Asoka, and a pillar was erected there on Sunday, the 12th waxing Nadaw, 1205 Sakkarâj. The eastern, western, southern, south-eastern and south-western pillars were erected on firm ground by Mahâminhlamindinyaza, Wun of Pagan, Sitkè Shwedaungyègaung, Nakan Shwedaungzeyasithugyaw, Nga Shun, Thugyi of Kawtha, Jailor Nga Swe Gyôk, *Myothugyis* Nga Kwe and Nga So Min, Po

* 1837-46 A.D.

Shwe Daung Kyawdinthu, Thinkyawthushwedaung, *Ywathugyi* of Tetnwègyaung village, Zeyathiri, *Ywathugyi* of Wetkyi-in village, Head Pagoda-slave Nga Shwe Maung and son Nga Pè, *Asiyin* * Nga Cheik and *Asuye* * Nga Paing. On the sandbank facing the northern wall the erection of a masonry pillar being impracticable, the boundary was marked with a large heap of stones on the 8th waning of Tazaungmôn, 1205 Sakkarâj. Then at a point 758 *tas*, one cubit, one *maik* and four *letthits* east of this and the same distance north of the central pillar facing the eastern wall, another large heap of stones was piled up on the 14th waxing of Nadaw, 1205 Sakkarâj. Then at a point 758 *tas*, one cubit, one *maik* and four *letthits* west of the central pillar facing the northern wall, and the same distance north of the heap of stones facing the western wall, a wooden post about 27 inches in girth was planted, and round it a heap of stones was piled up on the 15th waxing of Nadaw, 1205 Sakkarâj. These heaps of stones were erected by the same men abovementioned. This inscription is placed in the *tazaung* in front of the Shwezigôn pagoda on Thursday, the 8th waning Nadaw, 1205 Sakkarâj, in the presence of those who were deputed to demarcate the land, namely, clerk Nemyoyazanawyata, Surveyor Nga Eik, *Wutmye* † clerk Zeyakyawywa, Head Pagoda-slave Nga Shwe Maung and son Nga Pè, *Asiyin* * Nga Cheik and *Asuye* * Nga Paing.

INSCRIPTIONS OF PAGAN.

II.—Found at Wetkyi-in.

No. (1).

Locality.—In inscription cave within the group of monasteries.

Date.—532 Sakkarâj (1170 A.D.).

Founders.—Yattapisi and wife.

Substance of inscription.—Dedication of slaves to Kalagyaung ‡ image.

"ON Thursday, the 3rd waxing of Tagu, 532 Sakkarâj, I, Yattapisi and my wife offered to the image called Kalagyaung in monk Kunte's monastery 18 slaves bought with the produce of our own labour and not inherited from our parents, namely, Nga Myo and his six sons Nga Tha Lôn, Nga Than Bôn, Nga Para Bôk, Nga

* Designations of petty officials.
† Land dedicated for religious purposes.
‡ This means literally an Indian monastery. All monasteries built of brick and mortar were so called at that time, thus showing that masonry was introduced from India along with several other elements of civilization.

Kan Gu, Nga Dwe, and Nga Myo; O Twe; O Bye and his three sons Nga Tan Lin, Nga Ka Yi and Nga Tin; O Wa, his daughter O Bya Hauk and his son Nga Pôn She; Nga Pyaung and his son Nga Ywe; and O Wun Mu. The witnesses present at the dedication were Saya Nga Kala Thin, Nga Thu Yein Thin, monk Nga Thanga Thin, Nga Se Ya Yin, Nga Pye Thin, Ta Hna Lôn Thin, O Mein Pa, mahout Nga San Pa, Nga Pyi Ya Thin, Nga Naing Ngan Thin, Bala Thingyan, Mi Ya, Nga Ma Ta Thin, Than Pa De, Pan But Ngè, Nga Pan Han Thin, Nga Hla Thin, monk Lawkapyinnya, monk Nadi. . . . ."

No. (2).

Locality.—Within the group of pagodas on the west bank of the stream.

Date.—552 Sakkarâj (1190 A.D.).

Founder.—Wife of Kyan Thaing.*

Substance of inscription.—Dedication of paddy lands and slaves.

IN accordance with the wishes of three monks, namely, Mahâthera Bajjabuddhi, Mahâ Pandita and Agga Pandita, Kyan Thaing's wife offered to the eastern and western monasteries the Apitan land measuring 30 *pès*, the Taungbyan land measuring 20 *pès*, and the Ngaradin land measuring 50 *pès*, allotting 50 *pès* to each monastery. The following slaves were dedicated to the large pagoda and the small cave, namely, Pantaya O Zwe; her daughters O Mi, O Myauk, O Byi Wa and O Lut; her aunts Pantaya O Na and O Paung Laung; Pantaya Ein and daughter O Chè Chein; Pantaya O Thaik; Pantaya O Su and daughter O Mye; her aunt O Swin and daughter; total 14 women. Besides these there were five men, namely, drummer † Nga Pôn Ti, drummer Nga Pôn Daw, drummer Kunama and sons Ngà Yauk Lwè and Nga Yin Ma. The slaves dedicated to the cave built by *Ywathugyi* Pataya were: Nga . . . . . . and wife O Chit Pwè; drummer Nga Kin Ga, his wife Thu Mattari, his son Nga Kauk Sit, his younger brother Nga Tat Pyi, and his sister O Kan That; Pantaya Thani and daughter O Hla Bu; Pantaya Kali; Pantaya Yatthi and daughter O Ma Hla; Pantaya U Mè and daughter O Myet Hla; drummer Nga Ti Ta and drummer Nga Kun Ta; total 16 slaves. Besides these the whole of the villagers of Pôndaw were dedicated. The slaves dedicated

---

* This is not an ordinary name, but the designation of a patrician, and from the date of the inscription, the bearer must have been a minister of the reign of Narapatisithu.

† These slaves had to beat the drum on festive days. They occupied whole villages in Burmese times. In the Pagan district there is a village called Sidi (drummers). Then there are others called Letlôk (sweepers and weeders), Sungyet (those who cook the rice-offerings), and Pagan-yat (those who wash the plates and cups).

to . . . . were Nga Pôn Bye, his wife Ma Bye, his daughter O Thwe, and his sister O Na Lôn; and two *pès* of paddy-land were also dedicated in order that these four slaves might make rice-offerings with the produce thereof. The slaves dedicated to . . . . were drummers Nga Myet Mè, Nga Pan Tu, Nga U, Nga Sein, Nga Pyinnya and Nga . . . . . .; Pantaya O Mi; Pantaya O Kyan; Pantaya Tan Bu; Pantaya . . . .

No. (3).

Locality.—Within the group of monasteries on the west bank of the stream.

Date.—585 Sakkarâj (1223 A.D.).

Founder.—Daughter of Kyan Thaing.

Substance of inscription.—Dedication of paddy lands and slaves.

HAVING no father or heir to inherit my estate, I dedicate on this the 11th waning Pyatho, 585 Sakkarâj, Monday, the whole of the villagers of Nga Myindaung, a tank and a paddy-field measuring 40 *pès* for the upkeep of the recumbent image on the eastern side of my cave and of the image erected by monk Pwagyi. For this my good deed may I in every form of existence be replete with truth, wisdom, diligence, charity, and desire to become a Buddha. May those who injure or destroy my offering suffer in all the eight principal hells, namely, Sañjîvo, Kāḷasutto, Saṅghâto, Roruvo, Mahâroruvo, Tapano, Patāpano, and Avîci. The witnesses present at the offering were: Saya Ka, monks Thetadithapamauk, Nyanateiktha, Thudamayinthi, Thatparotheikki, Taunglat, Anandanyanabôkdi, Thudamalinga, Tilawkasaduyin, Dhammayazathiri. . . . .

No. (4).

Locality.—On the south side of a road which is about 200 feet from the two Kunsaw pagodas on the west bank of the Wetkyi-in stream.

Date.—592 Sakkarâj (1230 A.D.).

Founder.—Banker Minyazathuyanzeya.*

Substance of inscription.—Dedication of paddy-land and pagoda slaves.

WITH a view to promote the interests of the three Gems, namely, Buddha, his law, and monkhood, the banker Minyazathuyanzeya

* This is not a name but a title. Those of the wealthy class who enjoyed royal favour obtained titles and insignia of rank.

dedicated on Monday, the 14th waxing Tazaungmôn, 592 Sakkarâj, the following pagoda slaves, namely, Nga Pyi, Nga Pa Ze Wa, Nga Letkana, his son Nga Pyi, his younger brother Pa Gôn . . . .

. . . .

A paddy-field measuring 60 *pès* was also dedicated, and the banker directed that . . . .

. . . .

The total number of slaves was nine. The dedication was made in the presence of monks Thingyi . . . .

. . . .

No. (5).—Obverse.

Locality.—In a brick monastery within the Wetkyi-in group of monasteries which is about 800 feet south-west of the Shwezigôn pagoda.

Date.—591 Sakkarâj (1229 A.D.).

Founder.—*Tagagyi** and his mother.

Substance of inscription.—Dedication of paddy-lands, slaves and cows.

On Thursday, the 10th waxing Pyatho, 591 Sakkarâj, *Tagagyi* and his mother made the following offerings to the pagoda, cave and monasteries at Kyauktadaing, and to Buddha, his law, and monkhood: namely, Môksogyôn paddy-land measuring 300 *pès*, Nwèin paddy-land measuring 100 *pès*; 21 slaves belonging to her adopted son Nga Hlauk Thin, namely, Nga Pan Dcik of Kalamè village and son Nga Pa Yin; Nga Pa Paw and two sons Nga Pyi and Nga Hmyin Lè; his uncle Nga Sein, nephew Nga Yauk U, uncle Nga Wa, brothers Nga Than, Nga Tôn, Nga Pa Ngè and Nga Twe; Nga San Tha, his wife Ya Bwe, son Nga Ta, brothers Nga Ma and Nga Yaung, sister O Kywin, daughter O Kyaung Che, aunt O Mwè and niece O Lôn. Besides these the following slaves were dedicated: namely, Nga Ra Ywa Pè, wife Ni Tan, son Ka Ta, brothers Nga Pyi, Nga Yaung, and Nga Chan, sisters Ya Zi and A Zi; Yin Mwe's wife; Yin Ta's wife; his son Tè Ta, brother Tin Za and sister Pin Wi; Kalabu, his wife Hi Tu, daughter Eik Si; Mu Bya Ngè's son Nga Pu Gan and his brother Nga Twe; Ko Tu, his wife Kan Nu, son Thôk Tara, and sister O Set Che; Thin Go Hè, his wife Thu La Na, daughter Ku Kan and granddaughter Chat

---

* Donor of a religious institution.

Tu; San Nu; Na Yan; Tat Taw; drummer Me Ta, Lin Ga and daughters Pu Ni and another; Ku Ki and son; Nga Pôn Sôn and wife O Sôn; O Pôn and daughter U Lôn; O Bu, her daughter O Chat Hmyo, sister . . . . (last line).

REVERSE.

"May the light of their eyes fail them, and may the earth swallow them into its bowels. Let none molest these my offerings throughout the period of the Religion. May all those who approve of my good deed partake with me of its merits. The offerings made by me are 400 *pès* of paddy-land, 66 slaves, and 40 cows." On Saturday, the 8th waxing Tagu, 594 Sakkarâj, Thakin Pwa, the monk, dedicated the following as pagoda slaves: Nga Sa Ba, his daughter O Sôn and son Nga Paung; Nga Pyi Wa; Nga Pyi Wa Nape; Nga Kala; Nga Palè; Nga Pwa; Nga Pè Gu; Nga Pya Tho; and Nga Than; total 11. On the 5th waxing of Kasôn, 600 Sakkarâj, Nga Pu's wife offered . . . . . . pieces of cloth and 20 *pès* of paddy-land; Nga Kya Chin Thin Be offered 200 *pès* of paddy-land; Nga Kya Chin Thin 10 *pès*. . . . . (last two lines).

NO. (6).

Locality.—In the ruins of a brick monastery about 700 feet west of the Shwezigôn pagoda.

Date.—654 Sakkarâj (1292 A.D.).

Founder.—Myinzaing Thinkaya.*

[This inscription is so obliterated that, with the exception of the date and the name of its author, nothing can be made out connectedly. It consists of only nine lines.]

NO. (7).

Locality.—On a hillock standing on the east bank of Wetkyi-in stream, about 500 feet south-east of the Shwegyaung group of monasteries.

Date.—758 Sakkarâj (1396 A.D.).

Founder.—Saw Taw U.†

Substance of inscription.—Building of a monastery and dedication of paddy-lands thereto.

* This is the eldest of the three Shan brothers who founded the States of Myinzaing, Metkaya and Pinlè in 1298 A.D. In proof of this fact the Hmannan Yazawin quotes this inscription.

† Lesser Queen of Minkyizwasawkè of Ava.

AFTER having acquired every virtue, conquered every enemy of darkness and passion, and saved every man and *devâ* deserving of salvation, while seated on the throne beneath the banyan tree which germinated the same day which gave him birth, the Buddha passed away to Nirvâna. On Monday, the 5th waxing of Tazaungmôn, 758 Sakkarâj, Saw Taw U, Queen of Minkyizwasawkè of Ava, the glorious and powerful king entitled Sîritribhavanâdityâpavarapanditâdhammarâjâ, with a view to avoid the dangers of *samsaro* and in order to promote the interests of the Religion during its period of 5,000 years, built a beautiful monastery with concrete flooring for the residence of the eminent *Mahâthera* Pinlè. The monastery was erected a short time after the queen was rewarded with the myozaship of Pagan. Moreover, the queen dedicated the following garden land for the maintenance of the presiding monk, at the request of an official named Thilwa. At the *zayat* called Yanaungmyin, which stands on the north side of the Shwezigôn pagoda, the queen entreated His Majesty to perform in her behalf the consecration ceremony, and His Majesty accordingly poured out the water out of a bejewelled gold cup weighing 30 ticals while repeating the prayer that he and the queen and their eight sons might always be together in their future existences. The garden-land thus dedicated is known as Padethanyin. It extends from Thettawshe monastery to Myaukseikpin west of the Eindawya pagoda; thence southwards to the main stream; thence westwards to the Tilaungpingo hill; thence further westward to the monastery built by Thamadarit; thence north-westward to the temple of the Kyauktaw *nat*. The northernmost limit is the landing-stage behind the Shwezigôn pagoda and the southernmost limit is the northern boundary of Kanga garden, namely, ... (last line).

NO. (8).—OBVERSE.

Locality.—Within the Tazaung group of monasteries.

Date.—770 * Sakkarâj (1408 A.D.).

Founder.—Tazaung Mibaya.†

Substance of inscription.—Building of a monastery and dedication of village lands and palm trees thereto.

May the Religion prevail!

ON Tuesday, the 5th waxing of Tabaung, 770 Sakkarâj, the queen built a monastery and dedicated to it the villages of Kanbè, con-

* This date is evidently wrong and is probably meant for 778. The Hmannanyazawin quotes this inscription and notices the mistake, for on the reverse the Mibaya 'wishes' her two former husbands to partake of the merit of her benefactions and her third and last husband did not ascend the throne until 778 Sakkârj. This inscription is quoted also in the Yazawin compiled by Mahasithu the Twinthin Wun.

† Queen of Tayapya, of Mingaung I, and lastly of Mohnyinmindaya of Ava.

sisting of two main villages of that name and two subsidiary villages called Pyuywa and Kyeganmôksoywa. The boundaries of this group of villages are: eastward up to the Myitkaing Queen's monastery land; northward to the Taungbya rocks; thence northwards to the Kônyo rocks; thence further north to the Cha stream; thence in the same direction to a grove of trees; and thence to the Letpan tank; thence westward to a heap of stones piled up on an abandoned plantation; thence to the Ingyin rocks; thence to the Taungngè hill; thence to a ridge; thence still westward to the twin *nabè* trees; thence to the Kônyandwin pillar; thence to a large *tapase* tree; and thence to Yedwet stream. The western boundary commences from the Yedwet stream; thence southward to a triangular prism-shaped pillar; thence eastward to a small hill; thence southward to the Nanteintaungshin pillar; thence in the same direction to a pillar close by a palm tree; thence still southward to the pillar near the twin *pauk* trees. The southern boundary commences from the pillar near the twin *pauk* trees to the pillar at the Thategyaung monastery; thence eastward to the ridge forming a boundary of the Myitkaingdaungma land. The tract enclosed within these boundaries includes 230 *pès* of low-lying paddy-land and 3,000 *pès* of high land, or altogether 3,230 *pès*. Out of the usufruct of this tract of land, 20 ticals of silver (per annum) is to be paid to the administrators thereof; one and a quarter baskets of sample paddy are to be given for basket hire * and one-sixty-fourth of the produce in kind as Government revenue. . . . . (one line). "In accordance with the usual practice, 50 "*pès* of land are to be set apart for the rice-offerings. Let the over-"seers of the land bring in their usual monthly supply of fuel and two "baskets of charcoal each in the winter months, and see that when "cattle and game are killed, the administrators of the land are given "the hide and ribs, *Pyizo* the rumps, Thugyi the humps, and the "*Kyeza* the throat. Should any dispute arise in respect of the "land, let the overseers act as my representatives and bear the "costs. This has always been the custom in the Kanbè group of "villages."

The three villages of Indaung, Kandein, and Chaunggauk, together with their subsidiary villages, namely, Kyauksaukngè and Inbingyaungngè, were also dedicated to the monastery, free from the incumbrance of an annual revenue payable to Government and amounting to 23·313 ticals of silver. The boundaries of the land pertaining to these villages are: north, the Kywèyat village; east, the Kyaungywa village lands; south, the Chaunggauk village; west, the Kanialat village lands. The boundaries of Chaunggauk village

* That is to say for the use of a standard basket for measuring the outturn of grain.

are: east, the Pwingawa and Pindalè lands; south, the Pindalè and Ngatabôn lands; west, Pwa Saw's monastery land, Shweônhmin land, and the Nanywa village lands. Each of these three villages contains about 3,300 palm trees. It is customary for the thugyi, the overseers, and palm climbers of these three villages to hear the sermons delivered at the royal monastery on the full-moon day of Wagaung. If they fail to attend at the monastery at the beginning and conclusion of Lent, they are deprived of the privilege of sharing in the produce of the land and palm trees. Should the presiding monk of the royal monastery visit them, they have to build for him a temporary residence and provide him with the necessaries of life as well as two lengths of rope * each, and two baskets of pickled tea and two cows or goats at the beginning and end of the toddy tapping season. Besides this, whenever any overseer or toddy climber dies, the presiding monk receives 30 ticals of silver, and in the case of any one subordinate to them, one-ninth of the amount. It is moreover customary for the men who erected the boundary pillars and marks to point out the palm trees to the climbers while leading the way lance in hand. These climbers are called Tandawathi. Each climber is rewarded with a quarter basket of refined treacle, another of good jaggery, one-eighth basket of cleaned rice and a fowl. The revenue collectors receive the palm buds.† The revenue is 20 per cent. The collectors are rewarded with five ticals of silver each. The collectors have to administer to the wants of visitors from the monastery and their relatives, and give 20 ticals of silver out of their fees and perquisites, as well as a portion of any cow or goat killed. The revenue payable from Chaunggauk consists of . . . .

Reverse.

The Kyakat village lands in Taungzin circle, together with the palm trees standing thereon, were dedicated to the Kyaungdawu pagôda for the purpose of making the daily offerings of lights to it. The boundaries of these lands are demarcated with masonry pillars at the four corners. When the toddy farmer of the village dies, it is customary for his heirs to give 20 ticals of silver, one basket of pickled tea, and a pig to the abbot of the monastery. The farmer has to pay his respects to the abbot at the monastery at the beginning and conclusion of Lent on pain of losing his position. This refers only to the toddy farmer of Kyakat village. "Whoever destroys these my offerings, whether king, queen, noble-

* These ropes are usually made with the fibre obtained from the midribs of the leaves of the toddy palm and are intended for use at the monastery wells.

† More correctly the half-developed leaves used for writing on.

man, official, or commoner, may he or she fall repeatedly into the saltwater pot in the Uthataret hell, suffer every form of punishment and incur the curses and imprecations of all kings. May his or her possessions disappear altogether from existence like salt thrown into the middle of a large river from a boat, or like a handful of refined cotton thrown into the fire. May he in his next existence find himself in the eight principal and 128 lesser hells, suffering a hundred, a thousand, a ten thousand, a hundred thousand, a million times more violently than Dewadat.* Should he again become a man, may he be leprous and diseased, poor and needy, failing in every undertaking, despised and shunned by all men. Should he become even a king, may his subjects rebel against him and may he fall in battle with disgrace. On the other hand, may my ancestors before me and descendants after me, as well as my other relatives, the monks and all other men, abundantly reap the benefits of this my good deed. May my two former husbands, Sinbyuyin † and Mingaung, partake of our merit equally with us. May every creature inhabiting every region, from the highest abode of *nats* to the lowest *avíci* hell, be benefited by this good deed. May our guardian *nats* also, and the guardian *nats* of the Religion, the earth, the trees, and all other *nats* of the universe, have their share of the merit. Poison cannot be said to be very destructive to life, because it can kill only one; but the poison of the monkhood can destroy all monks and laymen and send them to the *avíci* hell.‡ If any one misappropriates any land offered to the monkhood, either by himself or by others, he will for a period of a hundred thousand *kalpas* become an ant or vermin in that land; the saving influence of 20 Buddhas will not reach him; he will have to pass through the 500 existences of ogres and will ultimately perish; . . . . (last line).

No. (9).

Locality.—Within the Tazaung *kyaungdaik* (or group of monasteries).

Date.—777 Sakkarâj (1415 A.D.).

Founders.—Mingaung I of Ava and his Queen Tazaung Mibaya.

Substance of inscription.—Building of two monasteries and dedication of 19 villages thereto.

---

* The brother-in-law and adversary of Gautama Buddha.

† Tayepya of Ava.

‡ This sentence is a variation of the 61st verse of the Lokaniti, which says that ordinary poison is not regarded as such; but that the property of the monkhood (if misappropriated) is deemed *the* poison, because ordinary poison kills only once, while the other kills repeatedly (that is to say, it affects the offender at every re-birth).

BEING desirous of attaining Nirvâna after enjoying their existences as human beings and as *devâs*, Their Majesties the King and Chief Queen of Ava erected two monasteries at the most auspicious moment* on the forenoon of Tuesday, the 5th waxing of Tabaung, 777 Sakkarâj. When the buildings were completed the king requested the queen to conduct the dedication. The queen replied saying: "O King! among the monkhood it is usual for the "disciple to follow the master; likewise for the children to follow "their parents, and for the servants to follow the lord." On hearing these words the king comprehended their import and conducted the ceremony in person. The following villages were then dedicated to the two monasteries, namely, Daungthitsi, Myaungsindè, Lèsha, Kanbè, Pyuywa, Minkyaganmôksoywa, Letpangan, Taganzin, Paukthaukpyetkan, Panlaingkuywa, Thapanyegyi, which is situated on the south-east of Popa hill, Indaung, Kandein, Chaunggauk, Kyaungngè, Inbin, Taungzin-Kyakat, Pakan-Nyaungdwin and Kanmè, total 19 villages. These were dedicated in the order named. The Governors of Pagan and Talôkmyo both claimed possession of the three Sindè villages, and as no satisfactory settlement of the dispute can be made, Their Majesties included these villages in the offering.† Out of the usufruct of these village lands, the keepers thereof shall receive 10 ticals of silver per village in addition to the usual court fees, harbour dues, cart tolls, stall rents, and petty taxes, also 50 pieces of lead for each female slave bought or sold and 100 for each male slave. Besides this they shall receive the equivalent of a leg of beef or pork whenever a top-knot-making or ear-boring or *nat* festival is held. The following scale should be followed when offerings are made to the presiding monks of the monasteries: in case of death of an overseer, namely, *kungan, pyizo*, thugyi or *myedaing*, 30 ticals of silver; *kundi*, 15 ticals; *kundidôn*, 7½ ticals; *tamaukkunzôn*, 3¾ ticals; *maungkunzôn* or *tamaungdôn*, 1⅞ ticals. When a presiding monk visits a village, the thugyi shall build for him a temporary monastery at a cost of 140 ticals of silver raised by subscription, his contribution being 75 ticals, and shall not include this sum in the revenue payable from the village, which he shall always pay in full in person. At the beginning and conclusion of the toddy-tapping season each village shall present to the presiding monks of the monasteries the equivalent of 3 viss of pork. The thugyis and other overseers of the village lands shall personally conduct all legal affairs regarding

* The Burmese are firm believers in astrology. Soothsayers of note always enjoyed the king's favour and they were consulted in all matters temporal and spiritual.

† A quaint form of deciding a judicial dispute to the satisfaction of all parties. Whoever has the last claim will reap in a future existence the merit accruing from the benefactions, the party who actually makes the offering coming in for a share.

their respective charges and the allowances payable to them shall be as recorded herein. The fees of the assessor shall be a piece of cloth and 25 pieces of lead in the case of a field having a sowing capacity of half a basket; 50 pieces in the case of *mayin* paddy-lands; 25 pieces in the case of vegetable gardens having a sowing capacity of one basket of soy beans . . . . . On Saturday, the 9th waxing of Pyatho, 778 Sakkarâj . . . .(last line).

No. (10).

Locality.—Within the Tazaung *kyaungdaik.*

Date.—778 Sakkarâj (1416 A. D.).

Founders.—Mingaung I, his Queen Tazaung Mibaya, and Thihapade, a nobleman.

Substance of inscription.—Dedication of paddy-lands to the Three Gems.

ON Sunday, the 13th waning of Nadaw, 778 Sakkarâj, Their Majesties dedicated to the Religion a piece of land whose ownership was long disputed by different parties. It measures altogether 55 *pès,* half of which is situated between Yabè, Kyabo, and Kadaung villages, and the other half in the last village. Its north-eastern boundary is a piece of land called Peikthana. It is bounded on the south by the Kaukla land and on the west by a fishery. This fishery and the paddy-lands adjoining it are included in the offering. On Wednesday, the 9th waning Nadaw, 778 Sakkarâj, the following land was separately dedicated to the "Law," namely, 35 *pès* of paddy-land south of Talaingdè village on the bank of the river. It is bounded on the south by the Kyabo road; north-west by a channel leading to a fishery; north by Myitkôn; north-east by Shwepaukpinzu; south-west by Kyebingwa; east by a large *tein* tree; and south by the Mahathaman land.

The offerings to be made out of the usufruct of this paddy-land are eight baskets of paddy, 400 pieces of lead, 40 pieces for the collector, four pots of rice-offering each containing one-sixteenth basket, and five smoked fish. On Monday, the 1st waning of Nadaw, 778 Sakkarâj, the Lèthangètaung fishery, situated on the north-west of Ywathitkyi village, together with its adjoining alluvial lands measuring altogether 300 *pès* and including 27½ *pès* of *mayin* paddy and 27½ *pès* of *than** paddy-lands was also dedicated to the "Law." On Tuesday, the 1st waxing of Pyatho, 778 Sakkarâj, Thihapade, the nobleman, offered the Minkyegan land containing 3,000 *pès* to his royal mother's † monastery. The land is bounded on the

* Archaic form of *kaukkyi* or main crop wet-weather rice.

† Pagan Mibaya, eldest daughter of King Mohnyin Mindaya, and wife of the then Governor of Pakan.

south by the Letpangan hill, and from a masonry pillar erected on this hill the boundary runs along the bank of a stream to another prism-shaped masonry pillar; thence to the Letpagan tank; thence northwards to a *thitnyo* tree on the southern bank of a stream; thence further northwards to a heap of stones; thence proceeding in the same direction to another heap of stones; thence to a masonry pillar at Ngapôngan; thence northwards to the twin *nabè* trees; thence to a large *tapase* tree; thence to the Pakanlan stream and along this stream to a masonry pillar at Saingdalin-Kyibinhla; thence southwards to a large tamarind tree north of Chaungmagaing village; thence further southwards to the headwaters of the Thanbongè stream; thence still southwards to the junction of three roads; thence in the same direction to a masonry pillar; and thence to the Natein range of hills. On Tuesday, the full moon of Pyatho, 778 Sakkarâj . . . . (last line).

NO. (11).—OBVERSE.

Locality.—Within the Wetkyi-in *kyaungdaik.*

Date.—804 Sakkarâj (1442 A.D.).

Founder.—Governor of Taungdwin* and his wife.

Substance of inscription.—Construction of monastery, offering to it of full text of the Tripitaka, and dedication to the same of garden and paddy lands, villages and slaves.

"I adore the Three Gems!"

THIRIZEYATHU, Governor of Taungdwin, is a most ardent devotee of the three incomparable "Gems." He is a grandson of Thihapade, nephew of King Mohnyin Mindaya and brother-in-law of the celebrated conqueror Mingyikyawzwa. He is the protector of the weak and distressed from all quarters of the earth, the promoter of the interests of the people, and an able upholder of the traditions of a long race of rulers. He has passed through several prosperous existences in the cycle of *samsaro* and is as glorious and resplendent as the sun in its zenith. From the time of his conception he was destined to excel in wisdom and foresight, courage and power, and proper discrimination in the performance of works of merit. Accordingly in the 1986th year after the Buddha's attainment of Nirvâna (1442 A.D.), the Governor and his wife,† daughter of Sinbyuyin Thihathu, being desirous of attaining Nirvâna, performed the following works of merit. In the year 800 Sakkarâj, during the reign of Mohnyin Mindaya, who ascended the throne of Ava on the morning of Thursday, the 10th waning of Nayôn, 788 Sakkarâj,

* Known in history as Minthirizeyathuya.

† His second wife, Sawbyichantha, granddaughter of Mingaung I.

a meeting of pandits from different parts of the empire, who were learned in the law, was convened in a large pavilion on a plain north of the palace in the presence of the royal family and ministers. High festivals were held on that occasion and lavish offerings of elephants, ponies, cattle, slaves, clothing and provisions were made. The king then, in consultation with the pandits, commanded the abolition of the current era.* At the most auspicious moment on the morning of Sunday, the 13th waxing of Tagu, of the 6th year of the new era founded by his royal uncle (Mohnyin) Mindaya and aunt Mibaya Saw, the governor erected a most beautiful monastery with several spires, turrets, roofs, and porches, on a highly favoured spot east of the Tetnwè stream and west of the Shwezigôn pagoda, in order that the Religion might flourish during its allotted period of 5,000 years. A wall was subsequently built round it and the building was decorated with various statues and paintings. In the monastery was placed for the benefit of students of the "Law" copies of the whole of the Tripitaka, which were purchased with the price of the hair from the head of the governor's second wife. On the full-moon day of the same month, while this good deed was being performed, the governor succeeded in annexing the country called Thokôk or Kale. On the 7th waxing of the following month he captured Thonganbwa, ruler of Maw territory, which includes the eleven principalities of Maingmyè and Maingmaw, Mohnyin, Chigyinwut near the seacoast, Maingkale, Manipur, Kachin Hills, Maingtein, Maingpyin, Maingti, Maingna, Maingmyin, Cha-o, Maingnyo, Mainglo, Maingthaw, Maingya, Maingchaing, Maingkôn, Maingpôn, Maingyo and Maingchi. Thonganbwa and the chief of Kale were soon afterwards taken by the governor to the presence of King Narapadi, who was then sojourning in a temporary palace on Minwun hill, and on Sunday, the 12th waxing of Kasôn, several elephants and ponies and a quantity of jewellery obtained from Kale were presented to the king. Narapadi was highly pleased with the governor's success, and as return presents awarded a young elephant called Chit Naung, a pair of mother-of-pearl bracelets set with precious stones, another of gold set with emeralds, and a village called Sinbyu in Pakan circle yielding a revenue of 40 ticals of silver. This village was subsequently dedicated by the governor and his wife to the monastery erected by them on the east bank of the Tetnwè stream in Pagan. Subsequently, on Wednesday, the 13th waning Tazaungmôn, 804 Sakkarâj, the governor's wife, wishing to reach Nirvâna, where all cease to exist, and to promote the cause of the Religion, begged of the king to grant her the Ngatayaw village in Pakan as

* This abolition does not seem to have been recognized for any length of time.

a boon. The presents brought by her on that occasion were: Chit Naung, the elephant which was obtained as a royal reward when Thonganbwa of Maw was taken captive; another elephant called Pyilalin; a pair of mother-of-pearl bracelets set with precious stones; a silver drinking-bowl weighing 70 ticals, which was borne to the royal presence by the Lawa Thugyi; and a jasper contained in a covered gold tray borne by the Thinthi Thugyi. At the time of the presentation the Heir-apparent Mahâthihathuya knelt on the right side of the throne, Thonganbwa of Maw was on the left, and Thirizeyathuya, the Governor of Taungdwin, was between them and in a line with them, while the ministers and court officials were in their proper places behind. His Majesty then commanded Naratheinga, a secretary, to approach, and after having questioned him as to the particulars of the boon prayed for, granted it to the governor and his wife, and to confirm the gift poured out a cup of water and celebrated it by the beating of drums and cymbals . . . . (one line).

REVERSE.

"By virtue of this our meritorious deed, may we, prior to our ultimate attainment of Nirvâna as Buddhas and chiefs of the three kinds of superior beings, and while we are still on the vast sea of *samsaro*, be successful in every undertaking; may all our wishes be easily fulfilled; may we in our next existence become suzerains of the universe, and rulers of the *devâs* in our subsequent existences; finally, may we become Buddhas able to ferry over all our relatives and friends as well as others to Nirvâna and ultimately to reach it ourselves."

"The dedicated paddy-lands in Pakan circle measure altogether 422½ *pès*; garden lands, 3,800 *pès*; pasture lands, 20,633 *pès*; *mayin* paddy-lands, 14,933 *pès*; palm trees, 2,633. The eastern boundary of the lands runs from Alègan to Lè-o, and thence to a large *tanaung* tree. The south-eastern boundary starts from the Sape land to Wadan, Ywabu, Wabu, Thamayo, Ywalèget and Lègaing. The southern boundary runs from the Kyauktaung land to Thitpu, Lintagaung, and Gyauknet. The south-western boundary runs along the edge of Wetpôk land to Kunlat-Kinmyin. The western boundary starts from the Yaw land to Thidutpin-Yedwet, Mônbin-Tetkaw, Ngapôntè and Thahin land up to the summit of Lindaung hill. The north-west boundary runs from the Sachi land to Kyauk-o, Chaungthwe, and Ngasat-in. The north boundary proceeds from the Kyaukmauk land to Kyauksin, Kyauktaga, and Kyaukpagôk hill up to the headwaters of the Pègyaung stream. The north-east boundary runs along the edge of the Pyathi land to

Siyin and Nyaungyin. Within the said boundaries there are many pieces of waste land. Whenever any of these are brought under cultivation they shall be included in the cultivated portions above mentioned. If the overseers concerned fail to do so, may they suffer every punishment according to the law promulgated by our Buddha. On the other hand, if they act honestly in regard to the reclamation of waste land, may they share in our merit. The Ngatayaw land in Pakan circle measures altogether 504½ *pès* and includes 2 *pès* of *mayin* land west of Letpanin village and south of Saukpuya fishery, 2 *pès* of the same kind of land north of the fishery, and ½ *pè* of wet-weather paddy land north of Inngè. It is bounded on the east by the land offered by Mingyikyawzwa and by Niyin land at Kaingywa; south-east by the Minywa village lands; south by the Sulaban monastery land; south-west by the land offered by King Sithu to the Kugyi pagoda; west by the land allotted to a number of natives of India* by the Gyaingnet monastery and Pabu monastery lands; north-west by the land allotted to the royal elephanteers; north by the Migyaungdin land; and north-east by the Tagaing land. These boundaries are thus recorded to obviate future disputes. Let not the Thugyis and other overseers of our lands conceal any portion of the same. Should they do so, may they suffer in the nethermost hell according to the law laid down by the Buddha. But should they report faithfully any reclamation of waste lands, may they share the merit with us."

A sedan chair, a cast-iron fire tray, a spittoon, a kettle, a lounge and a cot were placed in the monastery for the use of the presiding monk. A white umbrella was erected over the image standing in front of the monastery. The necessary repairs are to be made out of the usufruct of the Myaing and Ngatayaw lands. One-fifth of the same should be set apart for offerings of rice to the image in the monastery and for repairs to the building itself. One-fifth of the remainder is to be offered to the presiding monk and the balance to the clerks and slaves of the monastery. All overseers shall be appointed by the presiding monk and subordinate monks in consultation, and they are in like manner to supervise the repairing of the monastery, the out-buildings and walls, and the replacing of damaged documents in the monastery library by new ones.

"May those who fail to follow these my instructions suffer in proportion to their knowledge of the 'Law.' On the other hand, may those who follow them share in my merit. The following

* Probably colonists from Southern India. The list of books given in this inscription contains several names of Sanskrit works.

books are placed in the monastery for the enlightenment of all comers":—

Pârajikakaṇḍa.
Pâcittyâdibikkhûnîvibhaṅga. 1442
Vinayamahâvagga.
Vinayacûḷavagga.
Vinayaparivâra.
Pârajikakaṇḍa aṭṭhakathâ.
Pâcittyâdi aṭṭhakathâ.
Pârajikakaṇḍa ṭîkâ.
Terasakaṇḍa ṭîkâ.
Vinayasaṅgaha aṭṭhakathâ (1).
Vinayasaṅgaha aṭṭhakathâ (2).
Kaṅkhâvitaraṇî aṭṭhakathâ.
Khuddasikkhâ ṭîkâ (old).
Khuddasikkhâ ṭîkâ (new).
Kaṅkhâ ṭîkâ (new).
Vinayagaṇṭhipada.
Vinaya uttarasiñcaya aṭṭhakathâ.
Vinayasiñcaya ṭîkâ (new).
Vinayakhandhaniddesa.
Dhammasaṅgaṇî.
Vibhaṅga.
Dhâtukathâ.
Puggalapaññatti.
Kathâvatthu.
Mûlayamaka.
Indriyayamaka.
Tikapaṭṭhâna.
Dukatikapaṭṭhâna.
Dukapaṭṭhâna.
Aṭṭhasâlinî aṭṭhakathâ.
Sammohavinodanî aṭṭhakathâ.
Pañcapakaraṇa aṭṭhakathâ.
Abhidhammâ anuṭîkâ.
Abhidhammatthasaṅgaha aṭṭhakathâ.
Abhidhammatthasaṅgaha ṭîkâ.
Abhidhammatthavibhâvanî ṭîkâ.
Sîlakkhandha.
Mahâvagga.
Pâtheyya.
Silakkhandha aṭṭhakathâ.
Mahâvagga aṭṭhakathâ.
Pâtheyya aṭṭhakathâ.

Sîlakkhandha ṭîkâ.
Mahâvagga ṭîkâ.
Pâtheyya ṭîkâ.
Mûlapaṇṇâsa.
Mûlapaṇṇâsa aṭṭhakathâ.
Mûlapaṇṇâsa ṭîkâ.
Majjhimapaṇṇâsa.
Majjhimapaṇṇâsa aṭṭhakathâ.
Majjhimapaṇṇâsa ṭîkâ.
Uparipaṇṇâsa.
Uparipaṇṇâsa aṭṭhakathâ.
Uparipaṇṇâsa ṭîkâ.
Sagâthâvaggasaṁyutta.
Sagâthâvaggasaṁyutta aṭṭhakathâ.
Sagâthâvaggasaṁyutta ṭîkâ.
Nidânavaggasaṁyutta.
Nidânavaggasaṁyutta aṭṭhakathâ.
Khandhavaggasaṁyutta.
Khandhavaggasaṁyutta ṭîkâ.
Saḷâyatanavaggasaṁyutta.
Saḷâyatanavaggasaṁyutta aṭṭhakathâ.
Mahâvaggasaṁyutta.
Ekadukatika anguttara.
Catukanipâta anguttara.
Pañcanipâta anguttara.
Chasattanipâta anguttara.
Aṭṭhanavanipâta anguttara.
Dasa ekâdasanipâta anguttara.
Ekanipâta anguttara aṭṭhakathâ.
Dukatikacatukanipâta anguttara aṭṭhakathâ.
Pañcâdi anguttara aṭṭhakathâ.
Anguttara ṭîkâ (1).
Anguttara ṭîkâ (2).
Khuddakapâṭha, text and aṭṭhakathâ.
Dhammapada, text and aṭṭhakathâ.
Udâna, text and aṭṭhakathâ.
Itivuttaka, text and aṭṭhakathâ.
Suttanipâta, text and aṭṭhakathâ.
Vimânavatthu, text and aṭṭhakathâ.
Petavatthu, text and aṭṭhakathâ.
Thera, text and aṭṭhakathâ.
Therî, text and aṭṭhakathâ.
Pâṭhacariya.
Ekanipâtajâtaka aṭṭhakathâ.

Dukanipâtajâtaka aṭṭhakathâ.
Tikanipâtajâtaka aṭṭhakathâ.
Catukapañcachanipâtajâtaka aṭṭhakathâ.
Satta-aṭṭha nava nipâtajâtaka aṭṭhakathâ.
Dasa-ekâdasanipâtajâtaka aṭṭhakathâ.
Dvâdasaterasapakiṇṇakanipâtajâtaka aṭṭhakathâ.
Vîsatijâtaka aṭṭhakathâ.
Jâtattakî-sotattakî-nidâna aṭṭhakathâ.
Cûḷaniddesa.
Cûḷaniddesa aṭṭhakathâ.
Mahâniddesa.
Mahâniddesa aṭṭhakathâ.
Jâtaka ṭîkâ.
Dumajâtaka aṭṭhakathâ.
Apâdâna.
Apâdâna aṭṭhakathâ.
Paṭisambhîdâmagga.
Paṭisambhîdâmagga aṭṭhakathâ.
Paṭisambhîdâmagga gaṇṭhipada.
Visuddhimagga aṭṭhakathâ.
Visuddhimagga ṭîkâ.
Buddhavaṁsa aṭṭhakathâ.
Cariyâpiṭaka aṭṭhakathâ.
Nâmarûpa ṭîkâ (new).
Paramatthavinicchaya ṭîkâ (new).
Mohavicchedanî.
Lokapaññatti.
Mohanayana.
Lokuppatti.
Aruṇavatî.
Chagatidîpanî.
Sahassayaṁsîmâlinî.
Dasavatthu.
Sahassavatthu.
Sîhaḷavatthu.
Peṭakopadesa.
Tathâgatuppatti.
Dhammacakka.
Dhammacakka ṭîkâ.
Dâṭhâdhâtuvaṁsa.
Dâṭhâdhâtuvaṁsa ṭîkâ.
Cûḷavaṁsa.
Dîpavaṁsa.
Thûpavaṁsa.

Anâgatavaṁsa.
Bodhivaṁsa.
Mahâvaṁsa.
Mâhâvaṁsa ṭîkâ.
Dhammadâna.
Mahâkaccâyana.
Nyâsa.
Thanbyin ṭîkâ.
Mahâthera ṭîkâ.
Rûpasiddhi aṭṭhakathâ.
Rûpasiddhi ṭîkâ.
Bâlâvatâra.
Vuttimoggalâna.
Pañcikâmoggalâna.
Pañcikâmoggalâna ṭîkâ.
Kârikâ.
Kârikâ ṭîkâ.
Liṅgatthavivaraṇa.
Liṅgatthavivaraṇa ṭîkâ.
Mukhamattasâra.
Mukhamattasâra ṭîkâ.
Mahâgaṇa.
Cûḷagaṇa.
Abhidhâna.
Abhidhâna ṭîkâ.
Saddaniti.
Cûḷanirutti.
Cûḷasandhivisodhana.
Saddattha (bheda) cintâ.
Saddattha (bheda) cintâ ṭîkâ.
Padasodhana.
Sambandhacintâ ṭîkâ.
Rûpâvatâra.
Saddâvatâra.
Saddhammadîpaka.
Sotamâlinî.
Sambandhamâlinî.
Padâvahâmahâcakka.
Nvâdi (Moggalâna).
Katacâ.
Mahâkâ.
Bâlattajana.
Suttâvali.
Akkharasammoha (chedanî).

Cetiddhînemiparigâthâ.
Samâsataddhitaaṭṭhadîpanî.
Bîjakkhyaṁ.
Kaccâyanasâra.
Bâlapabodhana.
Aṭṭhasâlinî.
Aṭṭhasâlinî nissaya.
Kaccâyana nissaya.
Rûpasiddhi nissaya.
Jâtaka nissaya.
Jâtaka ganṭhi.
Dhammapada ganṭhi nissaya.
Kammavâcâ.
Dhammasatta.
Kalâpapañcikâ.
Kalâpapañcikâ ṭîkâ.
Kalâpasupratiññâsaku ṭîkâ.
Priṇḍo ṭîkâ.
Rattamâlâ.
Rattamâlâ ṭîkâ.
Roganidâna.
Dabraguṇa.
Dabraguṇa (Dravyaguṇa) ṭîkâ.
Chandoviciti.
Candaprutti.
Candrapañcikâra.
Kâmaṇḍakî.
Dhammapaññâpakaraṇa.
Mahosatthi.
Subodhâlaṅkâra.
Subodhâlaṅkâra ṭîkâ.
Tanogabuddhî.
Taṇḍî.
Taṇḍî ṭîkâ.
Caṅkadâsa.
Caṅkadâsa ṭîkâ.
Ariyasaccâvatâra.
Vicitragandha-saddhammanpâya.
Sârasaṅgaha.
Sârapiṇḍa.
Paṭipattisaṅgaha.
Sûlasâra.
Pâlatakka.
Trakkabhâsâ.

Saddakârikâ.
Kasikâprutti.
Palinî.
Saddhammadîpaka.
Satyasatvâvabodha.
Bâlapabodhanapruttikaraṇa.
Atthabyâkhyaṁ (Arthavyâkyaṁ).
Cûḷaniruttimañjûsâ.
Mañjûsâ ṭîkâ byâkhyaṁ.
Anu ṭîkâ byâkhyaṁ.
Pakiṇṇakanikâya.
Catthapayoga.
Matthapayoga.
Rogayatrâ.
Rogayatrâ ṭîkâ.
Satthekavipasvaprakâsa.
Râjamattanta.
Parâsa.
Vakôladdhaja.
Brihajjâtaka.
Brihajjâtaka ṭîkâ.
Daṭhâtuvaṁsa Dâṭhâdhâtuvaṁsa (ṭîkâ).
Patigaviveka ṭîkâ.
Alaṅkâra ṭîkâ.
Calindapañcikâ.
Vedavidhinimittaniruttivaṇṇanâ.
Nirutti byâkhyaṁ.
Vuttodaya.
Vuttodaya ṭîkâ.
Malinapaññâ (Milindapañhâ).
Saratthasaṅgaha.
Amarakosa (Amarakosha) nissaya.
Piṇḍo nissaya.
Kalâpa nissaya.
Roganidâna byâkhyaṁ.
Dabbraguṇa (Dravyaguṇa) ṭîkâ.
Amarakosa (Amarakosha).
Daṇḍî ṭîkâ (1).
Daṇḍî ṭîkâ (2).
Daṇḍî ṭîkâ (3).
Koladhvaja ṭîkâ.
Alaṅkâra.
Alaṅkâra ṭîkâ.
Bhesajjamañjûsâ.

Yuddhajeya.
Yatanaprabha ṭikâ.
Viragdha.
Viragdha ṭikâ.
Culâmaṇisâra.
Râjamattanta ṭikâ.
Mrityuvañcana.
Mahâkâlacakka.
Mahâkâlacakka ṭikâ.
Paraviveka.
Kaccâyanarûpâvatâra.
Pumbharasâri.
Taktâvatâra.
Taktâvatâra ṭikâ.
Nyâyabindhu.
Nyâyabindhu ṭikâ.
Hetubindhu.
Hetubindhu ṭikâ.
Rikkaṇiyayatrâ.
Rikkaṇiyayatrâ ṭikâ.
Barittaratâkara.
Shyârâmitikabya.
Yuttisaṅgaha.
Yuttisaṅgaha ṭikâ.
Sârasaṅgaha nissaya.
Rogayatrâ nissaya.
Roganidâna nissaya.
Saddattha (bheda) cintâ nissaya.
Pârâ nissaya.
Shyâmitikabya nissaya.
Brihajjâtaka nissaya.
Rattamâlânayayuttisaṅgaha nissaya.

INSCRIPTIONS OF PAGAN.

III.—Found at Hngetpyittaung.

No. (1).—Obverse.

Locality.—North of Nyaungu village.

Date.—804 Sakkarâj (1442 A.D.).

Founders.—Thinkaya, Governor of Taungdwin, and his wife.

Substance of inscription.—Dedication of village lands and palm trees to monastery.

On Saturday, the 2nd waning of Nayôn, 804 Sakkarâj, the Governor of Taungdwin, Thinkaya, and his wife obtained as a boon from the king, Mahâthihathuya,* the village of Yinsante, together with the lands pertaining to it, and the palm trees growing thereon. At the time the boon was asked the following presents accompanied the supplicants, namely, an elephantess called Shwethalun, a gold basket set with rubies and two bunches of gold sprays. These lands were dedicated to the royal monastery at Myittha, Pagan. The following personages were present at the time of the supplication of the boon, namely, Sithuya, Thugyi of Kale, brother-in-law of the Chief of Maw, the lord of three white elephants; Princes Nawyata, Uzana, and Sagumin; the ministers; the Shan chiefs and other courtiers. The boundaries of the land are as follows: south, Obyunyaung, Tanaungwun and Wathèbôk; thence to the junction of the Zayet and Kanmya streams; thence to a spot on the Thamôn hill marked with a stone dragon facing west; thence to a stone pillar underneath a *kôkko* tree; thence to a stone dragon placed under a large *nabè* tree at Yaukchi; thence to a stone pillar erected underneath a *gyo* tree on the east bank of the Kanthit stream; thence to a recumbent dragon in front of Nga Chaing Thin's tank; thence to Nyaungbindo, and then along the boundaries of Thittaung and Einshanzauk lands up to the main stream; thence to the Tabutkan pond used by buffaloes; thence to a *yingat* bush overgrown by a *kôkko* tree; thence to the small village of Ngapyitsin; thence to a stone dragon, facing west, built in front of a *nim* tree; thence to a cave; thence to Lindathamya; thence to the stream behind Einbwèswè . . . . Besides the land included within these boundaries, the palm trees standing thereon are also dedicated to the monastery erected by Princess U Min in order that the Religion might flourish for 5,000 years, and in order that the cause of the Three Gems might be promoted.

"May we by virtue of this our present meritorious deed, be enabled to act as guides to the kings and queens of this earth, as well as every nobleman and commoner, and every creature inhabiting every region between the lowest hell and the highest heaven. May we moreover be enabled to disperse every evil. Our daughter joins in our prayer. May those who destroy my offering themselves, or aid and abet others who destroy it, suffer every kind of punishment in the present; and in the future may they pass through the eight principal hells and suffer like the Buddha's tormentor Dewadat, whose bulk of body in hell is equivalent to a distance of 100 days' journey, and who is placed in an iron cage in *avīci* hell facing west and secured with iron spits about the size of an average log and piercing his body crosswise from side to

* This is the title by which King Narapadi was known while he was yet a Prince and 'eater' of Prome.

side and from front to back. May they fail to have the benefit of the saving influence of every succeeding Buddha. May they, even in their present life, be separated from their families and friends, become a deformed *peta* like the steward of Athasha Thate,* who coveted the alms given to the poor, and may they always incur the wrath of the king, be molested by thieves, and be in constant danger from fire . . . . (last line).

No. (2).

Locality.—Within the porch of a pagoda about 500 feet north of the southern group of pagodas.

Date.—577 Sakkarâj (1215 A.D.).

Founder.—Daughter of Nagayit.†

Substance of inscription.—Dedication of pagoda slaves.

On Saturday, the 6th waning of Tazaungmôn, 577 Sakkarâj, the daughter of Nagayit dedicated her personal slaves to the Religion, saying that she had no right of possession over even her own offspring.‡ The names of the slaves are: Sigôn Than, his daughters O Myet Mè, O Lat, U Lôn and Akyun; a young grandson; Nga Kya Thin and his wife O Wa Hnin, daughter O Pa O, sons Nga Pwè, Nga Pyin, and Nga Tha Lôn; O Dôn Ngè and her daughters O Kyi and O Lat, sons O Sôn, O Naing, O Ngè, and O Gala; Nga Pyi; O Lôn and his brother Nga Mwe, sons Nga Pya Lôn and Nga Lat; uncles Nga Ka, Nga Chat Dôn, and Nga La. Besides these personal attendants, other slaves were dedicated, namely, an old woman called Sa Ya; O Kywin; O Paung; O . . . . and O Pet. This dedication was made in the presence of monks Thabyi, Taunglat, Bôkdala . . . . . . , Narasinghakavi, Pananarasi, and Lakkhanâ.

No. (3).

Locality.—About 100 feet west of Kyunbogan monastery.

Date.—636 Sakkarâj (1274 A.D.).

Founders.—Five thugyis or revenue collectors.

* According to a current legend said to have emanated from Gautama Buddha himself and repeated by his disciples, this *thate* or rich man was a citizen of Dvâravatî (the modern Sandoway). One day he held a charitable festival and directed his steward to distribute alms lavishly to the poor and crippled who flocked to it. The steward sent many applicants away empty-handed and his avarice was rewarded with instant deformity and exile in the jungles.

† Nagaraj, an officer in charge of the royal elephants in Zeyatheinka's reign.

‡ This lady was evidently induced to part with her slaves. She could, however, of her own accord dedicate them for religious service as she could dispose of them in whatever way she pleased. Besides slaves, prisoners of war were frequently so dedicated. Religious slaves are always looked down upon and treated as outcasts.

Substance of inscription.—Building of pagoda and caves and dedication of paddy-lands and pagoda slaves.

On Friday, the 14th waning Tawthalin, 583 Sakkarâj (1221 A.D.), Thugyi Kyizin and his wife offered to the monk Winido a complete set of the Tripitaka together with 20 *pès* of paddy-land called Podettheinmyit. On the same day they bought Tauknwèthi, daughter of Ein Thi, as a slave. They moreover dedicated the following slaves to the "Law,"* namely, Nga Set Pa and his son Nga Set, Nga Pwe, Nga Ya, Nga Swa, Nga Pôn and his son Nga Pa Gyi, Nga Naung Ngè, Nga San Pyi, and Nga Yo.

"May those who destroy these our offerings suffer in the *avîci* hell."

On Thursday, the 9th waxing, Tazaungmôn, 596 Sakkarâj (1234 A.D.), Thugyi Shwe Nyaung and his grandson Nga Nyaung Bin dedicated to the image kept in monk Winido's monastery 30 *pès* of paddy-land west of Hngepyittaung hill and mentioned in Thugyi Nga Yit Thin's revenue register, and 20 *pès* in Magyidein village which are mentioned in Thugyi Tithanaw's register; total 50 *pès*.

"May those who destroy our offerings suffer in the *avîci* hell. May they never have the opportunity of beholding any of the succeeding Buddhas. On the other hand, may those who approve of them have a share of our merit."

On Monday, the 7th waxing of Tabaung, 598 Sakkarâj (1236 A.D.), Thugyi Kaungsin built a cave and dedicated the following slaves to look after it in his behalf, namely, Payan Gyi and his brother Payan Ngè. He further dedicated 70 *pès* of paddy-land in Taunglabat village, south-east of Myingôndaing.

"May every one, from the king downward, have a share of my merit accruing from this good work. May those who destroy it be burnt in the *avîci* hell."

On Thursday, the 7th waxing of Kasôn, 602 Sakkarâj (1240 A.D.), Kingathingyan, the Thugyi, built a masonry monastery, and his wife dedicated the Sagu paddy-land measuring 15 *pès* to the three "Gems."

On Thursday, the 3rd waning of Nadaw, 615 Sakkarâj (1253 A.D.), Kingathingyan and wife erected a cave and placed a large image in it. The cave had 4,000 small images on its four sides as well as representations of the Buddha's anterior births. The thugyi and his wife subsequently dedicated to the three "Gems" the following slaves, namely, Ta Ngôn and his son Nga Tha Din, his brothers Nga Pana and Nga Myitsa, Ma Tein Baing and her mother O Thet She, O Ma Kin Thin, and O Kyi Zu Mi. To monk Winido's

* That is to say, to look after the manuscripts and the place where they are kept, as well as the lands, if any, pertaining thereto.

monastery they dedicated the following paddy-lands, namely, 12½ *pès* behind Sadaung village, and the Madaya lands, measuring 350 *pès*; total 412½ *pès*.

On Tuesday, the 11th waning of Nadaw, 636 Sakkarâj 1274 (A.D.), Nga Thit Thin, son of Kingathingyan, the Thugyi, dedicated to the three "Gems" the following paddy-lands on behalf of his deceased wife,* namely, 30 *pès* behind Hngetpyittaung hill and mentioned in Thugyi Nga Yit Thin's revenue register, and 25 *pès* on the east bank of the main irrigation channel south of Ngansun village and included in the Kyetsein village lands. The witnesses to this dedication were Naratheinzi, Manawyaza and son Nga Sizeinthin, Atwinywe, and Nga Leinma Thin. The water-pouring ceremony was performed in their presence.

"May the king and every one else obtain a share of my merit, and may I be gifted with omniscience."

No. (4).

Locality.—Within the double tiered cave south-west of Hngetpyittaung.

Date.—633 Sakkarâj (1271 A.D.).

Founder.—Letkanaletwè.†

Substance of inscription.—Dedication of paddy-lands and pagoda slaves.

In the year 590 Sakkarâj (1228 A.D.) Letkanaletwè obtained from the king, as a reward for his success in war, 173 *pès* of irrigated paddy-land called Pandeinmwe in Mahadankyadu, and 27 *pès* of similar land called Ngasutabo. These he dedicated to the Payagyi pagoda in the presence of the monks Taminga, Tharapwe, and Winido.

On Friday, the 4th waning of Wazo, 607 Sakkarâj (1245 A.D.), 200 *pès* of paddy-land were dedicated to the same pagoda when the monk Bôkdalingawaranyanèyinthi, to whom the land was previously offered by the king, renounced the world and chose the life of a strict ascetic in a cave.

On Thursday, the 5th waxing of Thadingyut, 633 Sakkarâj (1271 A.D.), Nga Pyinnya Thin dedicated to the same pagoda his two personal slaves Nga Ya Kaing and Nga Thaung Ga, in order that he and they might escape the horrors of *avíci* hell. The slaves willingly submitted to this dedication while they were resting their heads on Nga Pyinnya's posteriors at a place called Ngataba.

---

* This sort of dedication somewhat corresponds with the practice in vogue in the church of Rome, where prayers are offered for the welfare of departed spirits.

† A minister of King Narathihapade or Zeyatheinka.

No. (5).

Locality.—About half a mile south of the Hngetpyittaung pagoda and a mile south-east of the Shwezigôn.

Date.—598 Sakkarâj (1236 A.D.).

Founders.—Yazathura and wife.*

Substance of inscription.—Dedication of paddy-lands, cows, and slaves to a monastery.

[This inscription is so fragmentary that nothing can be made out of it beyond the facts noted above.]

No. (6).

Locality.—On the south-west side of the Mahathaman group of monasteries.

Date.—614 Sakkarâj (1252 A.D.).

Founders.—Mahathaman and wife.

Substance of inscription.—Building of pagoda, monastery, rest-house, and covered walks, and dedication of paddy-lands, gardens, cows, buffaloes, and slaves.

"I adore the Buddha!"

In the year 1796 of the Religion, in the reign of King Uzana of Pagan, the minister plenipotentiary, who was a very pious devotee of the three "Gems" and whose wife was replete with virtue and wisdom and charity, erected a large monastery surrounded by a wall enclosing a beautiful garden containing young fruit trees, a tank, a beautiful covered walk and rest-house, on a piece of high land east of Pagan and in order that this offering, which was made to the monkhood might last throughout the whole period of the Religion, dedicated to it many slaves, male and female, paddy-lands, gardens and plantations, cows and buffaloes, and caused a large barn to be erected for the storage of grain. The following were the slaves dedicated by the minister and his wife in the presence of the monks Mahakathapa and Dhammathirithubutisan, to their monastery, which was completed on Wednesday, the 5th waning of Nadaw, 599 Sakkarâj; Nga Kan Tu and his sons Nga Pyi Wa, Ma Than and Nga U Pi; Nga Pyi Wa's son Nga U Hla; Nga San Thi's son Nga Myat; Nga Pyi; Nga Kin Bun Thin; Nga Ta Ba and his wife O Chat La, daughters O Myaik, O Si Gôn, O Yeik Tha, and O Let Kauk; Nga Pu Te and wife Eindaw, sons Nga Pôn Sa and Nga Kywè; Nga Pôn Sôn and wife Yadu, sons Be Hlan, Pè Ka, Nga Pana Ya, and Nga Tè, daughters Kali, Bôkka and Matuya; Nga Wun Bè and wife O Bôn, granddaughter O Lôn; Ma Lemi and daughters Ma Lè, O Bôn Ne, O Pi

*Yazathura is a son of Narapadisthu, by Queen Usaukpan, and uncle of Kyazwa, who was reigning at the time the inscription was erected.

Ku and O Pè Hla; Nga Yôn and son Nga Pyi Zôn, grandson Nga Si Zein; blacksmith Nga Pauk Ka and assistant Nga Min; O Tha Do; Meta; Madaw and wife Hi Tôn, daughter Paw Mi; Letkaw and wife Zanu, daughter Pu Tè; Ana Kataya and wife Ala Mu, sons Nga Pyinnya and Nga Dòk Cha; Nga Twe Ba; Nga Twe Mi . . .

. . . .

. . . .

The following lands were dedicated, namely, 40 *pès* of paddy-land behind Pinônyaing village in Mapinzaya circle, which was purchased by Mahathaman out of the 100 *pès* offered to the Brahman astrologers by King Mingyikyazwa; 50 *pès* of similar land in Kandu village purchased from Kinumi; 50 *pès* of similar land in Mabya purchased from O Chat Thin, a maid-of-honour; another 50 *pès* in Mabya obtained as a gift from the king; 30 *pès* of similar land in Mawbwe purchased from Sandaraein; 200 *pès* of similar land in Pakan called Letpanmye and Teindaunggwè, purchased from Dewapanzôn; . . . . . . *pès* of land obtained in payment of a loan out of 100 *pès* in Yatamaik, belonging to Kyamabat's son; and 1,500 *pès* between upper Dipeshin and Panbwe fishery which was obtained as a gift from the king. Out of these lands, 30 *pès* at Panbwe, 52 at Tanaunggyi, 30 out of Kinumi's land, and 100 at Dipeshin are dedicated to the Buddha and his "Law." Fifty *pès* out of Dewapanzôn's land and . . . . . . *pès* at Yatamaik are dedicated to the monkhood. The garden of young fruit trees situated north of the Ôktama-Kyauktuma forests was bought (here the inscription ends abruptly).

No. (7).

Locality.—Within the southern group of pagodas.

Date.—605 Sakkarâj (1243 A.D.).

Founders.—Minmeinma and Thugyi Thamantagôntan and wife.

Substance of inscription.—Erection of pagoda, cave, monastery, covered walk, rest-house and library, and dedication to the same of paddy and garden lands, slaves, and cows.

On Thursday, the 7th waxing of Tabodwè, 605 Sakkarâj, the eminent and charitably inclined lady Minmeinma, sister of the celebrated Tagagyi * in conjunction with Thugyi Thamantagôntan and his wife erected a pagoda, a cave, a monastery with masonry walls, a covered walk, a rest-house, a library, and 20 schools within the monastery walls, in order that the Religion might last its full period of 5,000 years. And for the upkeep of the same 300 *pès* of paddy

* Founder of inscription No. (5) found at Wetkyi-in, Pagan.

land, 30 slaves and 50 cows were dedicated to the three "Gems" by the Thugyi and his wife. Minmeinma, sister of Tagagyi, dedicated the following, namely, ... (here follows the names of the slaves, which are only partly decipherable). The dedication was made in the presence of monk Winido.

No. (8).

Locality.—Within the central group of pagodas.

Date.—617 Sakkarâj (1255 A.D.).

Founder.—Sachibo.*

Substance of inscription.—Building of monastery, cave, and rest-house and dedication of garden and paddy-lands-and slaves.

"I adore the Buddha!"

ON Wednesday, the 11th waxing of Nayôn, 617 Sakkarâj, Sachibo erected a monastery, a cave, and a rest-house, and dedicated the following slaves to the three "Gems," namely, Nga . . . . . . and son Nga Pa Thi; Nga Tha Lôn; O Kaung Myo and daughter . . . . . . ; O Kya Bwe; O Pyat; O Lauk Tet; O Kyan Byit and son Nga U Pi; Nga Kyaung; O Hla; Ma . . . . . . and daughter Chit Mye; O Daung Thu and daughter O . . . . . . ; Nga Pôn Byit; Nga Pôn; Nga Pôn . . . . . . ; Nga Mun; Nga Tagaung and son Nga Kwe; total 23 slaves. The paddy-lands dedicated are the following, namely, 30 *pès* south of Kyazinkyaung in Myingôndaing circle; 5 *pès* of garden-land in Pauktaw; 5 *pès* . . . . ; 5 *pès* of paddy-land in Lawa village, purchased out of the Pinmyaing lands; . . . . 60 *pès* behind Daukhlaga village, Mapinzaya circle; a portion of the *payan* gardens; . . . . ; 60 palm trees at Ngathayauk.

No. (9).

Locality.—At the source of the Wetkyi-in stream.

Date.—621 Sakkarâj (1259 A.D.).

Founder.—Somingyi, widow of Prince Minthalat.

Substance of inscription.—Building of monastery and dedication of slaves thereto.

"I adore the Lord of the three lokas!"

ON Monday, the 5th waning of Nayôn, 621 Sakkarâj, Somingyi, daughter of Mahathamangyi, † in compliance with the wishes of her

* Secretary to a Military Commander, corresponding to the modern *asuye.*

† Founder of inscription No. 6, *ante.*

princely husband, erected a monastery, and pouring out water jointly with her father, dedicated the same to the three "Gems." The lands attached to the monastery are the following, namely, 300 *pès* of *mayin* and 130 *pès* of *kaukkyi* land called Yagwetaya, and 100 *pès* of *mayin* and 900 *pès* of *kaukkyi* land called Kunthazeik in Pyônlaing circle; 1,000 *pès* of *kaukkyi* land called Tanaungwun in Masè circle; 70 *pès* of *mayin* land called Ingyintayazôn in Itingôn circle; 20 *pès* of *mayin* land in Ngazun circle; 20 *pès* of *mayin* and *kaukkyi* land called Kalazinga which is included in the Ôksana lands in Pyinmana. Out of these, 170 *pès* of *mayin* and 1,430 *pès* of *kaukkyi* land are set apart for the Buddha, his law, and monkhood, and 100 *pès* of *mayin* and 400 *pès* of *kaukkyi* land are reserved for the presiding monk of the monastery. The slaves dedicated were the following, namely, Nga Wun Ta and son Nga Tun; Nga Thit Kwe's wife and her sons Nga Kwe Ya and Nga Pagan Mi, daughters O Zu Yi and Apè; Apè's daughter O Mi U; Nga Thet She; Nga Kan Tha; Nga Kwe Ya and sons Nga U and Nga Pangè; Thin Da; Nga Pyi Ya's sons Pu Taya, Nga Sa Zo and Nga Pyu; total 16 slaves.

"By virtue of this good deed, may I enjoy the pleasures of this world and the world of *devâs*, and of Nirvâna; and may every one from the king downwards obtain a share of the merit. On the other hand, may utter ruin befall those who destroy my offering, and may they be burnt in *avîci* hell."

NO. (10).

Locality.—Within the double-tiered cave pagoda.

Date.—661 Sakkarâj (1299 A.D.).

Founder.—Anandapade.*

Substance of inscription.—Building of monastery and dedication of paddy-land thereto.

ON Thursday, the 8th waxing of Nayôn, 661 Sakkarâj, Anandapade obtained permission from the young king and built a monastery at Tharabwe. He further obtained as a gift from the king and dedicated to the monastery in the interests of the Religion 100 *pès* of paddy-land known as Kanbuntawgan, and 100 *pès* at Kyantu which was originally allotted to Santarathu's son Nga Twe for military service; total 200 *pès*. The following personages were present when the lands were applied for, namely, Thugyis Athincha, Yazathingyan, and Theingathu; nobles Tetkana, Saduyingapyitsi, Etkapade, Eindapyitsaye, Pônnyathu, Paritpyetkathu, and Mahathaman.

---

* A minister of King Sawnit of Pagan.

"May those who approve of this my offering have as many rewards as the grains of sand between Nyaungu and Thiyipyitsaya;* and may those who do not, and those who destroy the same, suffer in *avîci* punishments which exceed in number the said grains of sand, and may they never have the opportunity of beholding any of the succeeding Buddhas."

No. (11).

Locality.—In the porch near the great image.

Date.—1119 Sakkarâj (1757 A.D.).

Founder.—Alompra.

Substance of inscription.—Building of monastery and prohibiting the taking of animal life within a radius of 500 *tas*.

"We hereby command that the five letters *abhayadâna* be added to the inscription on the Hngetpyittaung seal, and that the officials and other inhabitants of Pagan and Nyaungu shall, on pain of severe punishment, refrain from indulgence in intoxicating liquors and drugs, and from taking any animal life or capturing any animal, within a radius of 500 *tas* of our monastery at Hngetpyittaung."—Given through Zeyayanaung, Governor of Pagan, on Saturday, the 4th waning of Tabodwè, 1119 Sakkarâj.

INSCRIPTIONS OF PAGAN.

IV.—Found on the north-east of Pagan.

No. (1).—Obverse.

Locality.—Within the walls of the Kemawaya pagoda.

Date.—569 Sakkarâj (1207 A.D.).

Founder.—King Nandaungmya.†

Substance of inscription.—Building of a monastery and library and dedication of lands.

"Reverence to the Blessed, Holy, and Enlightened One!"

On Thursday, the 1st waxing of Tagu, 569 Sakkarâj, King Nandaungmya, wishing to attain Buddhahood, built a cave, a library, and a monastery, and celebrated the dedication ceremony with dancing and music, and made offerings of gold and silver flowers. The following lands were then dedicated to the monkhood, namely, 1,050 *pès* of land with palm trees thereon and situated on the south-west of

* Old Pagan.

† Better known in history as Zeyatheinka and Uzana, which are his royal titles. Nandaungmya means a frequent supplicant of the throne. It is recorded that he succeeded in obtaining the throne from his father Narapadisithu, owing to the good offices of his mother.

Taungpeinnè; 300 *pès* adjoining the above and 700 *pès* of paddy-land at Kaungza. Besides the above, 10,000 *pès* of land on the banks of the southern Nabè stream were dedicated. This piece of land is bounded on the east by a piece of high land called *thakakan-tupya*, south by the Obôkku village, west by the Lintagaung land, and north by the Kanthit land. The other lands dedicated were: 300 *pès* of paddy-land at Ngapaukku; 50 *pès* at Myethabin; 700 *pès* at Maneik; 1,000 *pès* at Kaing, 500 *pès* at Salin-Kyaikpadaung-gyi, 500 at Pinmyaing, 500 at Yangôn, 1,500 *pès* called the Yebôk-kanzwè land, 50 *pès* at Pakan-Nwèni, 10,000 *pès* at Satheinywa-byu near Yaw territory, which is bounded on the east by the Sinzein land, on the south-east by the Gyaingzauk land, on the south by a line at a distance of a peacock's crow beyond the Nyaungdipa abyss, on the south-west by the Thabyedo land, on the west by the Chabin-gwabôn range of hills, on the north-west by the Kyunthanbyin land, on the north by the Yebyaletpan land, and on the north-east by a line which is a peacock's crow beyond Satthwa stream. His Majesty poured out the water of dedication amid the blowing of trumpets and beating of drums in the presence of an assembly of ministers and monks who acclaimed their approval.

"May all those, from the rulers of the earth downwards, who misappropriate or destroy my offering, suffer the eight kinds of punishment during their existence as human beings, and after death may they be burnt in the eight principal stages of hell; moreover, may they become *petas* like the man who, during the period of the Religion of Kakusandha Buddha, altered, through covetousness, a boundary pillar demarcating a piece of religious land and was punished by being immersed waist-deep in a slab of rock 60 days' journey square and upon whom the saving influence of three successive Buddhas has been exerted in vain. May they have no opportunity of beholding any future Buddha. On the other hand, may those who approve of my offering, who refrain from appropriating any portion of it to their own use, or who in any way maintain its continuance, become rulers of the universe, rich and prosperous men."

Reverse.

Date.—609 Sakkarâj (1247 A.D.).

Founders.—Monk Pwa Gyi and grandson.

Substance of inscription.—Re-dedication of slaves who were attached to the Anuyuda* monastery and the Lawkananda pagoda in 569 Sakkarâj.

A DISPUTE having arisen between the governor and the head pagoda-slave Ôksa in connection with the slaves dedicated by Monk

* Anuruddha.

Pwa Gyi and his grandson to the pagoda and monastery built by them respectively on Friday, the 5th waning of Thadingyut, 569 Sakkarâj, this inscription is recorded. The following slaves are re-dedicated to the Anuyuda monastery, namely, Mandaleik's son Pingaw; Namateik's nephew; Pingaw's son Apôk; Hitu's infant daughter; Mandalik's brother Tumu and nephew Leitkein; Mandaleik's wife Malika and sons Thoye and Nga Put; and Thabeik's wife Kingu. Only these ten remain out of those originally dedicated. "May those who molest these slaves suffer in all the four "departments of *avîci* hell, and perish together with all their kins-"men." The slaves re-dedicated to the Lawkananda pagoda are the following, namely, Nga Pan Tha's son Kadaw; Nga Pa Nwè, brothers Nga Yauk and Nga Kan Tu, uncle Nga Tha Din, cousin Nga Pa U, uncles Nga Pôk Pya, U Dôn and Nga Pyi Zôn, cousin Nga Pa Yin, uncles Nga Ka Ywè and Nga Chit Twè; Tanabyu's son Kauk Ka A; Amandan Thaw; Setthu; Tingu and daughter Ein Chan Tha. Out of 21 slaves originally dedicated, only these 17 are surviving. "May those who molest them suffer in all the four departments of *avîci* hell and may they perish together with all their relatives."

No. (2).

Locality.—Within the porch of the Einyagyaung pagoda, Pagan.

Date.—604 Sakkarâj (1242 A.D.).

Founder.—Wife of Kingathu (a noble).

Substance of inscription.—Building of monastery and dedication of slaves thereto.

I adore the Buddha, his Law, and Monkhood!

ON Thursday, the 14th waning of Nadaw, 604 Sakkarâj, the daughter of Nyaungyangyi * and wife of Kingathu* built a monastery and dedicated to it the following slaves, namely, Nga San Pè and wife O Tan Laing; sons Nga Kwe and Nga U Pi; cousin Nga Pyi Wa, Nga Pyi Zin, Nga Min Ngè, and son Nga Pa Zin; uncle Nga Hnit Laing and nephew Nga Aung Myin; Nga La Ma and sons Nga Twe and Nga Yauk U; daughters O Pôn and O Pi; Nga Ne and sons Nga Kyaung and Nga Lat; Nga Kyaung's son Nga Pa Sin; Nga Pa Zin and brother Nga Pan The; Nga Pyi Nyi; Nga Lo Hnit and son Nga U; Nga Hmyè and wife Ma Hla; daughters Mi U and Thudama; uncle Nga Pôn; Nga Pin Gaung, a mortar mason; clerk Nga La and son Nga Twe; Nga Pôn Lut; Nga Ban Mwe and son Nga U Lwè; nephews Nga U Pi and an infant; Nga Kyet Yôn's sons Nga Mutu, Nga U Lwe and Nga Pale; Nga Lôn

* Ministers of King Narapatisithu, Uzana, and Kyazwa, of Pagan.

and sons Nga U Hla, Nga Kanaw; Nga U Gyi and brothers Nga Kyun and Nga Myo, wife O Hnaung, brother-in-law Nga San; Nga San Le's sons Nga Kyi and Nga Chat; O Ket Pya and sons Nga Mi Lut, Nga Tet Pyi and Nga Dwe Byu; Nga U Pa and son Nga U; Nga U's wife Ma Thein and son Nga Mye I, daughter O Tage, sons Nga Kante and Nga Pa Gyi, uncle Nga Twe; O Nyo; O Gywe; O Mauk and niece O Lôn, husband Nga Le, son Nga Nyo, sisters O Bôn, O Byi, O Chat, and O Byi Wa; O Mauk's niece O Bôn and her daughter Mi Kin, sister O Pônza; Nga Pôn and brother Nga Môn, sons Nga Kwe, Nga Kaung, and Nga Aung Byi, daughter O Mun, nephew Nga Pôn He; Nga Tu Yin; Thit Taung's cowherd Nga Tôn; Nga Ta E and son Nga Than Gè; O Myin; Nga San, grandson of Nga He Thin's younger brother; Nga Twe's son Nga Mun; Nga U Lôn and son; goldsmith Man Te and two children; Nga La Gaung, a garden slave; O Na Lôn and daughters Mi U and O Kan Tu, sister O Nya Yan, niece Ma Ni; Nga Ta and sons Nga Kôn an infant, brothers Nga Nyo, Nga Chet Su, and Nga Ke; O Kin and daughter O Pun, nieces O Byi Ya and O Daing; washerman Nga Pyi and sons Nga Thaukkya and Nga Kaungyan; O Môn, a tinsmith's servant, and daughter O Bôn; Nga U Gyi and son Nga Pyi, brother Nga Swa, brother-in-law's son; O Yin's daughters O Lat and Mi U; Thit Sut's servant Nga Kun, deceased . . . . 's son Nga Nyo and wife O Nyet and their sons Nga Yin Di and Nga Mye; O Sin Kyè and daughter O Sat; Nga Pyi's younger brothers . . . . (one line) and 10 slaves who were dedicated along with the Wayindôk paddy-lands. Besides the above, there are Nga Sa Po and son Nga Min Se, brother Nga Ma Thein, nephew Nga Tin Byi, brothers Nga Aung Myin and Nga Pyit Sin, uncle Nga Mywin, cousins Nga San Ga, Nga Pu, Nga Ma Lauk, and Nga Twe, uncle Nga Pyi Zin and sons Nga U Lôn and an infant, uncle Nga Ti and son Nga Sein, uncle Nga Chan Tha, uncle Nga Aung and sons Nga Than Pa and Nga San, uncle Nga Myo; O Ka La Thin, O Kywe, O Hla, and all their relatives; O Ta, O Kala, O Pôn, O Kywin Yit and their relatives; O Pyi Thin's slave O Det Pyi and all her relatives and companions; the chief queen's slaves Nga Pôn, the boatswain and sons Nga Naing, Nga Sôn, and Nga San, brother Nga Taba; Nga Pi, and son Nga Yaung, and all their relatives, Nga Wun Pyi and sons Nga Paung and Nga Pin Gaung, brother Nga Chat Kaung, nephew Nga Pyi Nyi, brother Nga Aung Tha and son Nga Sôn; Nga Lôn Ma and brother Nga Naung Tha; Nga La Tha; O Taung Laung; total, 181 slaves. These are placed under the control of the Monk Thera, seven being scholars in his monastery.

"May those who molest these slaves, whether king or subject, monk or layman, man or woman, live short and inglorious lives as human beings and die an unnatural death caused by fire, water, lightning, axe, elephant, horse, donkey, leopard, orang-outang, or by some incurable disease while spitting clots of blood. May they, after death, be burnt in the great *avici* hell, and may they have no opportunity of beholding any of the future Buddhas. If perchance they are reborn as human beings, may they be leprous, lame, blind, deaf, dumb, or otherwise deformed or rendered infirm in consequence of their evil deed, and may they also suffer as *petas* beneath this earth. On the other hand, may those who approve of my offering and support it in any way in the interests of the Religion, have a share of its merit equally with me and my husband. May they, among men, ... " (last line).

No. (3).

Locality.—Within the porch of the Einyagyaung pagoda, Pagan.

Date.—604 Sakkarâj (1242 A.D.).

Founder.—Wife of Kingathu.

Substance of inscription.—Building of monastery and dedication of paddy-lands thereto.

Reverence to the Blessed, Holy and Enlightened One!

On Thursday, the 14th waning of Nadaw, 604 Sakkarâj, Kingathu passed away. On Sunday, the 3rd waxing of the following month of Pyatho, the daughter of Nyaungyangyi, appreciating fully the unstability of things temporal, and in order to perpetuate the memory of her beloved lord, dedicated several pieces of paddy-land to her own monastery, to that of the monk Mahâkassapa, and another, built by O Det Pyi Thin, her husband's aunt. The lands dedicated to the said monasteries are the Kanti land, measuring 200 *pès*, granted to Kingathu by King Sithu; 100 *pès* of *mayin* paddy-land called *kauknan*; the Pandin land, measuring 6 *pès*, obtained in exchange for a boat from A Twe, son of Warit; 200 *pès* of land called *mapo*, which was originally granted by King Sithu to Nyaungyangyi's wife; 50 *pès* of paddy-land obtained in payment of the price of an elephant called Ayanbye; 1,000 *pès* out of the 2,000 granted to Kingathu by King Kyazwa; the Tanyaukyit land, measuring 20 *pès*, granted to Nyaungyangyi's wife by King Kyazwa; and 1 *pè* of garden-land granted by the same king to Kingathu. The offerings made to the monks at the funeral were gold flowers worth 2,506 ticals of silver and the Tagaung garden-land measuring 8 *pès*, worth 1,494 ticals; and the Wayindôk paddy-land, measuring 125 *pès*, were offered to the image on Banker Minyaza's monastery. The total area of the lands thus offered is 1,710 *pès*. Out of this 10 *pès* of the Kanti land and 10 of the Kaukkan land are set apart for the maintenance of the presiding monks and inhabitants of the monasteries. The lands are placed under the control of the monk Thera.

" May the calamities mentioned in the inscription placed north of this befall those who misappropriate or destroy these offerings. On the other hand, may those who are devoted to the three 'Gems' be benefited by my good wishes and so attain Nirvâna."

No. (4).

Locality.—Within the porch of the Tazaung pagoda.

Date.—604 Sakkarâj (1242 A.D.).

Founder.—Wife of Kingathu.

Substance of inscription.—Building of monastery and dedication of slaves thereto.

Reverence to the Blessed, Holy and Enlightened One!

On Thursday, the 14th waning of Nadaw, 604 Sakkarâj, Kingathu passed away to the abode of the *devas*. On Sunday, the 3rd waxing of the following month of Pyatho, the daughter of Nyaungyangyi, knowing that all things on this earth are prone to change and destruction, and in commemoration of her deceased husband, dedicated the following slaves to the monastery built by O Det Pyi, her husband's aunt, namely, O Leinma's daughter O Kaung Maing and granddaughters O Chan, O Hla Wun and O Tha Din; O Si Gôn and daughter O Nyo; Nga Twè's son Nga Chit Kin, grandson Myet Ya; Chit Kin's brothers Nga La Pa, Nga Pôn and Nga Yôn; Nga Shan and sons Nga Pôn and Nga Sôn; Nga Aung Byi, son Nga Pu and grandson Nga Let Swè; Nga Sôn and sons Nga Tet Pyi, Nga Pin Di, Nga Hli and Nga Hlauk; Nga Sôn's brother Nga Taung Yan; Kalan Byu's sons Nga Pa Yin and Nga Pauk, grandson Nga Pa E; Nga Ti's son Nga Yaung; Nga Mye and son Nga Kin Pa; Nga Mye's brother Nga Thauk Kya and nephew Nga Aung Din; Nga Ti San and sons Nga Swa, Nga Chit Ya; Nga Swa's brother Nga Kyin and nephew Nga Wa; Nga Kwe and sons Nga Hli and an infant; Nga Kwe's brother Nga Yauk Pôn and nephews Nga U and an infant; Nga Yauk Pôn's brother Nga Pôn Zôn; Nga Sôn's sons Nga U Yin and Nga Hli Myi; Nga Taung Yan and sons Nga Mauk and Nga Taba; Nga Pe's son Nga Kala; Nga Yôn's sons Nga Sat The, Nga Chit Pa, and grandson Nga Lat;

Nga Twe's son Nga U Hla, O Kan We, daughter O In, and an infant granddaughter; O Kan We's sister O Lwi; Kyo Mache; Nga Chit Mun's son Nga Thanbaya; mortar mason Nga Thuma and two sons. . . . .

"Let these slaves utilize the usufruct of the paddy-lands for the upkeep of the monastery. Let the male and female head slaves enjoy the produce of 15 *pès* each without fear of future punishment in hell."

No. (5).

Locality.—Within the porch of the Tazaung pagoda.

Date.—604 Sakkaràj (1242 A.D.).

Founder.—Wife of Kingathu.

Substance of inscription.—Building of monastery and dedication thereto of paddy-lands, boat, elephants, cows, buffaloes, goats, and slaves.

Reverence to the Blessed, Holy and Enlightened One!

ON Thursday, the 14th waning of Nadaw, 604 Sakkaràj, Kingathu passed away. On Sunday, the 3rd waxing of the following month of Pyatho, the daughter of Nyaungyangyi and wife of Kingathu, being mindful of the ephemeral nature of all earthly things, and in order to preserve the remembrance of her husband, made the following offerings to the monastery erected by O Det Pyi, her husband's aunt, namely, 300 *pès*, including fishery and waste lands, at Ngapyetin, 10 *pès* of paddy-land at Puttaingkyaung, 100 *pès* at Sagu, 100 at Prome, and 11 *pès* of garden-lands; 300 out of the 500 *pès* of paddy-land east of Kyintharit; one male elephant called Thamizan, one female elephant, 10 cows, five buffaloes, 10 goats, and a small boat. The slaves dedicated were:—Nga Pi and wife O Byu, daughters O Nyo and O Than Ba; O Nyein and daughters O Kwe, O Nye U; O Nyein's sisters O Kaung Yauk, O Mun, and O Twe, and nieces O Kè Laung, O Tin; O Ke and daughter O Pin Myaing, and a granddaughter, name unknown; O Pin Nyaing's sister O Thin Twe; O Ke's sister O Twe; O Twe's nieces O Myet Pwin, O Chit Mi, and O Nyein Thi; O Tin Ke's daughter O Mwein, granddaughters O Than Pa and an infant; Nga Pyi Zôn's son Nga Pyit Sin; Nga Yauk and his brothers Nga Laung Laung and Nga U Hla, nephew Nga Kwa; Nga Kyi and son Nga U Pi; Nga Kaung A and sons Nga Kyan Bin and Nga Chit Swa; Nga Hla Byi and son Nga Pôn Za; and Nga Sein's son Nga Kywin.

No. (6).

Locality.—In Taungpi village about 600 feet north-east of Pagan.

Date.—656 Sakkarâj (1294 A.D.).

Founder.—Eindapyitsaya.*

Substance of inscription.—Building of pagoda, monastery, and cave, and dedication of lands, cows, and slaves thereto.

Reverence to the Blessed, Holy and Enlightened One!

IN the year 1837 of the Religion, or on Thursday, the 6th waning of Tazaungmôn, 654 Sakkarâj, Eindapyitsaya, the minister, wishing to attain Buddhahood in order that he might be able to save men and *devâs* alike from the miseries of *samsaro*, built a beautiful masonry monastery, a cave, and a pagoda surrounded by double walls. On Saturday, the 13th waxing of Wagaung, 655 Sakkarâj, Eindapyitsaya obtained the king's permission and dedicated the following lands, namely, 50 *pès* more or less at Salin, 50 *pès* more or less at Kanti, 50 *pès* more or less at Sagu, 20 at Mapinzaya, and 30 at Kanzônkyu; total 200 *pès*. These lands were registered by Minister Mahathaman. In the year 656 Sakkarâj, 40 natives of India, including 30 females, were dedicated as slaves; and 50 cows were at the same time offered for the maintenance of the monkhood throughout the period of the Religion.

"May every creature from the king of the *devas* downwards have a share of my merit. But may those who destroy my offering have no opportunity of beholding any of the succeeding Buddhas. May they become *petas* even should they be so fortunate as to remain as human beings, otherwise, may they be burnt in *avîci* hell and become its dregs. May the next Buddha be enabled to foretell when I shall attain Buddhahood."

No. (7).

Locality.—Within the group of monasteries west of the Myazigôn pagoda.

Date.—870 Sakkarâj (1508 A.D.).

Founder.—Minsithu and wife.

Substance of inscription.—Building of monastery and dedication of lands thereto.

I adore the three Gems!

IN the year 2052 of the Religion of Gautama Buddha, who acquired omniscience after a probationary period of 4 *asankheyyas* and 100,000 *kalpas*, Minsithu, King Narapati's Chamberlain and his wife dedicated to the monkhood their beautiful monastery which stands on the bank of the Irrawaddy north-east of Pagan, with the view that they might enjoy their lives as human beings and as *devas* and sub-

* A Minister of King Kyaswa of Pagan.

sequently attain the bliss of Nirvâna. The building of the monastery, which was of brick, was commenced on Saturday, the 10th waning of Nayôn, 865 Sakkarâj, and when it was completed, offerings were made for the maintenance of the presiding monks throughout the 5,000 years of the Religion. On Friday, the 10th waxing of Nadaw, 870 Sakkarâj, one tame female elephant with golden howdah, one pony with golden saddle and trappings and silver stirrups, one gold drinking pot, and one gold bottle were presented to the King by the Royal Chamberlain in the presence of the Ministers and the Governors of Tabayin, Pakan, and Pindalè, and permission was obtained from His Majesty to dedicate to the monastery the Tetnwègyaung village lands, including the landing-place, and the Kyaukmè village lands. Calling upon the guardian *nats* of the universe to witness his act, the King himself poured the water of dedication out of a gold cup. The boundaries of the landing-place are . . . . (last line).

No. (8).

Locality.—West of the Myazigôn pagoda.

Date.—874 Sakkarâj (1512 A.D.).

Founder.—Minsithu, Royal Chamberlain.

Substance of inscription.—Building of a monastery.

[THE latter portion of this inscription is so obliterated that there is only sufficient matter to show that the monastery abovementioned was built in memory of the founder's deceased son, who was a Governor of Shwedaung.]

INSCRIPTIONS OF PAGAN.

V.—Found on the east of Pagan.

[Inscriptions (1) to (8) have not been deciphered. They appear to be in Talaing-Burmese.]

No. (9).

Locality.—Within the porch of the Tainggyut pagoda.

Date.—506 Sakkarâj (1144 A.D.).

Founders.—King Kyazwa and daughter of Governor of Pagan.

Substance of inscription.—Dedication of lands and slaves to pagoda.

ON Saturday, the 5th waxing of Tabaung, 501 Sakkarâj, Nga Pu Thin, son of Ayimat,* applied to the king for permission to dedicate certain lands to the Tainggyut pagoda. He was asked to mention such lands as were available for the purpose, and he accordingly named 50 *pès* at Nakakan, 130 *pès* in Môksobo circle, 100 *pès* ad-

* A Minister of King Alaungsithu.

jacent to the Kyungaung lands, 70 *pès* known as the Myaungwun lands south of Yègyin village, 200 *pès* south-east of Ngalatwè village, and 100 *pès* in Peiksè circle; total 750 *pès*. The King Sithu commanded these lands to be dedicated.

On Sunday, the 5th waxing of Kasôn, 502 Sakkaràj, Queen Yadanabôn* built a cave near the Tainggyut pagoda and dedicated to it 30 *pès* of paddy-land at Myitkwè, north of Pyinmana. The royal betel server, Ein Pôn Thin, also built a cave and dedicated to it 10 *pès* of paddy-land at Salin, 30 *pès* called Tanaungkyi, 20 *pès* at Metkaya which are entered in Thugyi Thè's rolls, and 10 *pès* at Ngalinbôk, entered in Thugyi Bu's rolls; total 70 *pès*. To the brazen image placed in the cave the following lands were dedicated, namely, 30 *pès* of paddy-land at Pinlè, 1 *pè* of garden-land, 30 *pès* known as Kamyu, and 10 *pès* called Taya; total 71 *pès*. Thamantathu, the Thugyi, built a monastery near the pagoda and dedicated to it 40 *pès* of paddy-land in the Kamaing fishery at Wayindôk.

"May those who approve of these offerings have a share of our merit." . . . . (six lines).

On Sunday, the 7th waxing of Tabodwè, 506 Sakkaràj, Thinapattayo† dedicated to the pagoda 30 *pès* of paddy-land in Ketlôn circle known as the Nga Lin fields. The Pagan Governor's daughter and King Kyazwa dedicated, as pagoda slaves, a family consisting of husband and wife, two sons Nga Mya Lu and Nga Twè, and a daughter I . . . .

No. (10).

Locality.—In the porch of the Tainggyut pagoda.

Date.—541 Sakkaràj (1179 A.D.).

Founder.—Abinandathu.

Substance of inscription.—Repairing of the pagoda and dedication of slaves thereto.

In Wazo, 541 Sakkaràj, Abinandathu,‡ a court official, regilt the Tainggyut pagoda, set a golden *ti* upon it, built a new offering-platform near it, and regilt the statues of Sāriputto and Moggalāno . . . . A number of monks were supplied with food and robes. Abinandathu then offered himself, his wife, and two sons as slaves to the pagoda.§ Other slaves were also dedicated, namely, Nga Kyan Gaung, Nga Kywin, Nga Letkana, Nga Swa, and Nga Lu Ngè; total 9 slaves; moreover, 5 *pès* of paddy-land called Tanaunggyi were offered in

* Queen of Alaungsithu.

† A Minister of Sawmunnit.

‡ A courtier of Narapatisithu's reign.

§ This is quite unusual, for, as previously noted, pagoda slaves are always looked down upon.

order that the produce might be utilized for the rice-offering at the pagoda.

"By virtue of this my meritorious deed, may I and my teachers, masters, friends, and relatives escape the miseries of life in the present and the future and ultimately attain Nirvâna; and may I become a Buddha."

INSCRIPTIONS OF PAGAN.

VI.—Found on the south-east of Pagan.

NO. (1).—OBVERSE.

Locality.—Within the Damayangyi pagoda, about a mile south-east of Pagan.

Date.—527 Sakkarâj (1165 A.D.).

Founders.—Thugyi Kwa and Pè Bôk, daughter of Thugyi Môn.

Substance of inscription.—Dedication of slaves, cows, and lands.

I adore the Excellent Buddha!

ON Monday, the 1st waning of Pyatho, 527 Sakkarâj, this inscription was sculptured. Thugyi Kwa of Southern Kalanlôn circle, and Pè Bôk, daughter of Thugyi Môn, dedicated the following pagoda slaves, namely, Kangôncha and wife Yawôk, daughter Ein Bwe, son-in-law Nyache, and granddaughters Ein Lut and Ein Kut; Nga Leik, daughters Ein But and Ein Maya, and granddaughters Ein Byin and Ein Thwa; Nga Pa Ein, wife Ein Hlauk, and daughters Ein The, Ein Byôn, and Ein Dôn; Ein Mun and sons Nga Twe and Nga Ke; Kywè Eintha, son Nga That, daughter-in-law Ein Yan Gye, grandsons Nga Tut Put and Nga Kan; Nga Pyu; Nga Kôn; Nga Bôn; Ein Bôntaya Wè, daughter Ein Kan Gu and husband . . . . grandson Nga Taw Thu; Ein San Zu; Nga Kan Dôk; Ein Pywè; Than Dan; Ein Pwe and brother Nga Cha Zi; Ein Yanngè and husband Nga Pun Taw, daughter Ein Katte To; Nga Kin and wife Ein Byi; Ein Myethwe Gwè and daughter; Nga Pyinnya and brother Nga Pe; Nga Hlaw; Nga San and wife Ya Gwè, sons Nga Kaya Bat and Nga Mwe; Nga Yaing; Ein Lun Gwè, son Thazi, daughter Ein Mywè; Ein Byu; Nga Ma Thwa and wife Yo Yut; Ein Pôn Gywe; Ein Bwin Gwe; Ein Thit Kauk Kywe and son Nga Yauk; Nga Nauk; Nga Yaung.

REVERSE.

and wife O Mya; Twe Ein Yin; A Ngè; and Pôk Nga Yaung; total 73 slaves. Besides the above the following slaves were dedicated, namely, Nga Kaw Myin, wife Ein Dôn, son Nga Wa Byi, brothers Nga Taing and Nga Ku; Nga Pin Bôk, son Nga Paw, younger brother Nga Paung; Nga Pwa, daughters Ein Di Kywe and Ein Bet, sister Ein Gye; Ein Ywe and younger sister Ein Ze; Nga Myin and wife Ein Yauk, sons Nga Tha, Nga Hayi; Nga Nyein and sister Ein Gya, daughter Ein Gu; Nga Man Mu and wife Ein Zu, sister-in-law Ein Gupantaya; Ein Paung Gywe, Nga Pun and wife Ein Mwe, daughters Ein Myat, Pantaya and Ein Yan; Ein Sôn and brothers Wa Su and Nga Swi; Nga Pyi and wife Ein Kaw Yôn, sons Nga Taung and Nga Aung; Nga Kyein and wife Ein Bye, daughters Ein Wun and Ein Dun, sons Nga Chein, Nga Yein, Nga Lut and Nga Cha; Nga Taung; Nga Pwe Bôk and sons Nga Ôk and Nga Ngè; Nga Yôn Bôk and sisters Ein Dein, Ein Ywa Pantaya and Ein Zi; Ein Bu; and Ein Kwe; total 54. Also 48 cows, a garden, a tank, and 3 *pès* of *mayin* paddy-land.

"May those who destroy these my offerings die unnatural deaths by poison or be devoured by wild beasts; and may they find themselves in a worse plight than that of Dewadat. On the other hand, may those who witness (and approve of) these offerings escape my imprecations."

No. (2).

Locality.—Within the porch of the Sulamani pagoda.

Date.—545 Sakkarâj (1183 A.D.).

Founder.—Narapatisithu.*

Substance of inscription.—Building of pagoda and cave, and dedication of lands and slaves thereto.

I adore the All-wise!

On Thursday, the third waxing of Tazaungmôn, 545 Sakkarâj, King Narapatisithu, whose glory is as resplendent as that of a *devâ* or as that of the rising sun, visited Tuyin,† and seeing a luminous spot at a distance asked his attendants what it was. They replied that it was a fire; but the king knew better and noting the spot proceeded to it on his elephant, and demarcated it as a site for a cave. Subsequently the articles to be enshrined were placed underground and a cave was built over them. Above this was then erected a pagoda, and over this again was built another, and lastly the third tier was put on. When the whole was completed the king entered the cave and stationing himself in front of the golden image, sent for the monk Maha . . . . and poured out the water of dedication. The paddy-lands offered to the Religion in order that it might last its full period of 5,000 years are—

* King of Pagan (1174—1211 A.D.).

† A hill east of Pagan.

171 *pès* in Pinlè district, consisting of Lèdawya 10 *pès*, Pônu 10, Shawthin 10, Ngashanmaik 10, Pyinzi 30, Malè 10, Theinngè 21, and Paungsin village land 70 *pès*; 195 *pès* in Pyinmana district, consisting of Ngapônthin village land 10, Yeinywa village land 10, Isiôk 5, Thein 10, Tase 5, Thadaing 70, Kyundanyauk 30, Kundalin 30, Kyamalè 10, Panzingywè village 10, and Thasegôn 5; 300 *pès* in Yangôn district, consisting of 100 in Kyunywa village and 200 in Thanbyin village, including Pagannġè 10, Nyaungywangè 40, and Kanpanipadi 30; 120 *pès* in Myingôndaing district, consisting of Ôkkyithinywa 60, Itan 10, Sazaunggyi 20, and Sèywangè 30; 100 *pès* in Panan district; 145 *pès* in Tamôk district, consisting of Tahat 60 and Ywahaung village 85; 330 *pès* in Thindaung district, consisting of Kyauktaung-Mawbwe village lands 100 *pès*, Sanhlu 30, Ibyin 10, Taungu 90, Yeshu 50, Ngathet 30, Kamaung 10, and Metkaya-Myinshe 10; 40 *pès* in Tabyettha district, consisting of Ngalinbôk 30 and Taingmyi village 10; 175 *pès* in Kamyu district, consisting of Letwè 100 *pès*, Ywalat 30, Legyan 5, Kyaunglaungngè 10, and Kyaunglaunggyi 30; total altogether 1,627 *pès*.

[From here to the end (14 lines) the inscription is fragmentary.]

No. (3).

Locality.—Within the porch of the Damayangyi pagoda.

Date.—615 Sakkarâj (1253 A.D.).

Founders.—Mahapandita, Royal Preceptor, Nga Môn Thin and others.

Substance of inscription.—Placing image in western cave of pagoda and dedication of lands, slaves, and bells.

On Thursday, the 7th waning of Thadingyut, 567 Sakkarâj, the king (Narapatisithu) offered the piece of land facing the western wall of the Damayangyi pagoda to Mahapandita, his preceptor, to be used as a site for a cave. The royal preceptor accordingly built the cave, placed the image in it, and dedicated to it the following slaves, namely, Nga Kala Ngè, Nga Pyi U, Nga Si Gôn, and son Nga Myè Thôn; Nga Let Tet, Nga Taya, Nga Myo, Nga Pauk Ki, and Nga Yamana, total 9 men. The paddy-lands dedicated were: the Maukti lands, measuring 300 *pès* and bounded by a row of palm-trees extending to the Paunggwe lands and thence westward to the Zinyaw and Pantan lands; 5 *pès* at Kanhun and the Kyagwetka fields purchased by Nga Than Yin Gyi. The articles offered were: two bells weighing 2½ viss and 90 ticals respectively. The slaves offered by Nga Tôk Thin, the monk's chief disciple, were: Nga U Hla and Nga Pôn Su. "By virtue of these offerings, may my every wish be fulfilled; and may the king obtain a share of my merit."

On Sunday, the 7th waxing of Tabodwè, 615 Sakkarâj, Nga Môn Thin and his wife dedicated the following slaves: O Mye, Nga Yan, and Nga Aung Zin, son of Nga Pôn Su, who was purchased for 5 viss of silver. They further offered a brass kettle and a brass offering bowl weighing 1 viss. The slaves who were born in Nga Môn Thin's lifetime are Nga Taya's son Nga Tha Din, and Nga Tha Din's sons Nga Kywit, Nga Pa Ngè and Nga Pan Zit. The slaves dedicated by Wadu's wife and niece of monk Nga Tôk Thin were Nga Auk In and Nga Pin Yin, and the king re-dedicated the same slaves, saying that he confirmed the act of his grandmother.* Nga Môn Thin also confirmed the dedication of his father Nga Pyu Thin. "Let not the presiding monk of the royal monastery and his successors exercise any control over these slaves, but let my descendants after me look after them. By virtue of this my meritorious deed, may I have the opportunity of beholding the next Buddha;† may I ultimately attain omniscience, and may I be able to succour both men and *devâs*."

No. (4).

Locality.—Within the porch of the Damayangyi pagoda.

Date.—578 Sakkarâj (1216 A.D.).

Founder.—Mitaya Theinzi.‡

Substance of inscription.—Dedication of lands, slaves, and elephants to pagoda.

On Thursday, the 13th waxing of Kasôn, 578 Sakkarâj, Mitaya Theinzi dedicated to the pagoda . . . . ; 3 *pès* of paddy-land, two elephants, and the following slaves, namely: O Bôn and son; Nga Pan Tha and wife; Chan Tha Bôn and mother; Aung Kane and wife and two sons; total 10. The witnesses to the dedication were monks Thingapyitsi, Thingathu, Thattayapyitsi, Letyapayit, Mahame, Anandathu, Ôktamape, and Nga Shan Thin; total 8. "Let the five monks who are in charge of the pagoda be maintained out of the usufruct of the paddy-land. May those who approve of my offering have a share of my merit; but may those who destroy the same live short and ignominious lives, and be burnt in the great *avíci* hell."

* The historians are silent as to this relationship, presumably because they dare not or would not indicate the king's plebeian origin on the maternal side.

† Mettevya.

‡ A Minister of King Zeyatheinka or Uzana of Pagan (1211—1234 A.D.).

No. (5).

Locality.—Within the porch of the Damayangyi pagoda.

Date.—581 Sakkarâj (1219 A.D.).

Founder.—Kinmi Pèpo.*

Substance of inscription.—Dedication of slaves to pagoda.

On Monday, the 3rd waxing of Thadingyut, 581 Sakkarâj, Kinmi Pèpo dedicated to the pagoda the following slaves, namely: Nga Pôn Zôn, O Ya and daughters O Pyi Nyi, O Ti, and O Hmyauk; total 5. "I have dedicated these slaves to the pagoda. If any of my descendants molest them or their descendants, may they live short and inglorious lives, and be burnt in *avîci* hell."

No. (6).—Obverse.

Locality.—At the Taungkuni pagoda, about 300 feet south of Damayangyi pagoda.

Date.—553 Sakkarâj (1191 A.D.).

Founder.—Theingathuya.

Substance of inscription.—Building of cave for reception of manuscripts and dedication of lands and slaves.

The cave built and furnished with manuscripts by Theingathuya, a minister of King Narapatisithu, with the view that he might escape the miseries of *samsaro* and attain Buddhahood, was completed on the full-moon day of Tazaungmôn, 553 Sakkarâj, and when it was dedicated the following eight monks were present, namely, Pyitzobutdi, Kuthawyadithe, Ingu, Mahapandeik, Etthikadamakanbi, Damaguru, Damanandi, and Nanga.

In the same year, 120 suits of yellow robes were offered to these eight monks.

"Before I attain Buddhahood, may I be rewarded with every delight music can bestow, and to this end I dedicate to the pagoda the following musicians as slaves, namely, Nga Thu Ka, Nga Ma Ta, Nga Ma Yan, Nga Pôn Sôn, Nga Thu Yin, Nga Pyu, Pulawlè, Nga Yu Man, Adi, O A, O Kaung, O Kyi, Nga Pôn Ya, Umiyani, Parinasi Dewi, Ngariwi, Pulawle, Nanmadi, Kutadandi, Nga Sôk, Pôktanni, and Nga Kyun; total 23. Again, in order that I may never be in hunger or want, I dedicate 300 *pès* of paddy-land known as the Tenga fields to the pagoda and the presiding monk of the monastery. Lastly, to avoid becoming a slave in my future existences, I dedicate to the pagoda and the monkhood the following 100 slaves, namely: . . . . (a line) Nga Kun Zin and wife O Pôn, Nga Pun, Nga Pi and sons Nga Mye, Nga Wun Bye and Nga Mo, Nga Tu and wife O Sut, daugh-

* A maid of honour.

ter O Tin; Nga Awe and wife O Ya, O Kywin and daughter O Wun, Nga Pôn and wife O Paung, daughter O Byu, Nga Pyu and brother Nga U Pi; Nga Pôn and sons Nga Tauk Tu, Nga Se, Nga Chat, O Pi and daughter O Pa O, O Mwe, Nga Hmya and son Nga Paung, Nga Kan, Nga Thin Dè, Nga Mata and sons Nga Kywè, Nga Ngè and Nga Taing, Nga Kywe and sons Nga Maung Ngè and Nga Ha Yan, Nga Ka Lan, Nga Ya and wife O Paung, daughters O Ku and O Mwe, son Nga Myit, grandsons Nga Nyo and Nga Wun Be, O Kan and daughter O La Wa, Nga Pa, Nga Môn, Nga Pwin, Nga Pwa, Nga Myet, Nga Mun, Nga Kye, Nga Pyit, Nga U Zu and son Nga Than Ba, Nga Taung E, O Ma and sister O Pôn, O Sôn, O Ma and daughters O San Thi, O San Bin, O Bwin, O Ku and O Twe; Nga Deik and son Nga Wun Byi, Nga Saung and son Nga Kalan; Nga Paung; Nga Laung, Nga Than, Yakabu and daughter O Kôn, O Sat, Nga Pyi and wife O Pi, Nga Thet, Nga Lwe, Nga Paw, O Mwe and son Nga Sein, daughters O Sein, O Kywet, O Chôn, O Myo and O U Yaung, Nga Yôn and daughters O Sat, O Swin, Ya Keik and daughters O Thi, O Hmo, O Pwa and O Pôn, Nga Pa, Nga Mwe and brother Nga Myaik; total 100.

"For this my meritorious deed may I become a wise and distinguished *Rahan* in the time of the next Buddha."

No. (7).

Locality.—Within the porch of the Myaukkuni pagoda.

Date.—603 Sakkarâj (1241 A.D.).

Founder.—Queen Asaw.

Substance of inscription.—Building of cave-pagoda, monastery, and rest-house, and dedication of lands, slaves, and cattle.

I adore the three Gems!

WITH a view to escape the miseries of *samsaro* and attain Nirvâna, Asaw,* Queen of Uzana † and mother of Thihapade‡ and Tayabya,‡ built a cave, and on Wednesday, the full-moon of Kasôn, 603 Sakkarâj, formally dedicated the same by water-pouring. At the same time the Queen dedicated 178 slaves, 260 *pès* of paddy-land and two gardens. The names of the slaves from Pagan are: Myin Te Bôk, Sathaya, daughter Ta Da and son Pya Gat, Thatawa,

* This celebrated queen was a daughter of a farmer of Seiktein-Kanbyu village, near Popa. She was raised to the throne at the age of 12 on account of her great intelligence and beauty. She was the chief queen also of Uzana's son and successor Nayathihapati.

† Not the son of Kyazwa, who ascended the throne of Pagan in 1250 A.D., but the son of Narapatisithu, who began to reign in 1211 A.D., is here meant. This Uzana was also known by the names of Zeyatheinka, Nandaungmya and Tilominlo.

‡ Theinpade and Tayamun of history.

wife Meik Ti and son Nga Yauk Thit; Ga Ya, wife Kein Dari and daughter Đôk Ki; Kithara Palapôk; Tha Panara; Sandarapôk; Tintapôk; musician Budaw, wife Thu Ki, sons Titaya, Hitaya, Nga Mun, and infant, and daughters Yale and Site; drummer Petka and son Nga Twe; Pali and son drummer Nga Yut; drummer Nga Pagan and sister Gumi; Byinki and son drummer Nga Masun; Hitu and son artisan Nga Yinga, son Nga Buda; Muki Kywe and daughters Thuki and Thide, grandson Nga U; Thanzi and daughter Thiwali; Gani and daughter Dewi; total 41. The slaves from Ywale are—Nga Kaung and brother Nga Laung, and Nga Pyi Wa; totai 3. The cattle dedicated were 100 head of cows from Myinmu in charge of 20 herdsmen. The following offerings were also made, namely, a plain *thingan* and head-gear for the lower image, an ornamented *thingan* for the upper image, a gilt lounge, a screen, a cot with mattress and pillows, a betel clip, a brass lamp stand, a brass spittoon, a large brass kettle, a bell stand, a large and a small golden alms-bowl, two brass trays, five brass cups with covers, one large pot cover, eight musical gongs, nine smaller brass gongs, three pairs of cymbals, and three small bells.

The slaves dedicated to the pagoda by Pisenga were O Thukya and daughters O Myama and Ma Oka. Thugyi Thayan also dedicated a slave called Nga Laung. The offerings made to the monastery consisted of 174 slaves from Kawdè village and 300 *pès* of paddy-land. The slaves from Pagan were Nga Ku Da, Nga Pôn Lut, Nga Myè, Kyunozaukpeikthama, Nga Kaung, Nga Lôk, O Kan Pa and daughter O Thu Kya. The cattle offered were 100 cows from Sinbyu village in charge of 10 herdsmen; and the furniture for the monastery consisted of one gilt lounge set with precious stones, one spittoon, one brass kettle, two brass trays with stands, five cups with covers and a pot cover.

"Let all these offerings be under the control of the presiding monk of the monastery, and let him execute all necessary repairs. Let 5 baskets of paddy a month be given for every ten scholars in the monastery. On the full-moon days of Kasôn, Wazo, Wagaung, and Thadingyut, let offerings be made to the *devas*, and let each offering consist of 1½ baskets of rice, four baskets of paddy and six baskets more of paddy for the purchase of fruit, betel, and other necessaries. For the rice-offering at the pagoda let three baskets of red rice, one of white rice, and seven and a-quarter of paddy be given for each Lenten period.

"In addition to this let five-eighths basket of paddy be given for the daily rice-offering, and let 10 nuts a day be supplied for the betel-offering. Let the two men who look after these offerings be given a *pè* of paddy-land each. Let 135 baskets of paddy be set apart for the musicians, and let the leader receive two baskets and the others one basket each. Let the four cymbal-players receive half basket each, the oldest drummer one basket, the oldest singer one basket, and let the other drummers and singers receive three-quarter basket, half basket, or quarter basket according to their age and position. Let this be done every year."

INSCRIPTIONS OF PAGAN.

VII.—Found within the City walls.

No. (1).*

Locality.—Close to the eastern wall of the Shwegugyi pagoda porch.

Date.—503 Sakkarâj (1241 A.D.).

Founder.—King Alaungsithu.†

Substance of inscription.—Building of the Shwegugyi pagoda.

"HONOUR and reverence to the Buddha, whose wisdom is as vast as the earth and is pure, and who has led in the paths of the excellent law all human beings, *devâs*, and *brahmâs* and other beings, who could not of their own accord find their way across the slough and the grove of desire. I adore this Buddha, whose law and monkhood are incomparable."

"The present world is honoured with five Buddhas. Four, who were more eminent than men, have already appeared, and of these I shall proceed to enumerate briefly the excellent attributes of Gautama Buddha, who was replete with all wisdom and who was a scion of the Sakya family of kings: Let the righteous hearken to me.

"The Buddha, who is of great renown and who is the object of worship of the three superior beings, acquired the 30 kinds of virtue not only in one, but in several existences, by performing the three kinds of meritorious deeds, namely, that for the world in general, for his relations, and for the attainment of Buddhahood. He was the fountain of mercy and was full of diligence. One of his virtues was the performance of the five kinds of charity in the interests of the world. As King Vessantara his constant delight was the furtherance of the welfare of others, and as he chose the chief of the ten kinds of virtue, he became, on his demise, an inhabitant of the highest abode of *nats* excelling them all in glory. While there, a host of *nats* from different parts of the universe approached him

* This inscription is in Pâli throughout.

† King of Pagan (1092—1167 A.D.). He was also known as Shwegu-dâyakâ after the erection of the Shwegugyi pagoda.

with the request that he might assume Buddhaship, and it being in accordance with his own wish, the embryo Buddha looked ahead with the five kinds of vision, and on his next birth became a member of the Sakya family. The glorious and wise embryo remained as a man in the abode of men for 29 years and then renounced the world to become a *Rahan* and thus acquire omniscience. He performed several acts of penance, and his origin was as good as that of the previous Buddhas. He resided at the foot of a banyan tree near the Nerañjarā river, and lived on the milk offered him as alms. Subsequently be approached the beautiful and excellent throne under the Bodhi tree and having seated himself thereon exercised the four kinds of diligence. While the Bodhisat, who was more excellent than the three kinds of superior beings, was thus occupied, he beheld the *nat* Mâra, with a host of mercenaries, approach him with the courage of the king of lions. But he was totally unmoved; he destroyed the gate of desire and thus overawed the evil *nat* and his host. The victorious, imperturbable, wise and diligent Bodhisat then passed the three watches of the night exercising his omniscience. During the last watch or that immediately preceding the dawn he reviewed all his anterior births. Being more excellent than the five kinds of *Muni* and having acquired omniscience, he merited the title of Buddha. The emitter of the rays of wisdom, having acquired the knowledge of every law, joyfully recited the stanzas beginning with *Anekajâti Samsâram* and passed seven days on the throne. He thus emerged from all sorrow, accomplished his task of becoming Buddha and ceased from all passion, and was content, glad, and joyful, with his mind set upon the welfare of men and *nats*."

The wise, righteous, and justly famous King Alaungsithu, who is able to disperse his own enemies and those of his people and Religion as the glorious and rising sun disperses darkness, fear, and cold, has been ruling Pagan in accordance with the ten kingly precepts. Knowing that in the three worlds it is exceedingly difficult to become a Buddha or a man and have the opportunity of hearing the law of the righteous preached, the wise King Alaungsithu had this beautiful and lofty cave-pagoda built and adorned with several small pagodas and statues of *nats* in honour of the excellent and virtuous Buddha Gautama. Being desirous of saving the three kinds of superior beings from the miseries of *samsaro*, the king further had a wonderfully beautiful and pleasing image made which exactly resembled the living Buddha, the adorable, the wise, and the possessor of the five kinds of clear-visioned eyes. After the completion of this pagoda and image, His Majesty caused a complete copy of the Tripitaka to be prepared, and during the dedication ceremonies offered suits of robes to several monks, and cheerfully ministered to their other material wants with his own hands. An intense desire to become a Buddha then seized the king and His Majesty accordingly expressed the following prayer :—

"Gautama attained Buddhaship by acquiring the ten kinds of virtue and was thus enabled to liberate all sentient beings from the bonds of desire. May I, in future, be in a position to do likewise.

"The all-wise Buddha comprehended the mysteries of the law and propounded them without effort. He was the disburser of gifts to the multitudes of suppliant *brahmas* and *devâs* who flocked to him from the ten thousand universes, while he was with Aññâlakoṇḍhañña Thera in the highly pleasant Isipatanamigadavum grove, the resort of the flying *rishis* and the feathered world, after he had himself travelled a distance of 30 *yojanâs* with incomparable diligence, and was thus the means by which many attained Nirvâna. May I be able to do likewise.

"The excellent Buddha, whose origin was as good as his predecessors, was well versed in the Yamakas and could therefore prophesy as only Buddhas can. From his body was emitted variously brilliant rays of brown, gold, red, white, and scarlet, and six other kinds of resplendent rays penetrated with great rapidity to all quarters in different ways, lighting up the darkness everywhere. He succeeded in persuading by various means several heretics who despised Nirvâna and were on their way to the four forms of destruction blinded with their own vain beliefs and misled by the thought that they were Buddhas themselves, but who were in reality far from the path leading to the abode of the *nats* and to Nirvâna. Moved by a heart full of great and tender mercy towards all sentient beings, the Buddha brought many who were in abject misery from several other universes to this, and exerting his power placed them in a line on Mount Meru, walked along on their heads, and thus healed them all. May I be able to work miracles of this nature.

"Having performed the above miracle, the Buddha proceeded to the slab of rock known as Paṇḍhakaṁpata in Tāvatimsā, the abode of the 33 Sakkas, and having seated himself thereon in divine glory, administered the draught of blessing to several *nats* and *brahmas* and preached the Abhidhamma law to an assembly of *nats* headed by the one who was previously his royal mother. May I have the opportunity of performing a similar deed.

"The Buddha, who resided on the summit of Mount Meru, attended by a brilliant retinue, performed several miracles for the enlightenment of the whole world. May I, in future, be able to do likewise.

"After having preached to the assembly of *nats* in Tāvatimsā, the Buddha descended to this continent and preached several sermons to men, *brahmas*, ogres, *nats*, brahmins, *nagās*, elephants, and heretics who thought themselves Buddhas. May I become such a Buddha.

"The Buddha, whose origin is as excellent as that of his predecessors, performed the whole of the five kinds of duties incumbent on all Buddhas. May I be able to do so."

No. (2).*

Locality.—Close to the western wall of the Shwegugyi pagoda porch.

Date.—503 Sakkarāj (1241 A.D.).

Founder.—King Alaungsithu.

Substance of inscription.—Building of the pagoda.

"THE excellent Buddha, whose virtue is as vast in volume as the earth, whose serenity is like that of the Himalayas, the king of mountains, and whose wisdom is like the firmament, is free as the wind from worldly attachments and lusts and desires. He has passed the region of uncertainty and doubt, and is beyond the influence of cause and effect. Owing to the absence of desire, he is subject no more to the three kinds of *vattam*. Having attained the state of supreme refinement himself, he undertook to educate multitudes of men and free them from misery and sorrow. He was in the habit of acquiring special attributes and virtues, and as he was himself free from the flame of desire, he constantly strove to confer the same freedom on mankind. Omniscience was his ardent wish, and he brought comfort to many and was the refuge of the wise. He was the recipient of the charity of those who sought happiness. He was free from marriage ties and his diligence was great. May I become such a Buddha.

"The Buddha, who was safe from the approach and attack of the enemy Desire, who was free from fear and trembling, whose fame was widespread, who was full of mercy and wisdom, who may be compared only with the previous incomparable Buddhas, who always dispersed ignorance, who was replete with the 32 greater and 80 lesser attributes, who was ever surrounded with a halo of glory about a fathom deep, who was the possessor of the 18 kinds of gifts, whose constant wish was the welfare of the three kinds of superior beings, and who was the head of them all, mastered the four cardinal truths and was the possessor of the 14 kinds of sublime wisdom. He was, moreover, free from the poisons of desire,

* This also is in Pāli throughout.

passion, and ignorance, and was incomparable and full of diligence. May I become such a Buddha.

"The multitudes of heretics, who being blinded by passion, crowded into the grove of heresy like shoals of fish which rush into a net with fine meshes cast by a fisherman, were encompassed by the far-reaching and pure wisdom of the Buddha, the omniscient, and were subdued by him. Every living thing on the earth as well as the birds of the air, the different species of visible sentient beings, those with spirits and those without, were encompassed by that same wisdom. The world of *nats* and men was in utter darkness, but the Buddha's wisdom enlightened it. Ignorance flies before him as darkness flies before the rising sun. The excellent preceptor of *nats* and men is as skilfull in guiding them as an expert charioteer (in driving a chariot). He is therefore worthy of their adoration. May I become as worthy a Buddha as he.

"By my present offering I have endeavoured to acquire merit in the interests of all sentient beings. I do not desire the pleasures of life in this world or in the world of *nagas*, *nats*, or *brahmas*, or even as an immediate disciple of a Buddha. But, may I, by virtue of my offering, become as it were a bridge by which all sentient beings may cross the sea of *samsaro* to the excellent land of Nirvâna.

"May I succeed in crossing the sea of *samsaro* myself and be able to succour those who are being drowned or are drifting in the same.

"May I be enlightened myself in order that I may enlighten others.

"May I be free from passion myself so that I may liberate others from its bondage.

"May I be able to arise from the stupor of passion and awaken others who are under its influence.

"May I escape from the fire of passion and be able to extinguish it in others.

"May I be liberated from the trammels of passion and be able to extricate others from the same.

"May I be surrounded with the precepts of the righteous and cease from sin myself, so that I may purify others.

"May I always be free from desire, passion, and ignorance.

"May my wealth and happiness, which I have obtained without oppressing others, be continuous.

"May I never encounter any danger from fire, robbers, and the three other kinds of enemies.

"May I always be free from the evils which arise from the senses of sight, touch, smell, taste, and hearing.

"May I be able always to adhere to the precepts of the excellent Buddha, which enable one to eschew evil, and keep mankind from going to the four regions of punishment.

"All wise men, who are more excellent than other mortals, renounce the world and its pleasures. May I be able to do likewise and attach myself to the Religion.

"The excellent Buddha, who had at heart the welfare of *nats* and men, ordained the Sikkhāpadas. May I, in future, be able to observe the whole of those precepts.

"During this present dispensation of Gautama Buddha may I, by virtuous conduct, occupy as honourable a position among the monkhood as the beautiful moon does among the stars in the firmament.

"May I be able to keep the law propounded by the Buddha and contained in the Sutta, Abhidhamma, and Vinaya.

"May I, in the present dispensation of Gautama Buddha, be able to promote my own interests as well as those of others.

"May I be able to leave undone all such acts as were prohibited by the Buddha.

"May I always be sensible of all acts of kindness done to me by others and be alive to the necessity of reciprocating them.

"May I ever be far removed from evil companions.

"May I realize the misery of the poor beings who are subject to re-birth, and be enabled to work out my own salvation from the vast sea of existence.

"May I, by virtue of this my offering, have the opportunity of hearing the sermons to be preached by the coming Buddha Metteyya on the covered walk which will be as beautifully adorned and highly imposing as Mount Meru. May I have the opportunity also of offering the four kinds of necessaries* to that Buddha and be then qualified to hear the prophecy pronounced by him before the assembly of *nats* and men that I shall on a certain day attain Buddhahood.

"The Buddha, who was the object of adoration of all *nats* and men, was the possessor of several estimable attributes. May I become such a Buddha.

"The Buddha liberated 24 *asankheyyas* of sentient beings from the bonds of *samsaro*, performed every duty incumbent on Buddhas, preached his 84,000 sermons for the benefit of those of his time and of subsequent times, shone like a mighty flame amidst his disciples in the three lokas, and demonstrated the unstability of all

* Food, raiment, dwelling, and medicine.

things material, thereby setting at naught the philosophy of the foolish, who advocate their permanency. He has attained Nirvâna, where there is no aging or death. May I be able to do likewise and attain the bliss of Nirvâna." Here ends the prayer.

This inscription is erected by King Alaungsithu, who was full of wisdom and prudence; who was a seeker after omniscience and Nirvâna; who was a devotee of the three 'Gems;' whose glory is as resplendent and whose power is as mighty as the rising sun, the dispeller of the great darkness and cold which was much dreaded by the first inhabitants of the earth; and who is able to subdue his own enemies as well as those of the Religion and the people.

The building of this pagoda was commenced on Sunday, the 4th waning of Kasôn, 503 Sakkarâj, at the most auspicious moment. It was completed together with its statues of guardian *nats* on Thursday, the 11th waning of Nadaw, 503 Sakkarâj.

No. (3).—Obverse.

Locality.—Within the walls of the Shinbinbawdi pagoda, on the east side.

Date.—550 Sakkarâj (1188 A.D.).

Founder.—Thingyi Saya (Monk).*

Substance of inscription.—Dedication of slaves to pagoda.

On Wednesday, the 11th waxing of Nadaw, 550 Sakkarâj, the following slaves were dedicated by Thingyi Saya, namely, O Tha Pin and son Nga Pan Kè; O Pwa; Hnit Thi Ya; Nga Chat Ya; Nga Ku Kè; Kaung Pi Myè; Nga Pyi; Nga Yauk; Nga Yanna; and Nga Ywa Kyu; total 11; also O Tan; Nga Pi; Nga Sin Kyè Wa; O Thi Ki; Mo Pôn Lut; Nga Ma So and sons Nga Taba, Nga Pyaung Zôn; O Do; O Pyan; O U Lôn; and O Chat Ya; total 12; grand total 23.

"May I, by virtue of this offering, obtain omniscience; be freed from the miseries of *samsaro*; be always imbued with piety in my future existences; and be able to refrain from sinful deeds. May those who approve of my offering have their wishes gratified. On the other hand, may those who destroy the same be burnt in *avîci* hell together with their relatives, and may they never have the opportunity of beholding and being saved by any of the coming Buddhas, though their number may reach that of the atoms in a heap of earth."

---

* The word သင်းကြီး (*thingyi*) meant a military officer as well as a Buddhist ecclesiastical dignitary. So the founder might have been either the preceptor of a military officer of Narapatisithu's reign or simply an abbot.

REVERSE.

Date.—558 Sakkaràj (1196 A.D.).

Founder.—Thakin Pwèthaung.*

Substance of inscription.—Building of pagodas and dedication of slaves thereto.

ON Tuesday, the 9th waning of Tawthalin, 558 Sákkaràj, Thakin Pwèthaung dedicated to the two pagodas erected by him the following four slaves, namely, Nga Naing and son Nga Ta; Palè; and O Than, a musician.

"By virtue of this offering may I escape the miseries of *samsaro* and hell. May my parents and other relatives have a share of my merit. . . . . ." (six lines).

NO. (4).

Locality.—Within the walls of the Shinbinbawdi pagoda, on the east side.

Date.—566 Sakkaràj (1204 A.D.).

Founder.—Daughter of Sominpyanchi.†

Substance of inscription.—Dedication of pagoda slaves and paddy-lands.

ON Sunday, the . . . . Pyatho, 566 Sakkaràj, the daughter of Sominpyanchi dedicated six pagoda slaves, namely, Ein Mi Da; Ein Byat; Ein Kwi Sein; Ein Byit; Nga Lein; and Nga Tan Laing. The paddy-lands dedicated were 50 *pès* to the Buddha, and 20 to his law.

"Whoever misappropriates these my offerings, whether it be my daughter, or my husband, or any other, may he fall into the four principal hells." [Here follows names of slaves, which can only be partly deciphered.]

NO. (5).

Locality.—Within the walls of the Shinbinbawdi pagoda, on the east side.

Date.—570 Sakkaràj (1208 A.D.).

Founder.—Nga San Thin.

Substance of inscription.—Dedication of slaves, cows, and ponies to pagoda.

ON Sunday, the 9th waning of Wagaung, 570 Sakkaràj, Nga San Thin dedicated to the pagoda the following 10 slaves, namely:

---

* Probably a Minister of Narapatisithu.

† This is evidently Prince Pyanchi, third son of Narapatisithu by Queen Usaukpan.

Nga U Pi and wife O Wun Pa, son Nga U. Hla; Nga U Lôn and sister O Taung Do; Nga Chat and wife O U Ya, son Nga Tha Lôn, daughter O Let Swe; and Nga Ket. The following offerings were also made, namely, one brass pestle; one flower tray; and six *pès* of paddy-land known as Thangaing; also 90 cows and 15 ponies to defray the cost of erecting a cave in the name of Nga San Thin's wife. The witnesses to these offerings were Monk Gunathagiya; Monk . . . . (11 lines).

No. (6).

Locality.—Within the walls of the Shinbinbawdi pagoda, on the south side.

Date.—574 Sakkarâj (1212 A.D.).

Founder.—Thingyi Dhammapâla-Dhammathwè.*

Substance of inscription.—Erection of pagoda, cave, and monastery, and dedication thereto of slaves and utensils.

On Wednesday, the 3rd waxing of Tawthalin, 574 Sakkarâj, Thingyi Dhammapâla-Dhammathwè dedicated the following slaves to the pagoda, cave, and monastery erected by him, namely, Thuma,† Matayepyanili; Kuta; Pyakadathi; Pyathut and wife Dedante; Mèmaw and wife Taunggi; Balada and wife Ginga; Pègaw; Kalayandi, daughter of Ayin; Hada; Padaga; Nga Tha Ya; Gawda; Udayandi and son Kôktayantan; Saw; Râmâ; Setkamâ; Nga Taung Bye; Pawti and wife O Pu Taw; total 24. The following offerings were also made, namely, 300 ticals of silver, one large lamp with stand, one large brass tray, one large pestle, and one large brass kettle.

"May those who destroy my offering be deprived of the opportunity of beholding any of the coming Buddhas."

No. (7).

Locality.—Within the walls of the Shinbinbawdi pagoda, on the east side.

Date.—575 Sakkarâj (1213 A.D.).

Founder.—Minyin Okatthinchin.‡

Substance of inscription.—Dedication of slaves and paddy-lands to pagoda and monastery.

On Friday, the 11th waxing of Nayôn, 575 Sakkarâj, Minyin Okatthinchin dedicated to the pagoda and monastery 200 *pès* of paddy-

* Burmanized form of Dhammasvâra.

† These slaves were evidently natives of India.

‡ A Minister of Zeyatheinka.

land, 20 slaves, one large brass tray, one large pestle, one large brass kettle, one spittoon and one . . . . The following five eminent monks were witnesses to the offering, namely, Zayaganbi, Tilawthaya, Pyinnyawethatha, Dithapamauk, and Etgapandeik. Nga Yauk Thin, a nobleman, was also present. The names of the slaves are Nga Ta Paku and wife Yo Bôn, sons Nga Pa, Nga Thet She, Nga Pwa, daughter O Shan; O Min Pa; O Myo; O Than Pa; Yanthagya; Nawazani; O Sin; O Sin Kalit, and son Nga Ma; O Bwin and daughter O Myaing Yin Ki; O Nga Paung; Nga Kaung; and Nga Kyi Zu.

"Of the produce of the paddy-lands, let three-fifths be utilized for the Religion and two-fifths for the monkhood."

No. (8).

Locality.—Within the walls of the Shinbinbawdi pagoda, on the eastern side.

Date.—589 Sakkarâj (1227 A.D.).

Founder.—One of the Ministers of Zeyatheinka.

Substance of inscription.—Dedication to pagoda of slaves, paddy-lands, and cows.

On Friday, the 1st waxing of Thadingyut, 589 Sakkarâj, the Thettawshe Minister, wishing to attain omniscience, dedicated the following slaves to the pagoda, namely, Nga Mye and son Nga Myit; Nga Kin Bun and son Nga Thet Hlut; Nga Pyi; I Zwè; Nga Kyôn and son Nga Wun Tha; So Bun Tha; Mi Pwa; and Nga Pyit; total 11. Besides these were dedicated 15 cows, four pairs of bullocks, and a piece of paddy-land. The witnesses to the offering were Makawya of Kyaungupôn, Sekya, a monk of Tèdaungyi, Chattayapyitsi of Kanya, Nga Che Thin of Tandawyaw, Nga Myat of Kinpa, Nga Mye Thin and O Ti Thin of Yinthapanbin, Nga Kyè Thin, Bi Thôk Thin, Pinthaung Waik, Thingattabi, Thinzaye of Thinthi village, Thôktaba, Pônthi's sister, Nga Kaing, and Nga Set.

No. (9).

Locality.—Within the walls of the Shinbinbawdi pagoda, on the eastern side.

Date.—591 Sakkarâj (1229 A.D.).

Founder.—Thin Nga Swè Thin's brother.

Substance of inscription.—Dedication of pagoda slaves and cattle.

On . . . . Tazaungmôn, 556 Sakkarâj, Thin Nga Swe Thin dedicated the following pagoda slaves, namely:

. . . . . ., daughter O Ka, granddaughter O Ku; O . . . .; O Pan; O Chan Tha; O Myet . . . . . . Pyin; . . . .; Nga Yan Si and son . . . .; Nga Sin's son Nga Thaik; Nga Tha Ku; . . . .; and Bôktadat. These slaves were to look after the pagoda. The paddy-lands dedicated measured 35 *pès*. The witnesses to the offering were Nga Yin, Si Thin, Nga Pyi Thin, Nga Yin Thin, and Nga Hlauk Thin.

On Sunday, the 4th waning of Tabaung, 591 Sakkarâj, Thin Nga Swe Thin's younger brother dedicated the following slaves to the pagoda, namely, Nga San Pe; Nga Put and sons Nga Myin Saw, Nga Hlun; Nga Put's brother Nga Ye; Nga Ya Ma Na; Nga Pôn Zôn; Nga Ywet Pôn and sons Nga Pyi Zôn and Nga Tet Pyi; Nga Pôn Daw and son Nga Hlauk; Nga Chan Tha; Nga Pyi Zwa; Nga Mun; Nga Ya Me and wife O Mya Yo; Taya Go and daughter O Myet Mye; O Lôn; O Wun Tha and daughter O Pôn Lut, son Nga Than Bôk. Besides, 20 cows were also dedicated.

"May those who destroy these offerings suffer worse than Devadat in *avīci* hell, and live a short and miserable life here. The witnesses to this offering are Gitsakarapati and two sons; Nga Mye Thôn Yin; Pyitsaya Thu; Yanna Thu, Nala Thin; Thamanta Gônkè; and Gônkè. By virtue of this offering may I become an omniscient Buddha."

No. (10).

Locality.—Within the walls of the Shinbinbawdi pagoda, on the eastern side.

Date.—593 Sakkarâj (1231 A.D.).

Founders.—Kyan Chin Thin and wife O Kywè Ho.

Substance of inscription.—Building of cave-pagoda, and dedication of slaves thereto.

ON Monday, the 7th waxing of Tawthalin, 593 Sakkarâj, the following slaves were dedicated by Kyan Chin Thin and his wife O Kywè Ho to the cave-pagoda erected by them, namely, Yayi Pinsha, O Chan and daughters O San Byi, O San Tha; O Bôn and daughter O Sôn; O Gaung and daughters O Det Pyi, O Ta Baung, O Ma Wè, and O Hlun; total 11. The witnesses to this dedication were monk Wiseiktaru Pandi; monk Pyinnyana Gapi, Nga Tin Thin; Kale; Pahu; Nga Ein Thin, Thinbunyaung; Thin kâyaung; . . . .; Thinthinga; . . . . The witnesses to the offering were Nga Chan Tha Thin; Lu Ku Yaung; Nga Pôn Daw Thin; . . . .; Thinyin Pabyat Thin; Yepi Thin; Nga Kaw Thin; Thin Yin Nga Byin; Nga Cho Thin; Nga Tha Yun Thin; Kalan Nyo; Nga Thin Tinbin; Nga Kyi

Thin; O Nyè Mi, daughter of Nga Taw Thin; O Nyè Ngè; . . . .; total 16 witnesses.

"These slaves were not inherited from our ancestors, but were purchased out of our own earnings. Should any of our relations during seven generations molest any of them, may they be burnt in the *avici* hell below this earth."

The above was composed by the wise monk called Narindakari . . . . (five lines).

No. (11).

Locality.—Within the walls of the Shinbinbawdi pagoda, on the eastern side.

Date.—593 Sakkarâj (1231 A.D.).

Founders.—Nga Myin Kin, Nga Myin Do, and their aunt.

Substance of inscription.—Building of pagoda and monastery and dedication thereto of slaves.

On Thursday, the 5th waxing of Thadingyut, 593 Sakkarâj, the brothers Nga Myin Kin and Nga Myin Do, sons of Nga Sin Thin, dedicated the following slaves to the pagoda and monastery erected by them, namely, Anan and son Nga Pa Naung; Ayaw and son Nga Sagu; Nga Kywin; Thin Kwe and husband Seinga, daughter Aye; and Nga Thwi; total 10. The brothers asked their aunt to witness the dedication, and she added two more slaves, namely, Nga Tha Ya and son Nga Thôk. The following offerings were also made in the same year, namely, one brass tray, one pestle, and one lamp-stand.

"May those who destroy our offerings live short and ignominious lives and fail to behold any of the coming Buddhas."

No. (12).

Locality.—Within the walls of the Shinbinbawdi pagoda, on the eastern side.

Date.—597 Sakkarâj (1235 A.D.).

Founder.—Monk Pitarit.*

Substance of inscription.—Dedication of slaves, cattle, land, money, and utensils to the three "Gems."

I adore the Buddha!

On Wednesday, the 3rd waxing of Kasôn, 597 Sakkarâj, Monk Pitarit dedicated the following slaves to the pagoda called Pyathat,

* King Kyazwa's spiritual adviser.

namely, Nga Naka and sons Nga Myi, Nga U Hla, Nga Pôk, Nga Lu, Nga Pyin, Nga Pa Ngè, and Nga Pa E; Nga Myi's son Nga Yauk Thit; Nga Naka's nephews Nga Aung, Nga Tagu, and Nga Tha Pin; Pi Mi; Ya San and daughter Ya Yin, sister Atisi, nieces Yasan, Yapywi; Thida and son Nga Tan Ma; Thiyewi; Nga Pein Taw and sons Nga Yaung Ywe, Nga Tabaung and Nga Kwe; Nga Yan and sons Nga San, Nga Tho, and Nga Aung Sin; musicians Ke Nwè, Nga La Hôk, and Taba Thi; Meta; Nga Kyaing and son Nga Yin; Nga Nayan; Nga Pa; Nga Hlaing and son; and drummer Nga Dôk Cha. The following slaves were offered to monk Pitarit, namely, Dhamma Wôkti and wife Kôk Pè, son Petki, daughter Pweinde, son Maung Ma Meik; Thetki's sons Nga Thin, Nga Thila, and Nga Dwit; Nga Than's sons Nga Pôn Saung, Nga Tin Sha, and Nga Pôn; Nga Thila's sons Nga Mun, Nga Min Ban; Nga Dwit's son Nga Min Byu; Pweindè's daughters Amein, and Mein Bwin, Mein Gywit, Mi Hla, and Tho Bôn; O Hla and sister Nagi, nieces O Thalôn, O Byi, O Sôn, O Sagu, and O Bwin; O Myauk and sisters O Kyaung, and O Chan Tha; total 73. Besides, monk Pitarit offered 100 cows, five buffaloes, five ponies, and 50 *pès* of paddy-land granted him by the king and which lies near the field belonging to Pwin Hla and his wife. Twenty *pès* of this land are meant for the Buddha, five for the law, ten for the monkhood, and 15 for the maintenance of students of the law . . . .

. . . .

two large brass trays; one cover; . . . .
one pestle; one copper kettle; . . . .
one spittoon . . . . (3 lines).

No. (13).

Locality.—Within the walls of the Shinbinbawdi pagoda, on the eastern side.

Date.—599 Sakkarâj (1237 A.D.).

Founders.—Nga Pyi Thin and wife.

Substance of inscription.—Dedication of pagoda slaves.

ON Wednesday, the 7th waxing of Thadingyut, 594 Sakkarâj, Nga Su Thin and his wife I Chan Thin dedicated Nga Yaung, I Mywe She, and daughter I Kywin as pagoda slaves. The monk Gunati poured out the water of dedication and it was during I Chan Thin's lifetime.

In 599 Sakkarâj Nga Su Thin dedicated seven more pagoda slaves, namely, I Myo, I Tin Ke, I Sa Ye, I Pyu, I Payan, Nga Pwin, and Nga Sha.

On Friday, the 11th waxing of Pyatho, 598 Sakkarâj, Nga Thi Kwa Thin dedicated the following pagoda slaves, namely, I Hlun and I Taung We.

On Tuesday, the 11th waning of Tawthalin, 599 Sakkarâj, Nga Pyi Thin and his wife dedicated the following slaves, namely, Nga Taba and Nga Pôn Zôn to look after the pagoda.

"May those who molest these slaves suffer in the *avīci* hell and fail to behold any of the future Buddhas." The witnesses to this dedication were monk Gunati; U Pagôk; Chatta Tathi; Myana Thago; Kanta Wadi; and I Lwa; total six witnesses in the same year, ... (4 lines).

No. (14).

Locality.—Within the walls of the Shinbinbawdi pagoda, on the southern side.

Date.—599 Sakkarâj (1237 A.D.).

Founder.—Nyana Pyitsi.

Substance of inscription.—Building of cave, monastery, and rest-house with well, library, bell, and out-houses, and dedication of slaves, paddy-lands, and cows thereto.

THE building of the cave was commenced on the morning of Monday, the 3rd waning of Pyatho, 598 Sakkarâj, and it was completed in 28 days. The walls were finished on the full-moon day of Tabaung. The golden cap of the cave was set up on the morning of Monday, the 7th waning of Tabaung. On Friday, the 10th waxing of Tagu, the painting of the cave was finished. On the following Monday the 14,619 small images and 550 statues * to be placed in the cave were completed. The monastery and out-houses were also completed on the same day. The bell attached to the cave weighed 106½ viss. The cap of the cave was of brass, weighing 55½ viss, and 46 ticals of gold was used in gilding it. Twenty ticals more was spent in gilding the main image. Five school-houses were also built and an image was placed on the monastery, near which three banyan trees were planted. Besides, there were three lavatories and a library. All these were dedicated on Friday, the 9th waning of Nadaw. On Monday, the 4th waning of Kasôn, 599 Sakkarâj, Nyana Pyitsi, the nobleman, dedicated the following slaves to the cave erected by him, namely, Nga San Ya and son Nga Lut; Nga Tôn; Nga Pu Ya and wife O Gôn; daughters O Kyaung and O Yauk; O Kè Laung; musician Nga Tôn Da; drummer Nga Pwa; Nga Ma Lo; Thanapwè, an Indian musician; Nga Pyauk and O Ma, an Indian couple; their son

* These represent the various anterior births of Gautama Buddha.

Nga Taung Mwe; Nga Kyaung . . .; Nga Mun; Nga Yauk; Nga Twe; Mi Tu and daughter Palu; drummer Nga Pu Thi; Pwa and Yi. The lands dedicated were :—50 *pès* of paddy-land offered by Yanyindi and called Petmanyo, 20 for the rice-offerings at the pagoda and 30 for the maintenance of the presiding monk of the monastery; 70 *pès* of paddy-land called Paukpinbyu, 20 *pès* called Ye-u, and a barn containing 300 baskets of paddy, which were offered by monk Katathu for the maintenance of the presiding monk. Besides the above, monk Katathu offered Yatathu and 19 other slaves to the pagoda. The 40 *pès* of paddy-land offered by Minhla was for the maintenance of the students at the monastery, and the 30 *pès* called Pyaukya, situated south-west of Lègwè village in Lègaing township, are for the presiding monk: so are the 300 *pès* called Masèpaung, offered by Hnaung. The 100 *pès* just beyond Pyinbi village are dedicated to the three 'Gems.'

"May those who appropriate any of these lands suffer in the *avīci* hell along with seven generations of their relatives; may they never behold any of the future Buddhas, even if their number be as numerous as the atoms in a heap of earth. May they always be *petas* in their future existences. On the other hand, may those who approve of my offering share the merit with me."

Thirty cows were also offered to the pagoda. Bôkdalinga, the mason, was rewarded with an elephant and four suits of clothes, and Seiktara Misin, the painter, with an elephant, a pony, and two suits of clothes.

No. (15).

Locality.—Within the walls of the Shinbinbawdi pagoda, on the eastern side.

Date.—600 Sakkarâj (1238 A.D.).

Founders.—Myingaba Pizè, his wife and son.

Substance of inscription.—Dedication of slaves to pagoda.

"THE attributes of the Buddha and his Law are beyond comprehension, so is the merit of those who honour him and his Law. May they receive praise."

On Thursday, the 3rd waning of Pyatho, 600 Sakkarâj, Myingaba Pizè, his wife and son Atulayat dedicated the following pagoda slaves, namely, Periyan and wife Ma Lauk, daughter Yasawi, grandson Mimithwi; Yasawi's sister Akwe, nieces Awithakwe and Môktalôn, nephew Nga Thauk; Nga Di Kyet; total 9.

The witnesses to the dedication were—monks Bôkdayinthe, Dhammalat, U Ôktamayazakawi, and Awiyazapandeik; Pattan Thawami; Puyithaman; Thiyipônnayikadanbi; Ngachatma Thin;

Nganaing Thin; Salawagôn; Wizayapè; Udayapè; Ngabyè Thin; Ngakun Thin; Myinthadit; and Mwanayan.

"Whoever destroys our offering, may he suffer in the uttermost depths of the *avîci* hell, and may he never have the opportunity of beholding any of the coming Buddhas."*

No. (16).

Locality.—Within the walls of the Shinbinbawdi pagoda, on the southern side.

Date.—604 Sakkarâj (1242 A.D.).

Founder.—Kingathu's † wife.

Substance of inscription.—Building of monasteries, and dedication thereto of slaves and lands.

ON Thursday, the 14th waning of Nadaw, 604 Sakkarâj, Kingathu, the nobleman, passed away. On the following Sunday, his wife, the daughter of Nyaungyangyi, having lost her beloved husband and realizing the impermanency of things, commenced to build three monasteries in the name of her husband and lord, her mother and her father, and with a view to promote the cause of the Religion. The monasteries were adorned with ornaments of gold, silver, copper, brass, and rubies, and offerings were made to them of boats, elephants, cattle, goats, ivory, slaves, paddy and garden lands after having invoked the guardian *nat* of the earth to bear witness to the act. To the Mahakatthapa monastery 100 *pès* of paddy-land known as Sin-u were offered. This land was purchased for 2,000 ticals of silver from Chatmamè Thin and Chatmayè Thin during the reign of Alaungsithu. Chatmamè Thin and Chatmayè Thin were the aunts of O Det Pye Thin. The Osènyè land, measuring 16 *pès*, is included in the Sin-u land. The Pinthit garden, which was also offered, was obtained in satisfaction of a debt of 4,000 ticals of silver due from Thula Piyit, his younger brother Anantanru and Lapiyit. Besides the above, the following offerings were made, namely, Chanthagaung field, containing 7 *pès*, which was purchased by Kingathu's wife for 150 ticals of silver from Malauklan, his sons Nga U and Nga Lat, and his sister Wunmani Thin; Kyauksit field of 5 *pès*, which was State land, granted to Kingathu; 5 *pès* purchased from Sinbu at 6 ticals per *pè*; the Hlibo land, consisting of Tahat field, 6 *pès*, Pandin field 6 *pès*, Eindaraseik field 6 *pès*, and U Sauk Pan field 6 *pès*; Kantuhaung field containing 20 *pès*, consisting of 15 *pès* purchased from Thingyikyôn,

---

* This would include the Buddhas of future *kalpas* also, for there is only one more Buddha to come for this *kalpa*, namely, Metteyya.

† A Minister in the reigns of Narapatisithu, Uzana, and Kyazwa of Pagan.

and 5 *pès* from Thingyi Pet; 50 *pès* offered to the Law by Kingathu; the Yônpôn field containing 100 *pès* and consisting of 40 *pès* called Kanaukyibôk, and 60 *pès* purchased from O Pôn Thin; 300 *pès* out of the Kyônthaye land containing 2,000 *pes*; and the Pyingamya land containing 20 *pès*; grand total 617 *pès* . . . . also 45 *pès* of garden land in Siywa village; 25 *pès* west of Myinmwè and 25 slaves.

No. (17).

Locality.—Within the walls of the Shinbinbawdi pagoda,* on the northern side.

Date.—609 Sakkarâj (1247 A.D.).

Founders.—Nga Hla Thin and wife.

Substance of inscription.—Dedication of pagoda slaves.

ON Thursday, the 1st waxing of Nadaw 609 Sakkarâj, Nga Hla Thin and his wife dedicated the following pagoda slaves, who were purchased with their own earnings, namely, Nga Pan; Ho Mauk; Nga Taung Mwe; Nga Kwe; Nga Pa Gan; O Tha Lôn; Nga Ma Yôk; O Chan; O Yauk; Aung Ma; O Kyitsaya; Nga Kan Ba; Nga Kan; Nga Myit; and Nga Chit Swe. The witnesses to the dedication were—monks Thanlè, Pyinnya, and Kaya Thin; O Kôn Dan Thin; O Twe Thin; and clerk Nga Let Pyi. The number of slaves was 15.

"May those who destroy my offering suffer punishment under this earth, like Devadat. But whoever approves of my offering, may he share its merit with me. The paddy-land with the palm-trees thereon is for the presiding monk of the monastery. May I be liberated from the bondage of *samsaro* . . . ." (two lines).

No. (18).—Obverse.

Locality.—Within the walls of the Shinbinbawdi pagoda, on the eastern side.

Date.—610 Sakkarâj (1248 A.D.).

Founder.—Banker Aing Hnin Thin.

Substance of inscription.—Building of pagoda and dedication of slaves, land, and cattle thereto.

ON Monday, the 12th waxing of Tawthalin 610 Sakkarâj, Banker Aing Hnin Thin dedicated the 13 pagodas built by him and at the

* Built by King Kyanyittha of Pagan (1064—92 A.D.).

same time offered the following persons as slaves thereto, namely: Nga Yin Sin, Aing La Bu, Aing Kun Bu, Aing Mun U,. Aing Wun Bye, Aing Mi, I Myi, Aing Sin Win, Aing Hlun, Paduma Mi; total 10. The offering was made in the presence of his three sisters and Banker Nga Sinzwa Thin. These slaves were not inherited from his parents, but were bought with his own earnings. The other witnesses to the dedication were Yinga Pahe and wife; Sattalin Kabo and wife; Samanta Pattara and wife.

"Whoever molests these slaves, whether it be my kinsman or any other, may he be burnt in the *avîci* hell . . . ." (one line).

REVERSE.

ON Friday, the 13th waxing of Nayôn, the following offerings were made to the old monastery, namely: . . . . ; 47 *pès* of paddy-land; 271 *pès* of garden-land; 20 slaves; a herd of cattle; 20 *pès* of paddy-land called Moti, and 100 *pès* of paddy-land at Minkyichauk. To the three images placed in the monastery at Myebôn the following offerings were made, namely: the Zidônpein field of 70 *pès*; 85 *pès* of paddy-land at Kyizin; 542 *pès* of garden-land; and 21 slaves. Fifteen slaves and a herd of cattle are offered to the monastery itself. For the maintenance of the monk Kalaba, the Kyizin garden, measuring 5 *pès*, was offered. At the same time 190 slaves were granted their freedom. Two-thirds of the cattle were for the old monastery and the remainder for the new. Out of the produce of the lands daily rice-offerings shall be made according to the following scale, namely, 1 *pè* of rice per image, the remainder to be utilized for the maintenance of the monks who look after the pagoda and images. The names of the slaves dedicated to the old monastery are: Nga Myo and sons Nga Pwa and Nga Hnat; Nga U Hla and sons Nga Minze, Nga Mè, and Nga Pyu; Nga Ye Môn; Matu Naing and sons Nga Kôk, Nga Ket, and Nga Nyan; Nga San Ga; total 20. The slaves dedicated to the image placed in the monastery at Myebôn are—O Ta, daughter O Kywin, husband Nga Pyi Wa; O Kywin's daughter O Sit; Nga Ta Mo; Nga Pyi Wa; Kantu Ita; O Kyat; Nga Pôn and wife O Chan Tha; Nga Pôn's brother Nga Kyin; . . . . . ; O Ku's daughter O Kyun; O Tan Laing and daughter O Man Tu; O Pyi; O Chit and son Nga Hli, daughter O Myo; mahout Nga Taung Mwe and brother Nga [illegible] E and 15 other slaves; total 36. The offerings consisted of altogether 322 *pès* of paddy-land, 813 *pès* of garden-land, 56 slaves, and a number of head of cattle; also the garden of 5 *pès* at Kyizin which was offered to monk Kalaba.

No. (19).

Locality.—Within the walls of the Shinbinbawdi pagoda on the eastern side.

Date.—620 Sakkarâj (1258 A.D.).

Founders.—Banker Nga Taing Bin Thin and wife.

Substance of inscription.—Building of pagoda and dedication of slaves thereto.

ON Thursday, the full moon of Tawthalin 620 Sakkarâj, Banker Nga Taing Bin Thin and wife dedicated the following slaves to the pagoda built by them, namely, Nga Yauk Pôn and daughter Yate, son Nga Kyaung Gyi; Yanyôngi; Yatimi; Nga Pyu; O Chun Mwe; Yakywe; and Mi U.

"May every one from the king downwards have a share of the merit accruing from the offering of these nine slaves, and may I, for my part, attain Buddhahood." The witnesses to the dedication were monks Ôktayanti, Dhammayit, Pavaradhammarajaguru, Hlakametkabyan, Thuyeinthin, Bidayet, Kantathi, and Thukamein Maukgalan; Nga Pan Deik; Nga Pa Ngè; and Nga San Thin. "I request these witnesses to look after my offering, and I liberate the three slaves Titalè, Tharapi, and Yaywit. May those who destroy my offering suffer in *avîci* and never have the opportunity of beholding any of the coming Buddhas."

Inscribed by Nga Hnit Leik Thin.

No. (20).

Locality.—Within the walls of the Shinbinbawdi pagoda, on the northern side.

Date.—622 Sakkarâj (1260 A.D.).

Founder.—Tayamyè.

Substance of inscription.—Dedication of slaves, lands, and cattle to pagoda and monastery.

ON Friday, the 4th waning of Tabodwè 622 Sakkarâj, Tayamyè made the following offerings to the pagoda and monastery, namely, 30 *pès* of *mayin* paddy-land at Wayindôk; 12 slaves, Nga Awyin Naing, Tadundo Pônzôn, and sons Kalaza and Nga Nyo Hmè; O Kyaung, O Kyun, O Kyi, Hnanlo Ya, O Pya, O Chwin Pi, and O Pyu Lwa daughters of O Pônzôn; 10 palm-trees at Tayin; and five cows. The rent of the land shall be utilized equally for the upkeep of the pagoda and monastery. The students shall be maintained out of the same fund and the presiding monk of the monastery will execute all necessary repairs to the pagoda. The witnesses to the offering were Dhammathaya Pandeik, Thutabôkdi, Kalapat, Tawthein, Ata, ...

"May those who destroy my offering be always miserable in the present, and may they (in future) be burnt in *avīci*. May those who approve of my offerings increase in wealth and happiness."

No. (21).

Locality.—Within the walls of the Shinbinbawdi pagoda, on the northern side.

Date.—Nil.

Founder.—Theinka . . *

Substance of inscription.—Building of monastery and dedication thereto of slaves and lands.

ON Wednesday, the full-moon of Pyatho . . . . . . Sakkarâj, Theinka . . ., the nobleman, offered 30 *pès* out of 100 owned by him at Myingyan to the monastery built by him.

"May my liege the king as well as my parents and other relatives obtain a share of the merit. May those who destroy my offering suffer in the hell within this earth. But may those who approve of it share its merit equally with me . . . ." (four lines).

Three slaves, Nga Chat, Nga U Ga, and . . . . were also offered. "May those who destroy the garden offered by me, fail to enjoy happiness in the abode of men and *nats*, and may they suffer as . . . ."

No. (22).

Locality.—Within the walls of the Shinbinbawdi pagoda, on the eastern side.

Date.—636 Sakkarâj (1274 A.D.).

Founders.—Nga Lat Maing and wife.

Substance of inscription.—Dedication of slaves and lands to monastery.

"MAY those who approve of this good deed from the king and queen downwards reap the merit thereof throughout all ages." This is the prayer of the nobleman Thiriwutdana and his wife Min Saw Lat,† who built the monastery for the monk Thamantapattara. Those who witnessed the dedication of the monastery were: the Governor of Kaungsin, Saduyingabo, Nga Mye, brother of Queen Asaw, and his wife, Eindapyitsaya, son of Thatharapo . . . . Talathi and wife, Amyit and wife, and Atweaman.

---

* This is merely a portion of the title of a nobleman. The full title would be either Theinkathura, Theinkapati, or Theinkapyanchi.

† Daughter of King Narathihapade.

"By virtue of this my good deed, may I enjoy a position similar to that of Queen Asaw, either in this world or in the abode of the *nats*. May my descendants share my merit with me. Should any of them be so charitably disposed as to add to the offerings of slaves and land made by me, may they obtain an *asankheyyaṁ* times more merit than I, and may those who encourage them to do so never even hear of the existence of hell. On the other hand, may those who destroy my offering never have the happiness of hearing the sermons of the future Buddhas, though their number may equal that of the atoms in a heap of earth extending from the Nyaungu river bank to Sīripaccaya (in Pagan), and may they become charred pillars in *avīci* throughout *samsaro*."

On Thursday, the 8th waxing of Kasôn 636 Sakkarâj, Nga Lat Maing and his wife, who was a maidservant of the nobleman Thiriwutdana, obtained permission to dedicate a piece of paddy-land to the monastery. Accordingly they purchased for 80 ticals of gold, and offered the land known as Princess Othin Kyè Thin's field, measuring 20 *pès* and situated north of the east Yebôk village in Taungbyôn township. This land was originally included in the service land allotted to the regiment of cavalry called Saduyingabo * and was obtained by Min Saw Lat for 80 ticals of gold and her gold belt. It was subsequently offered to Seintarathinka, Kalapcyitsi and Sandatipa. On Sunday, the 3rd waning of Tazaungmôn, 625 Sakkarâj, Monk Saleti, the spiritual adviser of the nobleman Thiriwutdana, dedicated to the monastery 100 *pès* of paddy-land at Dipeshin which was . . . .

No. (23).

Locality.—Within the walls of the Shinbinbawdi pagoda, on the eastern side.

Founders.—Nga Min Thin and wife.

Substance of inscription.—Building of cave and dedication of slaves thereto.

On Wednesday, the full-moon of Kasôn . . . . . . Sakkarâj, Nga Min Thin and his wife dedicated the following slaves to the cave erected by them, namely, ... and daughter O Pyit U, son Nga Pyi Wa; Ahla . . . ; O Chat and son Nga Hla Byi; Dama and wife Hiti, son Pyi Hla, daughter Gate; Nga Tan Gyi and brother Nga Tan Gu; Nan Bi, Kuta, and Gada; total 16. These

* Plots of land were granted to soldiers in lieu of pay, and these were either worked by them or sublet, the Government retaining the right to resume the same.

slaves were not inherited, but were purchased by Nga Min Thin and his wife with their own earnings. The witnesses to the dedication were—Monk . . . ; Thuma Than ; Gôn Thakin Ka ; Nga Pyu Thin ; Lawha Pikyan ; Nga Nyo Thin ; and Thingyi . . . . . Chathin ; . . . .

"May those who destroy my offering suffer in the *Pyinsanandayeik* hell, and then. . . . ."

NO. (24).

Locality.—Within the walls of the Shinbinbawdi pagoda, on the northern side.

[ONLY a few words of this inscription of 17 lines remain legible. They serve to show that a brick monastery was built in 754 Sakkarâj (1393 A.D.) and that 50 *pès* of land were offered for the maintenance of the presiding monk.]

NO. (25).

Locality.—Within the walls of the Shinbinbawdi pagoda, on the northern side.

[THIS is merely a list of names, apparently of pagoda slaves.]

NO. (26).

Locality.—Within the front porch of the Shwegugyi pagoda.

Date.—913 Sakkarâj (1551 A.D.).

Founder.—Hanthawaddy Shinbyuyin.

Substance of inscription.—Confirming the dedication of offerings to monasteries throughout the country, and the assessment of the usual port dues.

I adore the three 'Gems!'

IN the year 913 Sakkarâj, which corresponds with the year of the Religion 2095, soon after his accession to the throne,* the king issued the royal order that all offerings made to monasteries throughout the kingdom shall remain *in statu quo*; that the assessment of port dues shall be in accordance with the usual rates; and that whoever contravenes this order shall be deemed to offend the Religion of the excellent Buddha and to injure the interests of the people.

* That is to say one year after the event.

INSCRIPTIONS OF PAGAN.

VIII.—Found on the south of Pagan.

No. (1).

Locality.—Within the walls of the Mingalazedi pagoda.

Date.—636 Sakkarâj (1274 A.D.).

Founder.—Narathihapade.

Substance of inscription.—Building of pagoda and monastery and dedication of lands thereto.

I adore the three 'Gems!'

ON Sunday, the 6th waxing of Tabaung 603 Sakkarâj,* King Narathihapade, whose title is Sîritribhavanâtityapavaradhammarâjâ, who is the supreme commander of the vast army of 36 million soldiers, and who is the consumer of 300 dishes † of curry daily, being desirous of attaining the bliss of Nirvâna, erected a pagoda. Having done so, the king enshrined within it 51 gold and silver statuettes of kings, queens, noblemen, and maids of honour, and over these an image of Gautama Buddha in solid silver 1 cubit high, on Thursday, the full-moon of Kasôn 636 Sakkarâj. On that occasion a covered way was erected extending from the palace to the pagoda. Bamboo mats were laid along this. Over these rush mats were spread, and over these again pieces of cloth 20 cubits each in length were spread ; and at each cubit's length of the way banners were placed. During the ceremony the princes, princesses and nobles threw a large number of pearls among the statuettes, and the pagoda was formally named the Mingalazedi.

I adore the three 'Gems!'

ON Monday, the 6th waning of Tawthalin 663 Sakkarâj,‡ the following paddy-lands were dedicated to the pagoda, namely, the piece of land round the pagoda bounded on the south by the

---

* This is clearly a mistake of the sculptor and should be 630 Sakkarâj. The inscription throughout shows evidences of indifferent workmanship and is evidently not the original one erected by Narathihapade. The Hmannan Yazawin mentions an inscription in verse about the founding of the Mingalazedi pagoda, and that, I think, is the original. It appears that the king commenced building in 630 Sakkarâj, but owing to a popular prophecy in vogue at the time that his kingdom would come to an end simultaneously with the completion of the pagoda, he deferred operations for 6 years until he was reproved by an abbot named Panthagu.

† It is related that Narathihapade bemoaned his cruel fate when one day, during his flight from the Chinese invaders, only a hundred dishes were set before him!

‡ The latter portion of this inscription was evidently inscribed by King Sawnit, grandson of Narathihapade, the original founder.

premises of the monastery occupied by the monk lately returned from Ceylon, west by the Chizwè monastery land, north by the Kantu pagoda land, and east by the Theinmazi pagoda land; 400 *pès* of land in Amyin, consisting of Sinza field and tank 100 *pès*, Kyegaung field and tank 100 *pès*, Ngaya field and tank 100 *pès*, Paungza field and tank 100 *pès*, and 40 *pès* of land in Nwèni-Pakangyi, consisting of Lèthitkyi field 10 *pès*, Lethitngè field 10 *pès*, Apôkkyi field 10 *pès*, and Tabyat field 10 *pès*.

No. (2).

Locality.—In the brick monastery within the walls of the Mingalazedi pagoda.

Substance of inscription.—Dedication of slaves to pagoda and monastery.

ON Monday, ... Sakkarâj, the following slaves were dedicated to the pagoda by . . . . . . , namely, ... ; Po Mu Lôn; Nga Hmin; Mana Thi; Silan Pawpi; Nga U; Mi Ye; Nga Kauk; Pakuni; Nga Pôn Yauk; total 16. The slaves who were dedicated to the monastery by banker Nga Tikyet Thin are—O Maing; O Mein; Pi Ngè; O Mun; Thin Nga; O . . .; Kin Ki; Nga Pa La; Pa Hmu La; Ama Lawa and son Nga Yauk Thit, brother-in-law Nga Sapi, daughter Than Sawi, and daughter-in-law Apyo Ngè; total 14; . . . . ; Wi Gyi; O Pyi; . . . . The slave dedicated to the pagoda was Nga Tha Din. Banker Nga Pu Yet Thin also dedicated Nga Sa Yi as a pagoda slave in the presence of Thukaba.

"Let my son go and trade with 200 ticals worth of cloth, and let the profits be utilized for the maintenance of the abbot of the monastery. Should this be found insufficient, let small subscriptions be raised and let my son undertake all necessary repairs to the monastery. Should my wife and my son prove disobedient to the abbot, let the property given to them be withdrawn."

The witnesses to the dedication were: the abbot Yewata; monks Talapanaik, Thiyathi, Thumana, Tanmadathi, Pyinnyawa, Tulapyinmya, Pannathi, and Pôktakawtha; Nga Nyein Thin; Nga Thari Thin; Pa Lein; Pata Thinyin; Nga Palè Thin; Kunbyauk Sauk and brother Nga Nyein Thin; and Nga Chit Mun Pa.

"May those who destroy my offering be burnt in *avîci*. I have accordingly broken the kettle.* On the other hand, may those who support it share the merit equally with me."

---

* A custom now extinct which was similar to that of the Chinese, who break cups and saucers in consummation of a pledge or contract.

INSCRIPTIONS OF PAGAN.

IX.—Found at Myin-Pagan.

No. (1).

Locality.—On eastern face of pillar within the walls of Myazedi pagoda.

Date.—446 Sakkarâj (1084 A.D.).

Founder.—Prince Râjakumâra.*

Substance of inscription.—Making of golden image, inscription, and dedication of slaves thereto.

"I adore the Buddha, who is worthy of all adoration!"

IN the year 1628 of the Religion, the king entitled Sîritribhavanâtityadhammarâjâ reigned in Pagan. His chief queen was called Trilokavadhamsakâdevî† and his son Râjakumâra. The king granted three villages of slaves to the queen. When the queen died the king handed over her jewellery and the three slave villages to the prince. After a reign of 28 years the king died, and in memory of his royal parents, the prince had a golden image made out of his mother's jewellery and dedicated thereto the three slave villages granted him by his father. The dedication was made in the presence of monks Mahati, Môkgalipôktateiktha, Thumedapandeik, Byamapala, Byamadi, Teya, Thingathena, and Wayapandeik. Having done so, the prince placed the image in a cave. The names of the three slave villages are—Thetmunalun, Shanbo, and Yabè. The following prayer and imprecation were then uttered by the prince:—

"By virtue of this offering may I acquire omniscience. May those who destroy my offering, whether it be my relatives or others, be deprived of the opportunity of beholding the coming Buddha Metteyya."

Nos. (2), (3), and (4).

[THESE inscriptions are on the other faces of the pillar on which No. (1) is inscribed. No. (2) is in Talaing, No. (3) is in some unknown character, and No. (4) is in Pâli and corresponds with No. (1). Apparently, therefore, Nos. (2) and (3) are identical with Nos. (1) and (4).]

---

* Son of Kyanzit Mingyi, and known also as Zeyakittaya, Governor of Daññavatî (Arakan) and the adjacent seven hill tracts.

† Commonly known as Queen Thanbula or Usaukpan.

Nos. (5), (6), and (7).

[These inscriptions are in a very bad state of preservation. So far as can be made out, they seem to correspond with Nos. (1) and (4). They are on the pillar within the Kubyaukkyi cave, west of the Myazedi pagoda. No. (5) is in Pâli, No. (6) in an unknown character and No. (7) is in Burmese.]

No. (8).

Locality.—Within the porch of the Mahadi pagoda, about a mile south of Pagan.

Date.—582 Sakkarâj (1220 A.D.).

Founder.—Thingathu's wife.

Substance of inscription.—Dedication of lands and slaves to pagoda.

"I adore the Buddha!"

On Thursday, the 5th waxing of Wazo 560 Sakkarâj, King Nandaungmya* dedicated the following lands to the monastery of his old tutor Dhammarâjâguru, namely, 100 *pès* in Myittha, consisting of 60 *pès* at Wayinnatha village, 30 at Ngo village, and 10 at Thamowada village; 140 *pès* offered by the king's sister Itminhlangè, consisting of 50 *pès* at Tetthe, 20 at Panan, and 70 at Ywatha; 100 *pès* offered by Queen Asaw, consisting of 70 *pès* at Petmanyo and 30 *pès* at Kyaukôk; the lands purchased by monk Mahadi, namely, 30 *pès* at Yangônsagyet, 25 at Thindaung, and 20 in Lègaing circle. Besides the above, Mahadi's brother-in-law offered 70 slaves from Mawlatha village and a piece of paddy-land. Mahadi also offered 70 slaves, 3,000 *pès* of paddy-land at Kyabin, 600 at Shanmo, and 40 at Sazathamyaung village. "These are offered by me to my pagoda . . . . May I be rewarded with the bliss of Nirvâna. May those who destroy my offering be burnt in *avîci*; may they be crushed to atoms when this world comes to an end, and may they find no place of refuge."

On Friday, the 7th waxing of Kasôn 582 Sakkarâj, Thingathu's wife dedicated to the Mahadi pagoda and monastery the following paddy-lands, namely, 40 *pès* at Kanhlaung, 50 at Pyedo, 20 at Taung, 40 at Nyaung-ubi, and 10 at Tabetswe. Grand total 4,175 *pès*.

---

* Also known as Uzana, Zeyatheinka and Tilominlo.

INSCRIPTIONS OF PAGAN.

X.—Found at Siripaccayâ.

No. (1).*

Locality.—Within the inscription cave on the premises of the Lokananda pagoda.

Date.—592 Sakkarâj (1230 A.D.).

Founder.—Mahâdânapati.

Substance of inscription.—Building of cave, monastery, and image, and dedication thereto of slaves, lands, cattle, and utensils.

THE prime minister of King Kyazwamingyi entitled Thiritribhavanâdicca was full of wisdom, forethought, equanimity, and piety, and was known far and wide for acts of lavish charity. He had a beautiful and spacious monastery built, as well as a cave adorned with various fine paintings and carvings, and placed within the latter an image of the Buddha, together with some of the sacred relics. On the morning of Wednesday, the 3rd waning of Tabaung 592 Sakkarâj, the prime minister made the following offerings for the maintenance of the monkhood and the upkeep of the image, namely, 108 male slaves, 1,000 *pès* of paddy-land, five golden alms-bowls, five brass trays, five double hot-water plates to hold rice-offerings, five beautiful lamp-stands, and 100 buffaloes. Having done so, he made the following prayer:—

"By virtue of this and other meritorious deeds done by me since my youth, may I, in my next existence, be far from the abode of the *petas* and lower animals and from hell, and be born in the *nat* country of Tâvatimsâ. From that position may I be able to promote the cause of the Religion and contribute towards the upkeep of the Cûlâmuni pagoda. May I exist alternately as a man and a *nat* and be able to perform various good acts; and having acquired the 30 kinds of virtue, may I become a *Rahan* during Metteyya Buddha's dispensation, able to observe his precepts; and may I ultimately attain Nirvâna. May every one from the king downwards, including my tutors, parents, descendants, and . . . . attain Nirvâna like me by virtue of this my good deed."

No. (2).

Locality.—Within the inscription cave on the premises of the Lokananda pagoda.

Date.—592 Sakkarâj (1230 A.D.).

Founder.—Mahâdânapati.†

* This inscription is in Pâli throughout. | † Prime minister of King Kyazwa.

Substance of inscription.—Building of cave, monastery, and image, and dedication thereto of slaves, lands, cattle, and utensils

ON Wednesday, the 3rd waning of Tabaung 592 Sakkarâj, Mahâdânapati made the following offerings to the image erected by him, namely, 78 slaves from Pagan, including natives of India, and 30 other slaves purchased by him, total 108 slaves; 150 *pès* of paddy-land at Salin, 200 at Kanti, and 650 at Yaungpagaung; total 1,000 *pès*; five golden alms-bowls; five brass trays with stands; and five lamp-stands. The names of the slaves are—Nga Myet Mè; Nga Pôn Zôn and sons Nga Su, Nga Chit Pôn, Nga Pyi Wa Thin; Nga Thi Yet; Nga Pyi Nyi; Nga Thu Me; O Bu; O Pôn Za; Tu Kè; O Na and son O Wun; Ma Pein San and daughter O Pyu; Ku Na Ka; O Bya Wa; Kan Myauk and daughther O Kwe Chi; Zan Bi; Thiriwi; Yari; Napi; San Mye; Maladu; Letki; Yathari; Tharapi; Pari; Thiriya; Yayi; Niru; Balaki; Ayaw; Nasi; Nakami and infant; Thunandi; Driwunti; Letku; Thazi; Satthi; Letkụ; Ata and infant; Thirya; Kari; Dari; Thabinki; Râju; Kanti; Thuti; Thuki; Râju; Mali; Satthi; Bravâ; Padumi; Madi; Nga Manaw; Nga Paya; Nga Maya; Nga Luka; Hlanmarâjâ; Mate and son Mahânam; Goyè; Thatawayè and infant; Nga Keikta; Dita; Thuma; Sugataw; Binwa; Kyasha; Apaya; Duma; Bilawa; total 78. Besides the above, 100 head of cattle and the Setkyalaung garden were offered.

"May my descendants, and not my ancestors, derive benefit from this good work."

INSCRIPTIONS OF PAGAN.

XI.—Found at Ledaunggan.

No. (1).

Locality.—On the southern pillar within the inscription cave near Lemyethna pagoda.

Date.—552 Sakkarâj (1190 A.D.).

Substance of inscription.—Apparently, dedication of slaves to Lemyethna pagoda.

THE following are the names of the slaves who have removed to a new village from Mashetywalun: Pôk Nga Se The and sons Pôk Nga Ku The, Pôk Nga Than Zin, Nga Pa Yan, Nga Pa Gyi, Nga Yan Gaung, Nga Hla Myat; Nga Chan Tha and infant son;

Nga Pyan and son Nga Kan Mye; Nga Thet Chwe and sons Nga Meikta, Nga Taya, Nga Chit U; Nga Tha Pin and sons Nga Nyo, Nga Sa Po, Nga Yeik Ko, Nga Yeik Tha; Pôk Nga Taung Mwe and son Nga Hwa; Pôk Nga Che The and sons Nga Lôn The, Nga Kado, Nga Pyi, Nga Pyan, Nga Pyi Nyi, Nga San; Apongè Thinyaungchan and sons Nga Pin, Nga Wun, Nga Shan; Nga Pyi; Pôk Nga Pè Thè and sons Nga Kala, Nga Kauk, Nga Yauk, Nga Myi; Nga Ko and nephews Nga Thin Yin, Nga Sha Bôk, Nga So; Nga Mwè; Nga Than Pa and sons Nga Su, Nga Hla Wun, Nga Kyan Chin, Nga Ko Ya, and infant; Pôk Nga Pôn Dwe and sons Nga Pe, Nga Kywin; Nga Kôn and son Nga Ya È; Nga Put; Pôk Nga Si and son Nga Lut; Pôk Nga Aung Zin and son Nga Wun; Pôk Nga Tôn Bè and son Nga Chit Pwè; total 57.

[The latter part of this inscription is fragmentary.]

No. (2).

Locality—On the same pillar as No. (1).

Date.—587 Sakkarâj.

Substance of inscription.—Lists of names of slaves apparently dedicated to Lemyethna pagoda.

On Wednesday, the 10th waning of Wazo 576 Sakkarâj, Nga U Yaung sold for 350 ticals of silver to Nga Chit Thin 11 male slaves who were inherited by him from his uncle Chit Ma Me Thin, deceased. These slaves were placed with others in Kunmasa village. Their names are—Pôk Kyan An and sons Myetya Nga Taung, Opuki Nga Ku, Sadat Nga Tu, and an infant; Nga Kalauk; Pôk Nga Pyi and sons Nga Sin Gaung, Nga Tha Ya, Nga Pa Tha; Nga Swe and son Nga Taung Yan; Nga Zin and son Nga Pôn Lut; Nga Kè and son Nga Wun Lôn; Nga Lu and son Nga Tu Gyin; Nga Than Lè; Nga Ta and son Nga Pyi Wa; total 20.

On Monday, the 3rd waxing of Wazo 587 Sakkarâj, the following slaves were dedicated, namely, Nga Ya Thin and wife O Pôn Thin, daughters O Tin Ke, O Kan Tu; Nga Mun and brother Nga Saung; Nga Thu Pa and brother Nga Lo; Nga Pôn Yauk Thin and brother Nga Wa Thin. These slaves were purchased from Nga U Yaung. The slaves who have to look after the paddy-land and garden at Thapanzeik are—Nga Myo and wife O Mauk, daughter O Kala, son Nga Yauk; Nga Dauk Cha and sons Nga Kywin and Nga Swin; total 7.

No. (3).

Locality.—On the northern pillar within the inscription cave, near the Lemyethna pagoda.

Date.—584 Sakkarâj (1222 A.D.).

Founders.—Maha Turingapyitsi* and others.

Substance of inscription.—Dedication of slaves, apparently to the Lemyethna pagoda.

On Thursday, the 6th waxing of Tabaung 584 Sakkarâj, the following slaves were dedicated by Nagara, namely, Pôkpeyama and son Hmuyakôkta; Kywèletki; Pôkkônza; Kywèmingyi; Kywèomyi; Kywèsanbi; Kywethuknayi; Kywekalôn; Kywethida; total 10. The slaves dedicated by Athayanpyitsi were—Susa and wife. . . . . .; Kywèayaw; Pôkkôkka; Kywèsawyi; total 5. The slaves dedicated by Môktabili were Letkana and wife Thittabi; Pôksarana and son Kôkta; Pôkkataw and brother Nga Pan The; Kywèpunayan and son Hmunabeyama, daughter Hmuyanaki; Kywèubè; Kywèmingyithe; total 10. The slaves dedicated by Kyan Thaing's aunt were—Pôkngataungwepye; Amipuzupye; Nga Pôn Zôn and 28 others; total 31. The slaves dedicated by Maha Turingapyitsi were—Thanbyayin; Ngawunbyi Thin; Kywèokisha and daughter O Pindi; Nga Lôn; Nga Hlun; total 6. Nga San and Nga Pyi Yaung offered three slaves, namely, Nga Sat, Nga U Pi, and Nga Pwè. Nga Lôn Thin and son Nga Pôn Thin of Yabôn offered two slaves, Nga Tôn and son Nga Ti. Nga Pwin Thin and son Nga Pôn Thin of Kanpi offered three slaves, namely, Nga Myin and sons Nga Maung Yin, Nga Pa E. Nga Kywin Thin, son of Ma Shet, offered two slaves, Nga Kala and son Nga Aung Sin. The slaves sold by O Sein Thin, Nga Lu and sons Nga Su, Nga Swin, Nga Taung Yan, and Nga Naing Gan. The slaves offered by Yadanathingyan were Nga Pyi and son Nga Myat; Nga Myat; Nga Lut; total 4. Nga Taung We Thin offered Nga Pôn. Thugyi Naung Tha offered Thilawi and brothers Nga Mwin Lwin, Yaman Byu, as well as Nga Pwè and sons Nga Shan and another. The slaves purchased through Bônmathinga were Nga Wet Kè, mahout Nga Myat, mahout Nga Nyo; and those purchased from Nga Pwè and wife were Nga Pôn, Nga Ku Ha, O Bye and daughter O Pu Ki, mahout U Pa Lun's wife, Wunmani and wife O Kaya, Nga U, Nga Yin Gaung, Nga Kyi and son Nga Ya Kan, son O Pu Ki, Nga Sin's brother, mahout Nga Naing's wife O Nanda, daughter O Bya. The slaves offered by Bônmapattaya were Nga Twe and Nga Ywe; grand total 20. The slaves offered on behalf of monk Bônmatheinga were Nga Mutu and sons Nga Pôn Zôn, Nga

* A minister of King Zeyatheinka.

Chit U, Nga Lôn, Nga Chan; O Thu Yit and daughters O Pôn Shi, O Kyin Mye, O Twe and an infant; Nga Nayi and son; O Pôn; Nga Ku Panathan; Nga Pwin; Nga Tet Pyi and son Nga Chin Ya; Nga Lôn and sons Nga San Lôn, Nga Pamyet; Nga Tabaung, son of Kyanpa; total 18, the grand total purchased through Dhammatheinga being 38. The slaves purchased through Lohathinga were Nga U and brother Nga Nyein; Nga Thauk and wife O Chat, son Nga Chan; O Twe and sons Nga Aung Bye, Nga Myo; Nga Pin Di and sisters O Bye, Hmu Ya O . . . . (last line).

No. (4).

Locality.—On the southern pillar within the inscription cave attached to the Lemyethna pagoda.

Date—585 Sakkarâj (1223 A.D.).

Founder.—Anandathuya and wife.

Substance of inscription.—Building of cave-pagoda, monastery, rest-house, and library, and dedication of slaves and lands thereto.

On Friday, the 7th waning Nadaw 585 Sakkarâj, the Prime Minister Anandathuya and his wife, being actuated by a desire to free himself and all the inhabitants of this and other universes from the miseries of *samsara* and to attain the bliss of Nirvâna, performed the following good deeds. A piece of land was planted with a number of palm trees and was enclosed with double walls. A cave-pagoda was then built and within it was enshrined a relic of Gautama Buddha placed in a receptacle composed of many graduated caskets, the bigger enclosing the smaller, and made of many metals and other materials. The innermost was fashioned out of a kernel of the seed of the *tari* palm and the rest were of glass, lacquerware, gold, silver, pinchbeck, ivory, copper, and marble successively. The receptacle was placed in a heap of gold and silver flowers, and the outside was painted and secured with brass wire. The top of the lid was of gold. A golden umbrella was placed over all and it was hung with pearls and coral beads. The umbrella was covered with seven layers of cloth and was ornamented with gold-leaf. Besides this there were a golden image weighing 30 *ticals*, a silver image weighing 50 *ticals*, and a painted marble image with gold and silver umbrellas over them. The image within the cave was lavishly bejewelled and it was surrounded with several small images. The walls within were adorned with paintings illustrating the 500* anterior births of Gautama Buddha. The different weights of metals

* The full number is 550.

used in ornamenting the cave-pagoda were 47·84 viss of brass, 39¼ *ticals* of gold, and 159 *ticals* of mercury. A masonry library was next built and a complete copy of the Tripitaka was placed therein for the enlightenment of all comers. Then a brick monastery was erected for the residence of an abbot, and several other smaller ones were built outside the first wall close by for the monkhood. Then a well was sunk and a tank was dug and gardens were cultivated all round it. Lastly, a beautiful wall was erected along the boundaries of the monastery land as well as rest-houses for pilgrims which might also be used by the people on festive occasions. A brick lavatory was also attached to the monastery for the use of the monks. All these meritorious deeds were performed in order that the Religion might last for 5,000 years.

The following slaves were dedicated by the nobleman and his wife for the upkeep of these institutions, for ministering to the wants of the monks, and for making the daily rice, light, and betel offerings to the pagoda, namely, Thanbyin (thugyi) Nga Lin and sons Nga La Gaung, Nga Myit Kaing, Nga Chit; Nga Pyit and sons Nga Pôn Lut, Nga Swin; Nga Pôn Daw Thin and wife O Pyit Thin, son Nga Pa Gin; Nga Ka Myè; Nga Pyi Wa and wife Yatin; Nga Naung and wife Mà Byè, daughters O Thin Lè, O Set Sôk; Nga San and wife O Pôn Ngè, son . . . . , daughter O Nôk; Nga Twe Bu and wife O Pu Dôn, daughter O Mye Bôn; Pôk Kyun Nga; Nga Ku and wife O Chat, daughter Yin Ki, sons Nga Pyi Zôn, Nga Mye, daughter O Aung Myin, and son Nga Yauk Lwè; artisan Nga Twe, wife O Kyaung and infant daughter; O Pôn Yôn; Nga Kywin, son of Nga U Lwè; Nga Naing and son Nga Aung Myin; Nga Pyi Wa; Sa Gaw and wife Môkta; Kayata and wife Padumi, lesser wife Wunbyiya, son Nga Pyit; Sandrapani and wife Zahlaw, sons Nga Chatta, Kata, daughters O Pagan and infant; Nga Tala and wife Hita, son Nga Kyi, daughter O Nyè; Nga Pyu, son of Kingaw; U Law and wife U Paw, daughter Pathi, son Yinka; Piya and wife Yupa; Tattwa and wife Urima, daughter Myet San Hla; Lawka and wife Tale; . . . . . (last line).

No. (5).

Locality.—On the same pillar as No. (4).

Date.—586 Sakkaràj (1224 A.D.).

Substance of inscription.—Dedication of slaves, apparently to the Lemyethna pagoda.

On Wednesday, the 11th waning of Nayôn 586 Sakkaràj, the following slaves were dedicated through Nga Kè Thin, namely, Nga

Tha Ya, son of Nga Shwin, deceased; Nga Tha Ya's brothers Nga Ku Ta, Nga Wun Tha; Nga Mun; Nga Pôn Bye; Nga Myat and brother Nga Myit, son Nga Tan Laing, a monk, son Nga Chan Tha, another monk, son Mataya; Nga Pôn Bye and brother Nga Paw, uncle Nga Kyi, cousins Nga U and Nga Mun, uncles Nga Pu and Nga Kyu; Nga Yaing Pu Su and son Nga Pyi Bye; Nga Pôn and son Nga Aung Din; Nga Eik Seik and sons Nga U, Nga U Lôn and an infant Nga Twe Tha; Nga Twe and brother Nga Pôn, son Nga Maung Yin; Nga Pa Gyi and son Nga Wun Byi; Nga Lun Bye and brother Nga Tan Byin Bye; total 32. The purchased slaves were—Nga Pi and sons Nga Pan Gywet, Nga Pyat; Nga O; total 4. The slaves dedicated by O Myet Mè Thin were—Nga Myin Kin and infant son, cousin O Chan Tha; O Tabye and nephew Nga Pu Yit and his infant son; Nga Pyit and brother Nga Mè; Pu Su and daughter Ma Lwè, and sister O Dwe Pu Su; total 11. The betel-vine garden at Taungbôn was also dedicated.

No. (6).

Locality.—On the northern pillar within the inscription cave near the Lemyethna pagoda.

Date.—588 Sakkarâj (1226 A.D.).

Substance of inscription.—Apparently, dedication of slaves to the Lemyethna pagoda.

THIRTY slaves were purchased and dedicated by Anandathu's wife and Nga Pyi Thin's two daughters, the former 10 and the latter 20. On Monday, the 6th waning of Nayôn 588 Sakkarâj, Nga Pyi Thin's daughters O Nyè Gyi and O Nyè Lat purchased, for 300 ticals of brass and 200 ticals of silver, 20 slaves from Ma Tit Thaik. O Wi Sin Thin and Nga Lun Gôn Thin weighed out the silver. The clerk who drew up the deed of sale was Nga Pyit Thin, and the witnesses were Damayaza Thinga, Bônma Thinga, and Zeya Yazathu. The two sisters dedicated their slaves with the prayer that they might obtain great merit from their offering. The other slaves dedicated at the same time were—Nga Sa A, Nga Taya De, Nga Sè, and Pôk Thatayo. The slaves kept in Kanaingzi village were—Nga Pa and sons Nga Paga, Nga Taung Thu and Nga Tayate; Nga Kabu and sons Nga Pet, Nga Than, Nga Ma Lauk; Nga Than Bôn and sons Nga Paing, Nga Nyet; . . . . (two lines).

No. (7).*

Locality.—Same as No. (6).

Date.—589 Sakkarâj (1227 A.D.).

NGA KÔN and brothers Nga Tôn Da, Nga San; Nga Myo, and sons Nga Wun Byi, Nga Hmè, Nga Pa U, Nga Pyi and Nga Ma Gôn; Nga Pa and son Nga Taung Mwe; Nga Chan Tha and sons Nga Pa Aing, Nga Meik Ta; Nga Aung and son Nga Than Ya, nephew Nga Than; Nga Wun Byi and son Nga Mye Lu; blacksmith Nga Mè and wife O Wun Tha; Nga Lôn and wife O Byu, son Nga Taung Mwe, daughter O Mwe; Nga Pyi Wa and wife O Kun, daughters O Pwe, O Wayin, O Pôn; Nga Put and wife O Taku; Nga Mun and wife O Sôn, daughters O Pinlè, O Kyakat, O Pè Ngè; Nga Môn and wife O Than Ba, daughter O Kyi, son Nga Lôn; Nga Kawè and son Nga Taba; Nga Môn and wife O Pôn, son Nga Yauk Sôn; Nga Twe; Nga Nyein and son Nga Mwe; total 108. The slaves purchased by Kittaya Thingyan were—O Chat, wife of Nga Taung Mwe, daughters O Taik, O Myo, sister O Gauk; Nga Paung and sons Nga Yauk Ya, Nga U Gyi, grandsons Nga Pa U, Nga Yan Aung; Nga Ya; Nga Wun Bye and wife O Mun, son Nga U, daughter-in-law A Nyè, granddaughter O Mein; Nga U Lôn and brother Nga U Lwè, sister O Maung Mya; Nga Kyi and wife O Lapa, sons Nga Taya, Nga Pun; Nga Yan Aung and wife O Tôn Da, daughters O Pyi Ya, O Than Pa; Nga Mwe and brother Nga Swè; Nga Saung and wife O Paung, daughter O Kyaung, son Nga Laung; Nga Naing Ngan and sons Nga Mun, Nga Hlun and an infant; total 36. On Thursday, the 7th waxing of Tawthalin 589 Sakkarâj, the following slaves were dedicated, namely, Nga U and sons Nga Pyi, Nga Ti; Nga Myit and son Nga Aung; Nga Taw and brother Nga Kaw; Nga Kwè Thein and son Nga Aung Myin; Nga Maw; . . . . .

No. (8).

Locality.—On the same pillar as No. (6).

Founder.—Thinyin Thiyat and wife.

Substance of inscription.—Dedication of slaves to an image in a brick monastery.

ON Saturday, the full-moon of Tawthalin . . . Sakkarâj, Thinyin Thiyat and wife O Pyi Thin purchased with their own earnings the following slaves and dedicated them to an image in a brick

* This inscription is apparently in continuation of the foregoing.

monastery, namely, Nga Myo and son Nga Tha Lôn; Nga Thin Bôn; Nga Tan Linmyithu; total 4.

"By virtue of this offering may I always be free from want. As a man may I be rewarded with the happiness of a Çakravatin, and as a *nat* with that of the king of *nats*. When the next Buddha Metteyya comes, may I without any difficulty obtain the position of a *Rahan*. May my parents and other relatives enjoy a share of my merit. I make this offering in the presence of Maha San Tin, Nga Kala Thin, Mala Thu, Mala Thingyan, Nga Shwe Thin, and Nga Naing Ngan Thin. May those who destroy it suffer in *avíci*, and never behold the face of any of the Buddhas."

On Wednesday, the . . . . of Wagaung, the following slaves were further dedicated to the image, namely, O Pyi Mè and daughter Thanbaya; O Wun; Nga Kan Gu; . . . . (two lines).

No. (9).

Locality.—In the inscription cave attached to the Lemyethna pagoda.

Date.—591 Sakkarâj (1229 A.D.).

Founder.—Thamantathu's wife.

Substance of inscription.—Building of cave and image and dedication thereto of slaves, lands, and cattle.

ON Sunday, the 8th waxing of Pyatho 591 Sakkarâj, the daughter of Kyanthaing Gyi and wife of Thamantathu* built a cave over the three images of her grandfather Sithu and placed on the east side of it her own image of Gautama Buddha, 5 cubits high. She then dedicated to it a number of slaves, eight pairs of bullocks, and 30 *pès* of paddy-land.

"By virtue of this offering may I, in my every existence, be replete with truth, righteousness, diligence, liberality, and desire to attain Buddhahood. May those who destroy my offering be burnt in the eight principal hells."

The witnesses to the offering were—monks Thetta Ditha, Nyana Teikthi, Thudamayinthi, Thatpuyithakawi . . . . (last line).

No. (10).

Locality.—Within the porch of the Zanthi pagoda, about 2,000 feet south of the Lemyethna pagoda.

Date.—595 Sakkarâj (1233 A.D.).

Founder.—Yazamaha Mingalapade.

* Ministers of King Zeyatheinka.

Substance of inscription.—Erection of cave and dedication thereto of slaves, lands, and cattle.

ON Monday, the 14th waxing of Wazo 595 Sakkarâj, Yazamaha Mingalapade built a cave, placed an image in it, and made the following offerings, namely, the Kanshe tank with its adjoining paddy-fields; the . . . . . tank and paddy-fields; the Kabin tank and paddy-fields; the Saukkyi tank and paddy-fields; the Tabyin tank and paddy-fields; the Tauklèma tank and paddy-fields; the Yetabôk tank and paddy-fields; the Ngatôkthin tank and paddy-fields; the Ngahmangan tank and paddy-fields; the Ywathagan tank and paddy-fields; the Kyedainggyi tank and paddy-fields; the Kyedaingngè tank and paddy-fields; the Ngatungan tank and paddy-fields; the Tauklèlèngè tank and paddy-fields; the Saukpagan tank and paddy-fields; the Pazinggyi tank and paddy-fields; the Yaungi tank and paddy-fields; the Thinbôk tank and paddy-fields; the Ngalônngè tank and paddy-fields; the Kanthitpyaung lands; the Thanit lands; total 3,000 *pès*. The cows offered numbered 200 head. The slaves were—Nga Kywin and son Nga Taung Yan; Nga Ke; . . . . . .; Nga Kaya; Nga Mayin and sons Nga Tin and Nga Pôn; Nga Pyi Gan and son Nga Myet Thi; . . . .; Nga Yahan and brothers Nga Kônma, Nga Kataw; Nga Yamanthanyat; Nga Than Lè and son Nga Than Gè;. . . . .; Nga Pauk and brother Nga Hlun; Nga Maung Yin and sons Nga Chan, Nga Naing Gan; . . . .; Nga Si; Nga Kôn; Nga Pi Dôn; Nga Gôn Dan; Nga Yaung; O Pyiki Saing and sister . . . .; O Myet Se; Nga Hnit Lo and brother Nga Chan, nephew Nga Pin Yin; . . . . The slaves from Pagan numbered 50 natives of India, including musicians, painters, woodcarvers, blacksmiths and masons.

"May every one from the king downwards, as well as every being inhabiting every region from Tâvatimisâ to *avîci* obtain a share of the merit accruing from this my good deed. May those who destroy it . . . . (two lines).

No. (11).

Locality.—In the inscription cave attached to the Lemyethna pagoda.

Date.—595 Sakkarâj (1233 A.D.).

Founder.—Anandathu.

Substance of inscription.—Showing how Anandathu obtained possession of the slaves dedicated by him.

THE slave Nga Mwè was presented to Anandathu by a blacksmith and his wife. Nga Ma Thin's son and brother-in-law claimed this slave, but their claim could not be proved. There were Nga Mwè and his son Nga Pan and 41 other slaves purchased from Nga Ba. The slaves from Kalôngyin were—O Pyi; O Pyit; Pi Thi; Nga Sôn and wife O Byu; Nga Kin Zun and sister Thattuma, brother Nga Lun; Tokala; Tohita and wife Yupi; Nga Ma Lauk; Nga Mun; Nga Kaung; O Pôn Bye; Wunthaya; Nga U Lwè and son Nga Tha Din; Nga Myet Pwin and son Nga U Pi; O Tan Ku and daughter O Chit La; O Scin Pi; Nga Yauk Kat and sons Nga Pyi Hmu, Nga Nyo Myi, Nga Twe Gyi; Nga Pyi; O Chat and daughter O Pè, granddaughter O Hla, great granddaughters Ma Pyè, Ma Pauk, O Wun, O Pyi Nyi; O Kyi and daughter Pa Lauk; O Tôn and daughter O Pyi; O Tin; O Lat. The offering was made on Friday, the 11th waning Thadingyut 595 Sakkarâj, in the presence of King Sithu, Thugyis Thitsayapade and Paditha, and Mahawè, in accordance with their decision that Anandathu was the owner of the slaves and not Nga Swè Thin. The witnesses to the decision were . . . . (last line).

No. (12).

Locality.—Within the walls of the Malabyit pagoda

Date.—600 Sakkarâj (1238 A.D.).

Founders.—Thanbyin* Thet She.

Substance of inscription.—Dedication of paddy-lands to the three "Gems."

On Wednesday, the 8th waxing of Tabodwè 600 Sakkarâj, Thanbyin Thet She dedicated to the three "Gems" 50 *pès* of paddy-land called Kwethe-Indin at Nwèni-Myittha. The ceremony was performed on a monastery east of Zayathla.

"Let the usufruct be utilized for the maintenance of the monks, and let none of my relatives appropriate any portion of it. My desire is to attain Nirvâna. Those who destroy my offering will go to *avîci.*"

The witnesses to the offering were—Thugyi Thet She's grandmother Nabatharit, monk Pyidwingyaung, and monk Sithawut, and Yadanamyemyan was the clerk, and Thuwunnatheinka, Nga Hla Thin and Nga Palè Thin were the surveyors.

No. (13).

Locality.—Within the group of monasteries built by Nyaungyangyi's daughter.

Date.—604 Sakkarâj (1242 A.D.).

* The office of a Thanbyin corresponds somewhat with that of the present-day thugyi.

Founder.—Kingathu's wife.

Substance of inscription.—Dedication of slaves and lands to the three "Gems."

"It is accomplished"

ON Thursday, the 14th waning of Nadaw 604 Sakkarâj, Kingathu passed away; and on Sunday, the 3rd waxing of the following month, his wife, who was the daughter of Nyaungyangyi, dedicated in his behalf the following slaves, namely, Nga Swè and wife O Pôn; Nga Twe and sons Nga Tanet, Nga Mun, Nga Pyi Zôn, Nga Thaukkya; Nga Ma Thein and brother Nga Pyi Daung; Nga Min Ngè; Nga Pyè; Nga Lôn Gyi and brother Nga Na Pu; Nga Nyan; Nga Naing; Tha Ngè; Nga Sein; Nga Twe; Nga Pale; Nga Pu and son Nga Nyo; Nga Yauk and brother Nga Aung Bye, nephew Nga Ya Gwe; Nga Pin Gaung; Nga Pyit Sin; Nga Taba; Nga Wun Byi and brother Nga Wun Tha, nephew Nga Swa; Nga Pôn and sons Nga Thanbaya, Nga U Hla; Yaman Gyi and brothers Nga Mun Ywe, Nga Tha Din, Nga Pôn, nephew Nga U Lôn; Nga Ywe and sons Nga Ke, Nga San Mye; Nga Maung; Nga Mun and brothers Nga Yan, Nga Lut; Nga Thaukkya and brothers Nga Meikta, Nga Than; Nga Taba; Nga Yauk Kat and two sons; Nga Pè and sons Nga Mun Ke, Nga Yan Zein, Nga Pa Gin; Nga Kaung Mun and son San Thi; Nga Peik and sons Nga Swa, Nga Pyu Sin; Nga U Nut and brothers Nga Naing, Nga Aung Din; Nga Pet and sons Nga U Lôn, Nga Tôn; Nga Thu Gaung and sons Nga Pauk Sin, Nga Thin Yin; Nga Pyi; Nga Tha Mya and sons Nga U Lôn, Nga Chit Kin; Nga Ke and brothers Nga Shan, Nga Yan Pa; Nga Shan and sons Nga Yan, Nga Pyu; Nga Min Ngè and son Nga Pan, grandsons Nga Pa U, Nga San; Nga Aung Bye; Nga Le; Nga Thauk Kya; Nga Chan; Nga Pôn; Nga Hmin; Nga U; Nga San; Nga Chit Ya; Nga Thein and brothers Nga Wun Byi, Nga Pôn, Nga Twe; Nga Ywe and brothers Nga Yan, Nga Nwe, Nga Shan; Nga Pyi Zôn; Nga Twe; Nga Pagyi and brothers Nga Maung, Nga Bala, Nga Pôn; Nga Saga; Nga Pyit; Nga Yan and son Nga San; Nga Yauk Mun; Thin Ka; Nga Pagyi's son; Nga Bala's son; Nga Wun; Nga Kyun; O Laung and daughters O Sein and two others; O Pôn; O Lun; O Pôn; Nga Kyun and brother Nga Tôn Pe; Nga Thanbaya and son Nga Twe; Nga Pan Zin and son Nga Nyo; Nga Chit Pa; O Myo and daughter O Kyaung; O Pyaung; O Gôndan; O Pyit and two daughters; O Pôn and daughter O Wazo; O Thin Kwe and daughter U Lwè; O Myi; Nga Yan; Nga Twe; Nga Aung Myin; O Pôn; and two others.

(Here follow fragments of the usual prayer and imprecations.)

No. (14).

Locality.—Within the porch of the Letputhan pagoda.

Date.—604 Sakkarâj (1242 A.D.).

Founder.—So Min.

Substance of inscription.—Dedication of slaves and lands to the three "Gems."

ON the 13th waxing of Pyatho 604 Sakkarâj, So Min, grandson of Thakin Pwagyi,* realizing his own impermanency, dedicated to the three "Gems" the Tipaunglaung paddy-land measuring 50 *pès*, the Pakan-Nwèni paddy-land measuring 50 *pès* and the following personal slaves, namely, Nga Pwet and sons Nga Pan Ya, Nga Pazin, Nga Pa Naung, Nga Twe; Putu and sons . . . ., Ku Ya; Thana Daw; Nga Teik and son; Nga Tha; total 13 weavers: Nga Kwe and sons Nga U, Nga Pwa; Nga Lôk and sons Nga Tha Lôn, Nga Lat; Nga Tha Din and two sons; Nga Chit Pwe; Nga Ha Yan; Nga Wun Byi; Nga Yauk; total 13 paddy-cultivators: Nga Kan Du; Nga Tôk and son Nga U Lôn; total 3 umbrella-makers: Nga U and son Nga Pè; Nga Myat and son Nga Kwe, grandsons Nga Tin Gu, Nga Lat, and two others; Nga Pu; total nine washermen.† The son of Nga Kywa was appointed head slave.

"May those who destroy my offering be burnt in *avici*. On the other hand, may those who approve of it share its merit equally with me."

No. (15).

Locality.—Within the walls of the old Shinkatthapa group of monasteries.

Date.—608 Sakkarâj (1246 A.D.).

Founders.—Prince Ôksana and others.

Substance of inscription.—Building of monastery and dedication of paddy-lands.

"I adore the Buddha!"

ON the 5th waning of Nadaw 606 Sakkarâj, Min Hla built a large monastery in front of Anandathu's, for the residence of monk Mahakatthapa, and dedicated to the monkhood the following lands, namely, 89 *pès* purchased at 15 *ticals* a *pè* from Nga Yauk

* A courtier of Kyazwa Mingyi's reign.

† The archaic form of ဝဝါသည် is given here as ကုလ္လာသည်.

Thin and situated in Kwinthuyaukka, Thindaung district; 55 *pès* purchased for 835 *ticals* from one Kyauktaung, and situated north of Kwinkwin, Ôkkyi village, in Myittha district.

In Pyatho 599 Sakkarâj, the husband of Thayeapwa dedicated 10 *pès* to the Law and 10 to monk Mahakatthapa.

On Sunday, the waning of Nadaw 610 Sakkarâj, 20 *pès* of land were dedicated. This land was purchased from Pyetgathu together with his family.

In Pyatho 604 Sakkarâj, 330 *pès* of land in Yiyaingyaing village were dedicated. It was purchased for 700 *ticals* from Nga Chit Sin together with his family.

On Friday, the 3rd waning of Kasôn 608 Sakkarâj, 3,332 *pès* of paddy-land at Maukkipauk were dedicated. These lands were purchased at a *tical* per *pè* by Prince Ôksana, Gôndan, Gunabattaya, Asalabiyit, headman of Sèta village, Kôn Kè, headman of Pinlè village, Shwetangè, Tuyingabattaya, headman of Yangôn village, Yazakônda, headman of Sètaywagyi village, Kannyayin, Chattarabo, headman of Myingôndaing village, and Pin Myaing, headman of Tamôk village, from the following persons, namely, thugyi San Ma and wife, son Nga Lat; Bônmachattaya and wife, son Nga Sein; An Din, and sons Nga U Pi, Nga San; Nga Kyan Thin's son and grandson Nga Pyi U; Nga Sôn; Nga Palè; Thinyin Bwin; and Nga Pyi Zin.

On Wednesday, the 4th waxing of Pyatho, 608 Sakkarâj, thugyi San Ma, Bônmachattaya, Pyi Zin Thiyin Bwin, again came and sold 1,010 *pès* of land at Sagyaukyatantit at the same rate and it was bought and dedicated by Princess Azit Twe.

On Friday, the 2nd waxing of Tazaungmôn 608 Sakkarâj, thugyi San Ma and Bônmachattaya again came and sold for 40 viss of silver 200 *pès* of paddy-land, consisting of 100 *pès* at Mèo, and 100 at Yabitha.

On Thursday, the 3rd waxing of Nadaw 608 Sakkarâj, thugyi San Ma, Bônmachattaya and Thinyin Mwin sold 300 *pès* more for 60 viss of silver.

The lands offered to monk Mahakatthapa by Itzanalôn, great granddaughter of Prince Ôksana, were—40 *pès* of *mayin** paddy-land at Ngapyunlaing; 100 *pès* of *kaukkyi*† paddy-land on the banks of the Pyunlaing stream; 60 *pès* of paddy-land round about Thathat tank, north-east of Musè village; 100 *pès* of *kaukkyi* paddy-land adjoining the Paungza land; . . . . (two lines).

* Rice cultivated in dry weather or recently inundated alluvial land.

† Wet weather rice.

No. (16).—OBVERSE.

Locality.—Within the porch of Princess Asawgyun's pagoda.
Date.—610 Sakkarâj (1248 A.D.).
Founder.—Princess Asawgyun.
Substance of inscription.—Building of religious edifices and dedication thereto of slaves and lands.

PRINCESS ASAWGYUN, daughter of King Dhammayaza Zeyathura,* by his chief queen,† being desirous of escaping the miseries of *samsaro* and of obtaining cessation of existence for herself as well as the innumerable sentient beings inhabiting the various universes on the advent of Metteyya Buddha, built a cave with images on its four sides, three libraries, a wooden monastery, a brick monastery, and a rest-house. For the upkeep of these institutions the following offerings were made by the founder: on Wednesday, the 11th waxing of Pyatho 610 Sakkarâj, Kyauksègyi land, 80 *pès* and 168 slaves; Kyauksèngè land, 330 *pès* and 195 slaves; Kyauktaga land, 80 *pès* and 51 slaves; Taungbyôn land, 5 *pès* and five slaves to the east Laungshe monastery, 20 *pès* and five slaves to the two images, and the remaining 25 *pès* and three slaves to the cave; Tanaungkyiywathit land, 100 *pès* and 50 slaves; Pindalè land, 30 *pès* and 17 slaves; Kantili land, 384 *pès* and 74 slaves; Myinmu land, 150 out of 500 *pès* and 100 slaves; Mamyo land, 1,000 *pès* and 50 slaves; Pakan land, 20 *pès* and 13 slaves; Kyantu land, 20 *pès* to the Tunan cave and the remaining 180 to this cave; Kyauksèmyegyi land, 50 out of 400 *pès* . . . . ; Salin land, 20 *pès* to the Tanhun monastery, and the rest, namely, 151 *pès*, as well as 187 slaves to the present edifices; Sagu land, 100 *pès*; Shaukhman land, 100 *pès* and 17 slaves; Ngamahi, Letsaungthami, and Paungpi lands, 100 *pès* and 61 slaves; Haranbo garden; Uyingye land, 100 *pès*; 116 Indian slaves from Pagan; 850 slaves from Thanithet; grand total 3,779 *pès* and 1,250 slaves. Besides the above, the Princess dedicated the following personal slaves, namely, O Saik Thin; O Hnalo Thin; O Pôn Thin; Chit Ma Lauk Thin; O Tun Thin; O Kala Thin; O Ma Hnan Thin; O Myet Thin; O Kyun; O Saung; O Taing; O Twe Ngè; O Pa; O Mi U; O Pyi Wa Ngè; O Mwein; O Chit and two children; O Na Lôn; and two tray-sellers; total 22 females: Nga Myat Thin; Nga Pôn La Thin; Nga Lat; Nga Taung Mwe Thin; Nga Chit Pwè; Nga Ma Lè; Nga Kyauk Sit; Nga San; Nga 'Hla U; Nga Pyi Nyi; Nga Mun; Nga Taba; Nga Pyu and brother Nga Kè; Nga U Ngè; Nga Myo; Nga Ôk; Nga Lat Ngè; Nga Pin Gaung; Nga Kwè; Nga Pôn; Sayi; Nga

* King Kyazwa of Pagan, whose title is here given as Siritribhavanapavaradityadhammarâjâjeyasûra.
† Thônlula or Thanbula.

Kaungyan Thin and brother Nga Meikta Thin; total 24 males. Nga Pyi Zôn; Nga Naing Ngan, and San Mye Zan were appointed head slaves. All necessary repairs to the buildings are to be executed by the Princess' descendants. The following materials were used in the building of the cave: 74 viss of silver, 113 pieces of cloth, 23 *ticals* of gold for gilding, and 92 *ticals* of mercury. The following provisions were consumed, namely, two baskets and 1,164 betel-nuts, ... chillies, and seven viss of salt. The apex of the cave was fashioned out of 66 viss of brass. The libraries cost 2,027 *ticals* of silver. The rice consumed was 504 baskets; the paddy, 2,309 baskets; salt, 110 viss; chillies, 5 viss; betel-nut, 10 baskets and 4,870 nuts. The monastery with spires and turrets cost 8 viss of silver, 68 pieces of cloth, 504 baskets of paddy, and 2,200 betel-nuts. The rest-house cost 215 *ticals* of silver. The brick monastery cost 36 viss of silver and 45 pieces of cloth; the walls, 20 viss of silver; cart-hire, 53 viss, 12 pieces of cloth and 182 baskets of paddy; the Cutamuni pagoda, 13 viss of silver and 30 of brass; the porches attached to the brick monastery 215 *ticals* of silver.

"I shall support these institutions to the end of my days, and thereafter let my two sons continue to maintain them."

REVERSE.

"May those who destroy my offerings live miserable lives in this world, and in the future may they never be reborn as human beings in any other world; may they never behold any of the coming Buddhas; may they become dogs and pigs; and may they fall ultimately into *avîci*. On the other hand, may those who take part in their maintenance share my merit equally with me."

No. (17).

Locality.—Within the cave near the Itzagawna monastery.

Date.—610 Sakkarâj (1248 A.D.).

Founder.—Minister Kyawzwa.

Substance of inscription.—Building of cave, pagoda, and monastery and dedication thereto of slaves and lands.

"I adore the Buddha!"

AT dawn on Tuesday, the 10th waxing of Tazaungmôn 610* Sakkarâj, Narapatisithu † commanded his Minister Kyawzwa to perform

* Judging from the context this should be 510. The numerals 5 and 6 were at that time written very similarly.

† Alaungsithu of history is also mentioned in inscriptions and legends as Narapatisithu, this title, which was formally taken later by his grandson, being supposed to have been given him by the King of the *devas*.

some meritorious act of charity worthy of His Majesty. The minister replied that he was willing to build a pagoda, but was in need of a relic of Gautama Buddha to build over; and on this account he was much troubled in mind and remained without food for seven days. Thereupon the king of *devâs* appeared to him in a vision saying, "Nobleman and supporter of the Religion! Be not anxious! Send a monk down to the province of Tenasserim." A monk, Shin Arahan, was accordingly sent, and when he came back with a relic, the minister enshrined it in a cave, and then approached the king with a request for a grant of land to be dedicated to the same. His Majesty was pleased to sanction the acquisition of a piece of land specially selected as being most suitable for the purpose. It contains 25 *pès* and is situated on the north-east of Myittha. The usufruct thereof is to be utilized for the upkeep of the cave and the maintenance of the monks connected with it. The present made by the minister when he asked the boon was a gold lotus weighing 50 ticals. The king then asked whether there was any other vacant land adjacent to the piece offered, and the minister Kyanmapat replied that there was one on the north of it. His Majesty accordingly dedicated that piece also, pouring out the water of dedication himself from a gold cup; total 130 *pès*. Minister Kyanmapat also offered at the same time and with the permission of the king and consent of Minister Kyawzwa a piece of land measuring 5 *pès* and named as Tauksha. Out of the produce of these lands, the monks are to receive the equivalent of two pots of rice-offering, two baskets of betel-nut, 1¼ viss of meat, two suits of robes, one water-goblet and one tray. The rice-offerings are to be made daily, morning and evening. The offering was made in the presence of His Majesty as well as Ministers Yaza-Thingyan, Ananda-Ṭhingyan, Mahathaman, Sitchio, Meiktila, and Kyanmapat. There was a heavy shower of rain at the time, and there was also an earthquake accompanied by rumbling sounds and the acclamation of the *devâs*.

"May those who destroy my offering suffer in *avîci* and in the other principal hells for as many years as there are atoms in the land attached to my offering. Even if they manage to escape those hells, may they never behold any of the coming Buddhas, and may they become hungry, thirsty, and naked *pelus*. If they succeed in becoming human beings again, may they be skinless and besmeared with blood. Should they become birds or beasts or fish, may they be without feathers, skins, or scales. On the other hand, may those who support my offerings be always happy and free from want and enjoy the merit equally with me. May they ultimately reach Nirvâna. May they be patronized by royalty. May my liege the king be able to extend his dominions. The pagoda and cave were completed on the same day, namely, Tuesday, the 10th waxing of Tazaungmôn 610 Sakkarâj.

No. (18).

Locality.—Within the walls of the Thanbula pagoda.

Date.—661 Sakkarâj (1299 A.D.).

Founders.—Princess Saw U and Minister Athincha.

Substance of inscription.—Building of cave, pagoda, monastery, and dedication of slaves and lands.

On Monday, the 5th waning of Tabaung 617 Sakkarâj, the chief queen of Ôksana and a daughter of King Kyazwa by Queen Thônlula, built a cave, a pagoda, a library, and a monastery, and dedicated thereto for the maintenance of the monks the Thandaing lands, 370 *pès* and 257 slaves; the Taungi lands, 88 *pès* and 235 slaves; Mapinzaya lands, 528 *pès*; total, 986 *pès* and 492 slaves. The Thandaing lands are especially dedicated for the maintenance of the presiding monk of the main monastery. The 30 *pès* of paddy-land at Ôksina are likewise so dedicated.

On Wednesday, the 10th waxing of Tabaung 631 Sakkarâj, Princess Sawpalè, daughter of Queen Thanbula and wife of King Ôksana, built a rest-house, and in support of the three "Gems" dedicated the Tahat lands, measuring 250 *pès* and 25 slaves.

On Wednesday, the 10th waxing of Kasôn 646 Sakkarâj, Princess Sawpalè offered 1,000 *pès* of garden-land to monk Taungu of Tetthachaing, and 200 *pès* of similar land to monk Tayatha.

On Monday, the 1st waxing of Kasôn 661 Sakkarâj, Princess Saw U, daughter of King Ôksana, and granddaughter of Queen Thônlula, dedicated together with Minister Athincha, 200 *pès* of paddy-land known as Taminye and situated at Minwun for the support of the three "Gems." Grand total, 2,666 *pès*.

No. (19).—Obverse.

Locality.—Within the ruined group of monasteries south of the Amana monasteries.

Date.—635 Sakkarâj (1273 A.D.).

Founder.—Minister Manawyaza's wife.

Substance of inscription.—Dedication of land to the three "Gems."

On Monday, the full-moon of Wazo 617 Sakkarâj, Nga Nyo Thin and Nga Yauk Kat Thin, sons of Minister Manawyaza,* de-

* A minister of the reign of King Ôksana of Pagan.

dicated the following paddy-lands to the three "Gems," namely, Kyantu land, 30 *pès*; Kanti land, 50 *pès*; Kan . . . . land, 15 *pès*; Kyôn land, 15 *pès*; Letpadaung land, 50 *pès*; Matè land, 50 *pès*; Pyithabye village land, 50 *pès*; Thattaya village land, 100 *pès*; Nga Nyo Ngè's land, 100 *pès*; Pôndaungtha land, 180 *pès*.

On Monday, the 1st waning of Tagu 633 Sakkarâj, Thamantapade* and his wife dedicated 100 *pès* at Ngamyangè and 30 at Pakan.

On the full-moon day of Kasôn 635 Sakkarâj, Manawyaza's wife Min Mi Gyi dedicated 1,330 *pès* of village lands, including Kankoywa 800 *pès*, and Yegyan-o 200 *pès*, Kanti 50 *pès*, Pye 50 *pès*, Wutchetkyun 10 *pès*, Kyantu land 30 *pès*, bought for 300 ticals of silver; Kanti land 50 *pès*, obtained from monk Asawminhla-achet; Letpadaung land 50 *pès*, obtained as a reward from the king by Nga Pu Dat and sold by him for 500 ticals of silver; Mantè land 50 *pès*, obtained from monk Sawdwe; Pyidetthabye land 50 *pès*, obtained as a reward from the king.

"I dedicate a slave along with each *pè* of land. May all those, including my relatives, who destroy my offering, come under the wrath of the king and live miserable lives as human beings. May they always encounter every danger from fire, water, thunder, axe, elephant, leopard, tiger, bear, and incurable diseases, and may they all die unnatural deaths. May they subsequently be burnt in *avîci* and never behold any of the coming Buddhas. On the other hand, may those who support my offering share its merits equally with me. May they live long and glorious lives and may they enjoy every happiness as men and *nats*, and may they ultimately become Buddhas and attain the bliss of Nirvâna."

REVERSE.

On Monday, the 1st waning of Tagu 633 Sakkarâj, Thamantapade and his wife built a monastery and dedicated to it the following lands, namely, 100 *pès* at Ngamyangè; 10 *pès* at Palangôn; 5 at Thitputhin; 5 at Nyaunghla; 2 at Myaunggwè; 2 at Kinônbyi; 5 at Ngasinthindôn, and 30 at Pakan.

"May all those, including my relatives, who destroy my offering incur the wrath of the king and live miserable lives in the present world. May they meet with every kind of danger from fire, water, thunder, axe, elephant, leopard, tiger, bear, and every incurable disease, and may they all die violent deaths. May they subsequently be burnt in *avîci* and never have the opportunity of be-

* One of Narathihapade or Tayôkpyemin's ministers.

holding any future Buddha. On the other hand, may those who support my offering share its merit equally with me. May they live long in prosperity, enjoying every happiness as men and *nats*. May they ultimately become Buddhas and attain the bliss of Nirvâna."

No. (20).—Obverse.

Locality.—Within the porch of the Sawlawun pagoda.

Date.—653 Sakkarâj (1281 A.D.).

Founders.—Yazathu and his mother Pwa Saw.

Substance of inscription.—Dedication of slaves and lands to the three "Gems."

"I adore all the Buddhas!"

On Friday, the 11th waxing of Tazaungmôn 626 Sakkarâj, King Kyazwa's great grandson Yazathu and his mother Pwa Saw,* being actuated by their great piety, dedicated to the three "Gems" the following lands and slaves in order that the Religion might last for 5,000 years, namely, Myegan-Myingan land, 200 *pès* and five slaves; Muthaw-Mônshan land, 10 *pès,* which is attached to the monastery erected by Yazathu's father.

On Thursday, the 7th waxing of Wazo 652 Sakkarâj, the following offerings to the three "Gems" were made by Yazathu on the occasion of handing over his father's monastery to monk Asalapôkte, namely, 150 *pès* of mango-gardens at Taungdwin and 10 slaves; Osuban-Tanyaukku land 300 *pès*. Besides the above, Yazathu supported several other institutions founded by his father. The Anan land, measuring 20 *pès*, and a number of slaves belonging to Yazathu's father were also dedicated to his monastery. On the occasion of the festival of the full-moon of Tazaungmôn, Yazathu and his mother dedicated to the monkhood the Sinzut-Ngamun land containing 2,000 *pès*, together with all the slaves attached to the same. This land was the subject of a lawsuit between Kyatthawut, thugyi of Pôktaik, and Thattabo, thugyi of Môndaung, and at the request of Yazathu's mother it was granted to her by the king. Pwa Saw subsequently obtained permission to dedicate it to the royal monastery, and it was done in the presence of the King and Ministers Athinkaya, Yazathingyan, Thingathu, Sattalingapyitsi, Tetkana, Eindapyitsaya, Pyetkathupônnya, and a number of thugyis and other notables.

On Thursday, the full-moon of Tagu 653 Sakkarâj, Yazathu and his mother made the following offerings to the three "Gems" in

* Queen of Narathihapade or Tayôkpyemin as is clearly mentioned on the reverse of this inscription as well as in inscription No. (25) following. This relationship is not mentioned in the histories.

order that the Religion might last 5,000 years, and that previous to their attainment of Nirvâna they might not experience any form of misery: Môkso village lands, 300 *pès* and 15 slaves; Talôk land, 30 *pès* and 30 slaves, which were the subject of a dispute in the reign of King Nandaungmya; Mingun land, 100 *pès* and 10 slaves; 600 *pès* adjacent to the Tanmaka circle; Kywèzein land, 200 *pès* and 7 slaves.

On Thursday, the 11th waxing of Nayôn 653 Sakkarâj, Yazathu built a pagoda. On that day his mother suddenly realized that her ancestors had to depart this life without taking any of their possessions with them, and that she would have to do the same in her turn and leave behind all that she had still after giving her son his due inheritance. She therefore resolved to give away her personal property in charity and accordingly made the following offerings with a view to further her parents, her children, and other relatives on their way to Nirvâna: Myemôn garden-land, 100 *pès* and 10 slaves; Kyauksè land, 100 *pès*, which was granted by King Nandaungmya in exchange for the Sinkyè land.

Reverse.

Sin-u land, 300 *pès*; O Ku Thin Yabagaw's land, 30 *pès*, together with the slaves attached to it; Thanbôk land, 30 *pès*, with its slaves; Kyetlet land, 100 *pès* and 30 slaves; Kyet-in land, 100 *pès*; Sagyat potter's land, 1,000 *pès* and 30 slaves; west Thettaunglwè land, 500 *pès*; Thetlègyun land, Thaubungyun land, Kyilègyun land, Sabaza land, Satthwa land, Mapyè-Thinthet land, Kanbunzôk land, Kègyin land, and Pyingan land; total, 800 *pès*.

On Wednesday, the 10th waxing of Nayôn 653 Sakkarâj, Pwa Saw dedicated the following personal slaves also, in the presence of Ministers Athinkaya, Yazathingyan, Thingathu, Sattalingapyitsi, Tetkana, Eindapyitsaya, Pônnya, Pyetkathu, and other courtiers.

"May my grandfather King Kyazwa, grandmother Saw Min Hla, my husband the king, my son the king, my parents, my two sons, my uncle Thingathu, aunt Thônlula,* elder sister Yadanabôn, my three brothers and two younger sisters, my deceased kinsmen, my attendants and servants, the ministers and other courtiers, and every being inhabiting every region between the highest heaven and the lowest hell, have a share of the merit accruing from my good deed. I have by virtue of my former good deeds survived all my kinsmen. May those who support my present offering made in order that the Religion might last 5,000 years, have the opportunity of beholding all the future Buddhas, who will be as numerous as the

* Daughter of King Kyazwa and Chief Queen of Ôksana.

atoms in a heap of earth extending from Nyaungu to Siripaccaya. On the other hand, may those who destroy the same never behold any of the said Buddhas; may they suffer torment like all heretics. May I, by virtue of this offering, become a *nat* in my next existence so that I may adore the Buddhas day and night continually, and before my ultimate wish is obtained, may I be enabled to acquire the 10 kinds of virtue possessed by every embryo Buddha."

Sut Nga Nun's land . . . . ; Kywèzein land, 200 *pès;* Thetthit land, Môkso village, 30 *pès;* Anan land, 20 *pès.*

No. (21).

Locality.—Within the cave near the Minwainggyaung pagoda.

Date.—631 Sakkarâj (1269 A.D.).

Founder.—Pwa Saw.

Substance of inscription.—Building of religious edifices and dedication thereto of slaves and lands.

"I adore all the Buddhas!"

On Wednesday, the full-moon of Pyatho 627 Sakkarâj, the grandmother* of Ôksana, the eminent, glorious, powerful, and pious King Sîritribhavanâdityapavaradhammarâjâ, the possessor of several white elephants and precious gems, built a beautiful cave with walls surrounding it from the reception of the three "Gems," placed a beautiful image of Gautama Buddha in the same and built a brick library containing a copy of the Tripitaka, in order that she might attain the bliss of Nirvâna. The palm-leaf manuscripts were placed in a gilt box near which there were three small gilt images. A large monastery, a rest-house, another with spires and a store-house were also erected. The lands and slaves dedicated for the upkeep of these religious edifices were: Tanhmyinmi land, 100 *pès* and 193 slaves; village paddy-lands, 170 *pès* and 159 slaves; another field 150 *pès;* Mapalan land, 25 *pès;* Theinga-Pigyan land, 204 *pès;* Nyaunggyun garden and 24 slaves; Mônbaung garden; Sataung land, 10 *pès;* Seikmalan land, 10 *pès;* 85 slaves from Pagan; 21 slaves from Kandaw.

On Wednesday, the full-moon of Tabodwè 631 Sakkarâj, Pwa Saw built a large brick monastery and dedicated to it the whole island of Kyalaung-Putlet; the island of Inzaya; 104 purchased slaves; 3,598 *pès* of paddy-land; 133 Indian slaves.

On Thursday, the 5th waxing of Tabodwè 616 Sakkarâj, the abovementioned Tanhmyinmi land of 800 *pès* was granted by King Ôksana

---

* The founder of this inscription is King Ôksana's grandmother on the maternal side. His paternal grandmother died seven days after his father Kyazwa's accession to the throne, and this inscription was erected during the reign of his son Narathihapade.

through Minister Mahathaman to Atulayit and Kyauktawu. On Tuesday, the 4th waxing of Tabodwè 623 Sakkarâj, this land was transferred by the king to the possession of Pwa Saw.

On Monday, the 10th waxing of Tagu 604 Sakkarâj, the above mentioned 193 slaves were offered to monk Pwayin by King Kyazwa, together with the said 170 *pès* of land. On Thursday, the 10th waxing of Kasôn 598 Sakkarâj, the said 159 slaves and 150 *pès* were granted by the king to Pwa Saw while she was residing at Kunbyaukngè. On Sunday, the 5th waxing of Wazo 598 Sakkarâj, the king offered to Pwa Saw all the lands and slaves which were offered to him at Pagan by Minister Theinga Thingyan and wife, namely, Sisaunggyi land, 30 *pès*; Ngakuthin village land, 20 *pès*; Nga Pauk Thin's field, 30 *pès*; Kyabin land, 20 *pès*; Kannyayin land, 20 *pès*; Nanibo land, 5 *pès*; Pauktin land, 7 *pès*; Pantawi land, 7 *pès*; Sônkalan land, 30 *pès*; Nuhat land, 5 *pès*; Sithinga land, 30 *pès*; . . . . land, 204 *pès*, 24 slaves; Nyaunggyun garden.

No. (22).

Locality.—Near the inscription cave attached to the Lemyethna pagoda.

Date.—628 Sakkarâj (1266 A.D.).

Founder.—Thingathu's daughter.

Substance of inscription.—Building of monastery and dedication of land thereto.

On Thursday, the 7th waxing of Wagaung 628 Sakkarâj, Thingathu's daughter* built a monastery within the precincts of Anandathu's monastery and dedicated thereto the Kangyôkthami land, containing 50 *pès*, which was purchased for her by Ministers Yamanngè and Mahathaman for 500 ticals of silver; also 1,000 palm trees at Magwe. On Monday, the 3rd waxing of Wazo 587 Sakkarâj, the whole of the revenue derived from the Wutchet and Thananlègyaung villages, including 2,000 *pès* of garden-land, was dedicated towards the making of daily rice-offerings and lights.

No. (23).

Locality.—Within the Amana group of monasteries.

Date.—628 Sakkarâj (1266 A.D.).

Founder.—Minister Thingathu's daughter.

Substance of inscription.—Building of monastery and dedication of slaves and land thereto.

* Lesser Queen of Narathihapade or Tayôkpyemin.

"I adore the Buddha!"

ON Thursday, the 7th waxing of Wagaung 628 Sakkarâj, the daughter of Minister Thingathu, being desirous of escaping from the miseries of existence, of old age, death, evil companionship, separation from loved ones, want, &c., and subsequently attaining the bliss of Nirvâna, built a large monastery at great expense, and for the maintenance of the monks residing therein dedicated to the same several slaves and pieces of garden and paddy land.

"May every one from the king downwards obtain a share of my merit. May they live long and be able to support my offerings. May the queen and her maids-of-honour also obtain a share. May they be happy in one another's love. May the present and all future kings, nobles, and commoners, who support my offerings, have their every wish fulfilled. May I for my part be free from enmity, be easily satisfied, slow to anger, compassionate, wise, far-seeing, unenvious, lavish in charity, faithful, and unforgetful throughout *samsaro*; and on the advent of Metteyya may I obtain the excellent gift of liberation from existence."

The lands offered were 100 *pès* in Mapinzaya-Kaunggamu; 39 *pès* in Sagu-o-seikthit, and the slaves attached to the same; .... *pès* in Salingyan, together with the slaves attached to it; 40 *pès* in Taungni together with its slaves; Myinzaing land, 30 *pès* and slaves; Matadè land, 40 *pes*; Taungbyôn land, 30 *pès* and slaves; Kyôn land, 250 *pès*; Kalun land .... *pès* and slaves; Ngamya land, 10 *pès*; Pathein-Gwintamit land, 2,764 *pès* and slaves; Sayun land, 50 *pès*; Pyitadaingzi land, ... *pès*; Pyiogwe-Tanbein land, 30 *pès*; Pyipitanaing land, 30 *pès*; Pyitathaye land, 30 *pès*; Pyitabin-Nakanet land, 50 *pès*; Pyichisi land, 500 *pès* and slaves; Tarakin-Pathein land, 100 *pès*; Kayaung land, 100 *pès* and slaves; Sakata land, 100 *pès* and slaves; Pakasanwet land, ... *pès* and slaves; Tayintanlu land, 600 *pès* and slaves; Uyathi land, 666 *pès* and slaves; Pègu land, 1,000 *pès* and slaves; Puttawdwin-Kyauktaung land, 100 *pès* and slaves; Myebônzaung land, 100 *pès* and slaves; Wunbogyauk land, 300 *pès* and slaves; Sawun-Sabyin land, 100 *pès* and slaves; Ngapogaing garden-land at Myittha, 7 *pès*; 6 *pès* obtained on behalf of Sithu's wife; 5 *pès* obtained in the name of the king; Pupa garden; Opaha-Minyinpaditha garden; Saluthamain garden and slaves; Nga Pyit's garden and slaves at Pilin; 100 *pès* of paddy-land adjacent to this garden; Nga Pyi Thin's garden at Mani; Dhammapyitsi's garden; Nga Te's garden and land; O Tôn's garden; Nga Maing's garden at Minduwa; Gyaingganaing garden; Tamyatha garden and slaves; Nga Kya Twè's garden; Mani garden; Tarakin-Pathein garden; Talaunggadè garden, and 30 *pès* of paddy-land adjacent to it; Tanut garden and slaves; Malalan garden and slaves. The slaves offered were: Nga Pônna and family; Kaya Thi and family; Nga Yauk Thin and family; Nga Sun Lun Thin and family; a family of slaves from Daing; a family of slaves from Pyôn; a family of slaves from Palè-u; O Pôn Thin and family; Nga Myaik Thin and family; a family of slaves from Munalun-Paunglaung; a family of slaves from Pyepaunglan; a family from Pyibaukseik; 20 slaves from Tamyi; 30 from Sein; a family from Shanbo; a family from Ngahmeik-Kaungyan; a family from Yandun-Yanthan; a family from Kyabin; Pegu thugyi's family of slaves; 40 other slaves from Pegu; 10 from Pyônlaing; 30 members of the families of Nga Saung, Nga Chan, and Nga Tha Daing. The slaves in Pagan were—Nga Chit Thi Thin; Thuyè, an Indian, and son Nasingyin, grandson Nga Kyun; Nga Tha Lôn; Nga Yauk; Nga Kwe; Daramu; Nga Pyit Kaung and son Nga Pan Du; Nga Chit Swa and son Nga Thet She; Kunmarasa and son Nga Kwe; Nga Kaung Hmu; Nga Yu Ya; Nga Lat; Nga Palè and sons; Nga Kyun and an infant; Nga Yut; Nga Ywa Haung and son Nga Pôn Malaung; Nga Ma and son; Nga La Gaung's son Nga Pôn Laung; Nga Nauk Kaung; Nga Hli Bu and son Nga Chit U; Nga Kala and son Nga Chit Kyi; Nga Sein; Nga Pyi Pa and son Nga Nyo; Nga Pôn Za and son Nya Hnaung; Nga Lat; Nga Shin; Nga Tha Bin; Nga Pyit Sin; Mi U; Yan Baw; O Kyan Zôn; O Pet Sut; Waze Makyan; O Tan Laing; O Kuyi and son; O Pe and two sons; Ma Kya Sa; Ma Pyet Si Mi; Ma Pyet Si; O Ma and child; Ma Tabe; Kalamyin and daughter Kotanmasaung, granddaughter O Kin; O Gyi and child; O Palè; O Pyi; Patheinthi and two children; O Lat; O Mathein and daughter Myat Chin Zwa; O Chit U; O Pegyi; O Mi; O Taku and daughter Chit Tat Swa; Mintamatan; O Lôn and child; Kanyayet; Kishamôn; Mathinmalaw; Mônkyinli; Kalabu; Akaungthun and daughter O Mye Me; O Lôn; O Paung Baw; O Pôn Saung and daughter O Tasat; O Shan; O Twe; Daramu; Nga Sagu, wife and child; O Mein; O Paunglaung and child; O Ein The; O Wun Pe; O Lat; O Mwe's daughter; O So; O Hlun; O Koh Pya; Nga U Lôn; Nga Tet The; Nga Naing Gan; Nga Chin and two children; Nga Lôn and son Nga Mun; Nga Lon's brother; Nga Chin Ya; Nga Payôn; Nga Pyi's son; Nga Chit Sin Go; Nga Tan Laing; Nga Tun; Pagunya; Nga U Lôn and son Nga Yauk; Nga Payin; Nga Lat; Nga Saik; Nga Pauk Wa Naing; . . . . . .; Nga Chit Mun; Nga Kaung Zôn; Nga Kwe; Nga Thana; Ma Twe Gyin; Chit Twe Macha; O Pyi Zin and child; Kaungmayôk; O Nyo; . . . .; Laung Mana Thin; O La; O Sin Kye; O Kyaung and child; O Chit Sat; O Yin; O Hla; O Pyu Sin; O Lat.

NO. (24).*

Locality.—Within the Amana group of monasteries.

Date.—630 Sakkarâj (1268 A.D.).

Founders.—Pyitsapade's mother and sister, Thingathu's daughter and Minsekywin.

Substance of inscription.—Dedication of paddy-lands to monastery.

A PADDY-FIELD at Salin, measuring 160 *pès*, together with the slaves attached to it, was dedicated to the Palin monastery. Also 200 *pès* of paddy-land at Kinmun. In the year 630 Sakkarâj, Pyitsapade's mother and sister dedicated 20 *pès* of paddy-land at Mapinzaya. Minister Thingathu's daughter also dedicated to the monastery 2,764 *pès* of both wet and dry weather paddy-land. The lands dedicated to the monkhood were—Sagyet, 40 *pès;* Puyin, 10 *pès;* Taungbalin, 10 *pès;* and Kalanbo, 10 *pès.* The land offered by Minister Pyitsapade was called Nyaungdaing, measuring 50 *pès.* Minsekywin, grandson of Minister Mingalapade, offered 500 *pès* of paddy-land at Chaungletto.

"May those who support my offerings share the merit equally with me. May those who destroy them suffer in the eight principal and 100 lesser hells for a period of years equal to the number of molecules in a heap of earth extending from Nyaungu to Siripaccaya."

NO. (25).—OBVERSE.†

Locality.—Within the porch of the Sawlawun pagoda.

Date.—653 Sakkarâj (1291 A.D.).

Founders.—Yazathu and mother Pwa Saw.

Substance of inscription.—Dedication of slaves, lands, and cattle to the three "Gems."

"I adore all the Buddhas!"

ON Monday, the 12th waxing of Tazaungmôn 631 Sakkarâj, Yazathu, the very pious and charitable grandson of King Kyazwa, made the following offerings to his father's monastery as well as to the three "Gems" in order that the Religion might last 5,000 years, namely, Kanyingôn land at Taungdwin, 180 *pès* and one slave; Mywin Thin's land at Mônshan, 10 *pès* and one slave.

On Thursday, the 7th waxing of Wazo 652 Sakkarâj, the following offerings were made to Asalabôkdi, the presiding monk of the said monastery, namely, a mango-garden measuring 150 *pès* and 11 slaves; O Su Pan's land, 300 *pès* and one slave; the whole of Kun Tha's slaves and Anan land 20 *pès.* On the conclusion of lent of the same year the mother and son jointly dedicated to the three

---

* This inscription is evidently in continuation of the foregoing.

† This is founded by the same parties and records the same facts, with a few additions, as the foregoing inscription No. (20).

"Gems" the Pôktaiknet, Sinzut, and Ngamun's lands, having an aggregate area of 2,000 *pès*, and 30 slaves. With regard to these lands Katwetkathu and Pônnya questioned Sinzu and Nga Mun in the presence of the king and monks Tipitaka, Adiyazagwin, Thamatapathatika, Asalabôkdi, and Minyatha, as to Pwa Saw's title to the same, and on their statement in her favour, the king formally passed an order in the audience hall by Minister Thiyiathinkaya, confirming Pwa Saw's title to the lands and the slaves attached to the same. Pwa Saw was thus enabled to dedicate them as above. The witnesses to the dedication were—King Kyazwa, Ministers Athinkaya, Thingathu, Byetgathu, Pônnya, Eindapyitsaya, and other courtiers. The royal order was read out by Minister Pônnya in the audience hall of the palace.

On Thursday, the full-moon of Tagu 653 Sakkarâj, Pwa Saw dedicated the following lands and slaves to her grandfather's monastery in order that the Religion might last 5,000 years, and in order that she might herself escape the future miseries of existence, namely, Môkso village land, 300 *pès* and 15 slaves; Talôk land, 30 *pès* and 17 slaves; Mingun land, 100 *pès* and 9 slaves; Itminhla land, Tamaga circle, 600 *pès* and 30 slaves; Kywezein land, 200 *pès* and 7 slaves.

On Thursday, the 11th waxing of Nayôn 653 Sakkarâj, Pwa Saw built a pagoda in memory of her beloved son (Yazathu) and realizing that her parents and ancestors and even her son had to depart before her leaving all their possessions behind them, she resolved to dispose of her estate in charity.

She accordingly dedicated to her father's monastery the following lands and slaves: Môn garden-land, 100 *pès*; Papa and Katanthaw lands in Myedu, 1,000 *pès*; Kyauksè land in Myitha, 150 *pès* and a number of slaves; Okuthin-Yabagaw land, 30 *pès* and slaves; Yabagaw-Thinbôk land, 300 *pès* and slaves; Yele-sin-u land, 200 *pès* and 100 slaves; Kyetlè land, 100 *pès* and 30 slaves; Kyetin land in Tabye, 100 *pès* and 47 slaves from west Petthet, 9 from Mappe-Thinthet, 5 from Thette, 7 from Aunglwe, 5 from Nabya, 30 from Wunbin-Myinbo, 3 from Sabaza, 4 from Satthwa, 7 from Kegyin, and 9 from Kinbunzôk. Besides this Pwa Saw offered all her personal ornaments and jewellery, as well as her dwelling-house . . . .

Reverse.

By virtue of these offerings, may the king,* the father of my two beloved sons, my grandmother Saw Min Hla, my parents, my two

* Narathihapade or Tayôkpyemin.

sons, my aunt Queen Thônlula, my elder sister Queen Yadanakôn, my younger sisters and brothers, and every one inhabiting every region from the lowest hell to the highest heaven obtain their fondest wishes. May those who support these my offerings, which are made in order that the Religion might last 5,000 years, have the opportunity of beholding the future Buddhas, who will be as numerous as the atoms in a heap of earth extending from Nyaungu to Siripaccaya. On the other hand, may those who destroy them never have any such opportunity, and may they have their portion with the heretics. May I, on my part, obtain every happiness as *nat* or man, beautiful, illustrious, charitable, and wise, and on the advent of Metteyya, may I be enabled to make the greatest charitable offering. May I ultimately reach the same state as Metteyya Buddha and be thus able to lead men and *nats* from *samsaro* to Nirvâna."

The offerings made to the presiding monk of the monastery were—Anan land, 20 *pès* and 50 Indian slaves; 10 *pès* at Mônshan; 30 *pès* at Talôk and slaves; 100 *pès* at Môkso and three slaves; 200 *pès* out of the Sinzut lands and five slaves; Kywetlè land, 100 *pès* and slaves; Okuthinyabagaw land, 30 *pès* and slaves; Tamaka land, 600 *pès* and slaves; and 30 *pès* at Pakan. Rice-offerings are continually made at my father's cave-pagoda, and my son's pagoda and library. During lent each superior monk is supplied with a yellow robe, and lights and other offerings are periodically* made to them at my monastery. Let the monks residing therein be attended on and furnished with every comfort in case of illness.

Let 150 ticals be set apart for the maintenance of the monks, and let the balance be utilized for the upkeep of the edifices. Let the monks be full of learning and good works, let those among monks who support my offerings share their merit with me. Let monk . . . . look after those slaves who minister to them.

No. (26).

Locality.—Within the Minwaing group of monasteries.

Date.—634 Sakkarâj (1272 A.D.).

Founder.—Queen Pwa Saw.

Substance of inscription.—Dedication of slaves, lands, and cattle to the three "Gems."

ON Saturday, the full-moon of Tazaungmôn 633 Sakkarâj, Queen Pwa Saw made the following offerings to the three "Gems,"

---

* Offerings of candles, candle-sticks, lamps, and oil are made in the month of Tabodwè (February), provisions and clothing in Tagu (April) and Wagaung (August), and holy-water in Kasôn (May).

namely, 29 gardeners, 300 *pès* of paddy-land, a garden, a grand staircase for her monastery, and a herd of cows and goats.

On Thursday, the 8th waning of Tabaung 634 Sakkarâj, Queen Pwa Saw made the following offerings which were granted her by her son King Ôksana, through Minister Mahathaman, namely, 29 gardeners, 300 *pès* of paddy-land, one garden, 127 slaves from Inzaya, and 133 Indian garden slaves.

"I dedicate these lands for the upkeep of my incomparable monastery, and these slaves for looking after it continually, keeping it always in good repair, for preparing the rice-offerings and the light-offerings and for ministering to the monks. I offer the cows in order that fresh milk, cream, butter, and ghee may be obtained for the monks. May my lord the king,* my son the king,† and my grandson the king,‡ and all their successors, as well as every being inhabiting every universe between the highest heaven and the lowest hell, obtain a share of my merit, and reach Nirvâna. By virtue of my good deeds may I, before attaining Nirvâna, become the happiest among men and the most beautiful and glorious among *nats*. May I be beloved by all men and *nats* and be the possessor of vast wealth. May I become a most famous and powerful ruler of kingdoms. May I, in my every existence, be wise and charitable and be possessed of every good virtue, and may I ultimately obtain the bliss of Nirvâna. My title to the lands, slaves, and cattle which I have offered is unquestionable, and no dispute regarding them is likely to arise hereafter. May those who destroy my offering live short and miserable lives. May they become *petas* separated from their families and friends and be deprived of all their possessions. May they incur the wrath of the king and be constantly in danger of losing their lives from lightning, fire, axe, water, &c. May they be burnt in *avîci* and in the seven other principal and 16 smaller hells. May their existence be alternately as *petas* and as inmates of those hells. On the other hand, may those who are so charitably disposed as to support my offerings, share my merit with me equally. May they live long and happily, be always free from every kind of danger, and be never troubled in body or mind. May they escape the miseries of *samsaro* and having enjoyed every form of happiness, may they ultimately attain the wish and reward of every Buddha, namely, the bliss of Nirvâna."

On Friday, the 10th waxing of Tagu 633 Sakkarâj, Queen Pwa Saw presented to the king a list of offerings made by her, and it was recorded. Minister Saduyingathu, ... (last line).

---

* Kyazwa. | † Ôksana. | ‡ Narathihapade.

No. (27).

Locality.—Within the southern brick monastery near the Dayinpato pagoda.

Date.—635 Sakkarâj (1273 A.D.).

Founder.—Thanbyin Letsaung.

Substance of inscription.—Building of monastery and dedication of slaves and lands.

ON Monday, the full-moon of Thadingyut 635 Sakkarâj, Thanbyin* Letsaung purchased a piece of land east of Amana and built a monastery thereon. He then dedicated to the three "Gems" contained therein the following lands and slaves, namely, 75 *pès* of inherited land; one betel-nut garden; 1 *pè* of paddy-land and 22 slaves; Taungmyin land, 100 *pès;* Myingôndaing land, 80 *pès;* 30 *pès* at Hlègu; Pakan land, 10 *pès;* total, 295 *pès,* 22 slaves, and one garden.

"May the king and every other sentient being have a share of my merit. May those who support my offering share my merit equally with me."

The amount spent in copying the Tripiṭaka was 3,000 *ticals* of silver, and the cost of building the monastery 3,400 *ticals;* total, 6,400 *ticals.*

No. (28).

Locality.—Within the walls of the Malônbyit pagoda.

Date.—636 Sakkarâj (1274 A.D.).

Founder.—Minister Taya.

Substance of inscription.—Building of religious edifices and dedication thereto of slaves and lands.

"I adore all the Buddhas!"

ON Thursday, the 10th waning of Nadaw 636 Sakkarâj, Taya, minister of the pious, excellent, all-powerful and glorious Sîritribhavanâdiccapavarahommarâjâ† spent large sums of money and jewellery in building a cave at Amana and a large image therein, a large brick monastery, a library, an ordinary monastery, a rest-house, and a store-house, in order that he might escape the miseries of *samsaro* and attain the bliss of Nirvâna, and for the upkeep of these institutions the following offerings were made, namely, 300 viss of silver obtained in payment of a loan made to Gingabyit and wife; 150 viss of silver similarly obtained from the sons of Oktama-

* A revenue officer corresponding somewhat with a thugyi of the present day.

† Narathihapade.

thu; Yangôn lands, 500 *pès*; 10 *pès* purchased from Taingmalôk's daughter; 36 *pès* purchased from Kangyat's daughter; 4 *pès* of garden and paddy land purchased from Seiktarapyitsi; 36 *pès* purchased from Kyanmapat's wife; 100 *pès* and 50 palm-trees obtained in satisfaction of a loan from Nakaralan's son; 20 *pès* purchased from Kingabyit; 300 *pès* obtained as the price of an elephant from Kingabyit; 40 *pès*, including a tank, purchased from Pôndithin's father; 300 *pès* and a tank purchased from Nga Pyizôn Thin.

"May every being from the king downwards, including the *nats*, obtain a share of the merit accruing from my good deed. May I before attaining Nirvâna be the most exalted among *nats* and men. May those who are so charitably inclined as to support my offerings, live long, enjoy immunity from disease, be beautiful and sweet-voiced. May they have every wish of theirs satisfied, and may they ultimately reach Nirvâna."

No. (29).

Locality.—Within the brick monastery, close to the north of Dayinpato pagoda.

Date.—638 Sakkarâj (1276 A.D.).

Founder.—Princess Asawpaditha.

Substance of inscription.—Building of monastery and dedication of slaves and lands.

"I adore all the Buddhas!"

On Tuesday, the full-moon of Tazaungmôn 638 Sakkarâj, Princess Asawpaditha* obtained the grant of a piece of land east of Hmana from the king and built thereon a monastery for monk Anandapyinmya. She then dedicated to the three "Gems" contained therein the following lands and slaves, namely, Tetthe land, 26 *pès*; Tanyauk land, 42 *pès*; Kanthit land, 200 *pès* and five slaves; Lathat land, 100 *pès* and two slaves; Sanet land, 200 *pès* and two slaves; Pyu land, 100 *pès*; Kyazwa-Putkaing land, 300 *pès* and 30 slaves; Kyedwin land, 30 *pès*; Kywèsinbyôn-Lainglet land, 428 *pès*; Atubadaya-Thintin land, 45 *pès*; Danathu-Thintin land, 45 *pes*; Danathu *mayin* land, 40 *pès*; Ôktaung-Omyè land, 50 *pès*; Tabyintaw land, 1,000 *pès*; Pusu-Thakadan land, 100 *pès* and 10 slaves; 100 slaves from Yegè; one betel-nut garden at Kanaingga-i, yielding 50 baskets of nuts; total, 1,366 *pès* of paddy-land, 1,100 *pès* of other land, and 149 slaves.

"I give all this property away because I love the reward of Buddhahood more. May every one from the king downwards have a

* A daughter of Narathihapade.

share of my merit. May those who support my offering share its merit equally with me. But may those who destroy it never have the opportunity of beholding any of the Buddhas, and may they be burnt in *avīci*.

No. (30).

Locality.—Within the Minwaing group of monasteries.

Date.—643 Sakkarâj (1281 A.D.).

Founder.—Queen Pwa Saw.

Substance of inscription.—Purchase of lands for monastery.

"I adore all the Buddhas!"

On Wednesday, the 5th waxing of Tazaungmôn 639 Sakkarâj, Queen Pwa Saw* purchased 1,000 *pès* of paddy-land to be attached to her monastery for 1,000 ticals of silver. The transaction was effected through Ministers Mahathaman and Wuthipyitsi, and the owners of the several pieces of land were Bônmakittaya, Bônmatheinga, Nga Pyit Thin, Bônmathu, Pyigwin, Bônmapade, Nga Ônletna, Nga Ya, and Nga Pônna, and the witnesses to the transaction were Thugyi Kya Mye and Nga Wun Sin Thin. The rewards made that year to those land-owners and others for the purchase of wearing apparel were—Bônmakittaya, 35 ticals of silver; Bônmatheinga, 3 ticals; Nga Pyit Thin, 10; Bônmathu, 10; Pyigwin, 3; Bônmapade, 2; Nga Ónletna, 1; Nga Ya, 1; Nga Pônna, 1; Panzin, 2; Nanda Thiri, 3; for the purchase of food and drink, 54 ticals; Nga Chan Tha Thin, 5; Nga Pan Daung Thin, 5; purchase of toddy, 2¼ ticals; grand total, including price of land, 1,137¼ ticals. This money was paid by the hands of Nga Tan Laing, clerk to Mahathaman; Thilapa, clerk to Wuthipyitsi; and treasurers Thin Gyi and Thin Yin. But the lands were not delivered that year and the land-owners agreed to treat the purchase-money as a loan and to repay 3,000 ticals subsequently in satisfaction of it.

On Sunday, the 1st waxing of Nadaw 641 Sakkarâj, Kittaya, Nga Kin Maung, Nga Pa Sin, and Nga Pôn were asked to hand over the land. On this Kittaya, saying that there were standing crops on the land then, he would undertake to pay 6,000 ticals instead of 3,000 if the land was not delivered in the following month. A document was accordingly executed, but at the time fixed Kittaya came to the monastery and having received a further reward of 73 ticals of silver, he made over the piece of land called Hawkanbyin and said that it contained 1,000 *pès*. Subsequently it was brought to the knowledge of Minister Saduyingabo that

* Chief Queen of Narathihapade and subsequently also of his son Kyazwa.

the measurement of the land was incorrect, and under his orders the land was re-measured properly and boundary pillars were erected. The expenses thus incurred by Saduyingabo amounted to 40 ticals of silver and 11½ viss of lead.

On Sunday, the 6th waning of Tazaungmôn, Minister Anandapyitsi had the land measured again in obedience to a royal order and it was found a little short of 1,000 *pès*. Thugyi Nga Yauk Pyi Thin, Kittaya, and others were then sent for, and in the presence of Minister Saduyingabo and several monks the deficiency was made good. On that occasion a reward of 100 ticals was made to Thugyi Nga Tet Pyi Thin, another 100 to Kittaya . . . .
. . . . (last line).

No. (31).

Locality.—Within the walls of the Lemyethna pagoda.

Date.—646 Sakkarâj (1284 A.D.).

Founder.—Ein Kyan.

Substance of inscription.—Dedication of lands to monastery.

On Tuesday, the full-moon of Wazo 646 Sakkarâj, Ein Kyan* made the following offerings to his monastery for the maintenance of the three "Gems" contained therein, namely, Laung land, 100 *pès*; Letwô land, 30 *pès* and a number of slaves; Mogyo land, 30 *pès* and slaves; Sôngyi land, having a sowing capacity of 15 baskets, 500 palm-trees and slaves.

"By virtue of this good deed may I, in my next existence, become a man able to promote the cause of the Religion. May those who destroy my offering live short and miserable lives, and when they die may they suffer ten thousand times more severely than Dewadat in *avîci* for as many *kalpas* as there are atoms in a heap of earth extending from Siripaccaya to Nyaungu. May those who are able to support my offering live long and happily; may they always be free from want in every existence throughout *samsaro*, and after having enjoyed every happiness as men and *nats*, may they obtain the bliss of Nirvâna."

No. (32).

Locality.—Within the porch of the Dayinpato pagoda.

Date.—656 Sakkarâj (1294 A.D.).

Founder.—Thanbyin Zeyathate.

Substance of inscription.—Dedication of slaves and lands.

---

* A minister of King Narathihapade.

ON Monday, the 12th waxing of Wazo 651 Sakkarâj, Thanbyin Zeyathate dedicated 150 *pès* of paddy-land at Kanti, out of which 10 were attached to the Dayinpato pagoda, 10 to the cave, and 130 to the monastery he built at Amana.

"May those who support this offering share its merit equally with me. On the other hand, may those who destroy it live short and miserable lives during the dispensation of every Buddha. May they suffer in *avîci* and other principal hells."

On Wednesday, the 11th waning of Pyatho 656 Sakkarâj, the king commanded the dedication of 100 *pès* of Kansi paddy-land to the monastery erected by Zeyathate. The following ministers and courtiers were present at the time, namely, Athinkaya, Mahabo, Yetkana, Etgapadi, Saduyingapadi, Pônnya, Eindaraseik, Alônhmauk, and Zeyathate.

"May those who destroy this offering suffer in *avîci* and other hells. On the other hand, may those who support it reap its reward equally with me."

The slaves were—Nga Pè, Nga Pè Gyi, and Nga Sin.

NO. (33).

Locality.—Within the Itzagawna group of monasteries.

Date.—653 Sakkarâj (1291 A.D.).

Founder.—King Kyawzwa.

Substance of inscription.—Dedication of garden-land to cave.

THE Mahâthera Dhammasîri was interred in the west cave. On Monday, the 9th waning of Tabaung, the king* dedicated to the cave a piece of garden-land extending from Tingôk to the Tankè land, together with the slaves attached to it. The witnesses to the dedication were two princes and five ministers, namely, princes Kyazwa and Yazathu, and ministers Sitthate, Athincha, Yazathingyan, Thihathu, and Mahabo.

On Monday, the 5th waxing of Tagu 653 Sakkarâj, monks Pitakawilatha and Thamantapathatika came and reported the demise of the Mahâthera to the king in the audience hall. On this the king offered the said cave to them in the presence of courtiers Hngetpyittaung, Wimalapati, Awiyazaguru, and Et.

"This offering is made in order that the Religion might last 5,000 years. May those who destroy it suffer for as many years as there are atoms in a heap of earth extending from Nyaungu to Letpanzeik. On the other hand, may those who support it be rewarded with merit as great as that heap of earth."

* Kyawzwa of Pagan, son of Narathihapade or Tayôkpyemin by Shinpa, a lesser Queen.

No. (34).

Locality.—Within the porch of the Ngazishin pagoda.

[This inscription is so obliterated that only a few names of slaves in the middle can be made out.]

No. (35).

Locality.—Within the group of monasteries built by the mother of King Ôksana.

Date.—704 Sakkarâj (1242 A.D.).

Founder.—Queen Minsawu.

Substance of inscription.—Building of monastery and dedication thereto of slaves and lands.

"Reverence to the Blessed, Holy, and Enlightened One!"

On Monday, the 5th waxing of Pyatho 704 Sakkarâj, the Queen-Dowager* built the Pagan monastery and dedicated to it a tract of land at Talôk, bounded on the *east* by Inma, on the *west* by the river, *south* by the Ngapônthe stream, *north* by the Zinyaw stream, and including the Tanzato-Kanauk field 150 *pès,* Tanzato-Kanwun field 60 *pès,* Thandasè field 80 *pès,* Pyogin field 30 *pès,* Tawzein field 410 *pès;* also a tract of land called Myônpangyè bounded on the *east* by Letthama tank, *west* by Saukwun land, *south* by Myaungdaung land, and *north* by the stream and containing 30 *pès* of high-land for nurseries, 20 *pès* liable to floods, Sama and Ôktara tank-fields 120 *pès,* Theinga tank-field 2 *pès,* Letpan tank-field 30 *pès,* Yatha-Myenè field 150 *pès,* Einpu-Nakauk field 20 *pès,* Lèu field 30 *pès;* total 1,055 *pès.* The slaves dedicated were—San Ma; Thattapagyan; Bônma Thuta; Bônma Kyan; Bônma Theinga; Bônma Sarabo; Bônma Thaman; Bônma Yasa; Bônma Thu's son; Bônma Kyan's son; Bônma Theinga's son; Bônma Sarabo's son; Nga Pandu Thin; Nga Lôn Pa; Mi Bauk; O Sein's two uncles; O Swe Yin's father; O Chit Aung's father; Wun Byit Ya's father; Nga Hla Ba; Nga Naung Hla's father; Nga Tôn; San Ma's two sons; Nga Pandu Thin's two sons; Thattaba Kyan's son; Nga Thalôn Thin; Nga Kin Mun's father; Nga San Ba; Nga Kin Mun; Nga Naing Gan; total 33. The Kyabolet field of 40 *pès* was attached to the monastery for its upkeep.

"By virtue of this offering may all my wishes be fulfilled. May my son the king, my daughters, nieces, and grandchildren share my merit equally with me. May every being, both on land and sea, have a share. May the guardian and other *nats* also have a share.

---

* Minsawu, daughter of Narathihapade by his fifth queen Shinshwe. She was raised to the throne by Kyawzwa and Thihathu successively.

On the other hand, may those who destroy my offering find themselves always in poverty and want and be afflicted with all manner of diseases and ailments. May the saving influence of a host of Buddhas equal in number to that of the atoms in a heap of earth extending from Pagan to Pinya, have no effect on them."

"This kingdom of Pagan is called so because it is the most pleasant and beautiful of all kingdoms. It is also called Arimaddana because it is inhabited by people who are warlike and brave and are able to vanquish their foes, who dread even the sound of its name. Its people always enjoy immunity from danger and are free from pain. They are well versed in every art and possess various industrial appliances. The country is full of useful things, the people are wealthy and the revenue is enormous. The kingdom may therefore be said to be more desirable than the land of the *nats*. It is a glorious kingdom and its subjects are known to be glorious and powerful. The monastery I have built stands to the east of the capital."

No. (36).

Locality.—Within the inscription cave attached to the Lemyethna pagoda.

Date.—737 Sakkarâj (1375 A.D.).

Founder.—Queen of Toungoo.

Substance of inscription.—Offering of an elephant for repairing a rest-house.

On Thursday, the 13th waxing of Tazaungmôn 737 Sakkarâj, the Queen of Toungoo offered a young elephant, 5 cubits high, on behalf of her deceased lord, in order to repair the large rest-house erected by Anandathu.

"May my husband the king* reap the reward of this offering. May I obtain for myself a share of Anandathu's merit accruing from his good deed."

No. (37).

Locality.—Within the inscription cave attached to the Lemyethna pagoda.

Date.—752 Sakkarâj (1390 A.D.).

---

* Pyanchigyi, who ascended the throne of Toungoo in 1367 A.D., assuming the title of Asawmyatswanawyata. Four years later, he repaired the Shwezigôn Pagoda, Pagan, and dedicated several slaves to it, recording the fact in a lithic inscription. He is also the founder of inscription No. (2) following, which was found on the south of Pinya. In the 8th year of his reign he endeavoured, with the assistance of the Talaings, to repudiate the suzerainty of the King of Pagan. Minkyizwasawkè therefore sent out an expedition headed by his brother Sawyannaung, Governor of Prome, and Pyanchigyi was defeated and slain in action.

Founder.—Saddhamma Thera.

Substance of inscription.—Offering of money to a *simâ*.

ON Thursday, the 5th waxing of Tazaungmôn 752 Sakkarâj, Saddhamma Thera being desirous of avoiding the misery of hunger throughout *samsaro*, offered to the *simâ* attached to Anandathu's monastery . . . . . . *ticals* of silver, the interest of which was to be utilized for breakfasts on Sabbath days and 1¼ *ticals* to be used in the same way for a pot of curry on each Sabbath day.

" May those who destroy my offering " (Inscription ends).

INSCRIPTIONS OF PAGAN.

XII.—Found at Thamati.

No. (1).

Locality.—Near the Thamati pagoda.

Date.—664 Sakkarâj (1302 A.D.).

Founder.—Queen Pwa Saw's sister.

Substance of inscription.—Building of new monastery, repairing of old one, and dedication thereto of slaves and lands.

"I adore the Buddha, the Law and the Monkhood!"

" BY this act of adoration may every one be benefited and have their wishes fulfilled. I dedicate my paddy-lands for the maintenance of the monks, in order that I may attain Buddhahood. May all rejoice at my offering and approve of it. Those who do so, or actively support the offering, do what is meritorious, and will obtain a share of the reward. May those, therefore, who are desirous of reaping this reward support my offering. Those who regularly make the rice-offering daily will ultimately attain Buddhahood."

On Saturday, the full-moon of Tazaungmôn 621 Sakkarâj, 1,000 *pès* of paddy-land in Dipeshin was obtained from Kanandat's wife in barter for an elephant by Nayathingyan in the presence of Nga Pwè Thin and wife, Athamingala and wife, Nga Sôn Thashin and Nga Sin Kyè, and was dedicated to monk Gunathagaya's monastery. This fact was recorded on stone on Sunday, the 9th waning of Thadingyut 627 Sakkarâj.

On Monday, the 9th waning of Nadaw 631 Sakkarâj, Nayathingyan and his son Nga Pazin sold to Kanandet for 3,000 ticals of silver the whole of the paddy-land called Kanhaung, including a piece of *mayin* land watered by an arm of the tank from which the land takes its name. The witnesses to the transaction were—

Atthamangala, Minse Nga Yit, and Ôktama Pwetha. Nayathingyan originally acquired the land in the following way: He purchased the timber standing thereon from Byôngya Nga Laing Thin, Guna Theikda, and Nga Yaung Thin, servants of Minister Theingapade, but when the minister bade him extract the timber he was unable to do so at the time and he was therefore obliged to buy the land also. The purchase was made in the presence of several officials and a feast was spread on the culvert of the tank. A bullock was killed* and 10 pots of toddy were served up. The partakers of the feast included Pyigwin, Nga Sandi and son Nga Kin Pa, Nga Kyan Thin and sons, Nga Thit and sons.

On Friday, the 12th waxing of Wazo 664 Sakkarâj, Queen Pwa Saw's sister built a brick monastery in place of the ruined one erected by her aunt, wife of King Kyazwa, and dedicated thereto the following lands and slaves, namely, Thanbyingyin land, 100 *pès*, which was granted her by the king after the death of her sister and when she was raised to the throne, together with slaves Nga Pôn Zaung and son Nga Lè Dè; Nga Ywe; . . . . Nga Pyu; U Lwè's daughter Ein Yauk, granddaughters Ein Than and Chan Tha U; O Chit Yin; . . . . ; O Sa Ye and daughter Eindaungthu, granddaughter Ein Gyi; Ein Bye; . . . . (three lines).

No. (2).

Locality.—Near the Thamati pagoda.

Date.—636 Sakkarâj (1274 A.D.).

Founder.—Banker Nga Wa Thin's wife.

Substance of inscription.—Building of pagoda, cave and monastery, and dedication thereto of slaves, lands, and cattle.

"I adore all the Buddhas!"

ON . . . . the most glorious king of Pagan being desirous of obtaining the bliss of Nirvâna built at . . . . . a pagoda, a cave, and a monastery . . . . 1,000 *pès* of land at . . . . demarcated on the *east* by a large *tein* tree, on the *south* by a *kôkko* tree, *west* by a *kanyin* tree, and north by a teak tree; 60 *pès* at Pyithaumyin Ngachè, demarcated on the *east* by a *pyinma* tree, *south* by a *môn* tree, *west* by a *kyôk* tree, and *north* by a *chè* tree; 50 *pès* at Kyaukôk, Lègaing; 50 *pès* at Pyaungbya; 500 *pès* of old *mayin* land at Muthasindan village, bounded on the *east* by a line extending from Magyitabin to Ngapaik bridge, *south* by the Mu river,

* Evidently the tenets of Buddhism regarding the taking of life had not yet taken firm hold on the mind of its devotees at that period. The rituals of devil-worship must have been still in full force.

west by Sapyathinbôn, and *north* by Magyimôn village, 70 *pès* north of Talôkyein village.

"May those who destroy my offering suffer in the eight principal and 128 lesser hells. May they never behold any of the coming Buddhas. On the other hand, may those who support my offering share its merit equally with me. By virtue of this offering may I always be a *Rahan* throughout *samsaro*." The lands dedicated to Queen Palèmè's monastery measured altogether 2,080 *pès*.

"I adore all the Buddhas!"

On Friday, the 13th waxing of Nayôn 636 Sakkarâj, banker Nga Wa Thin's wife made the following offerings to the royal monastery, namely, Madaya and daughter O Myi E; O Taung Ma; O Sin; O Gôn; O Chi Thin; O Li and child; O Mun; total 9 slaves, 300 *pès* of paddy-land at Dipeshin, and three pairs of bullocks. These offerings were made in the presence of the following monks, namely, Kyanmapat, Saduyingabo, Sithawut, Mingalagyi, Tamati, Pahlwe, and Mingyaungngè.

"May all those, including my own relatives, who destroy these my offerings never behold any of the future Buddhas; may they be burnt in *avîci*. On the other hand, may those who support my offerings have their wishes gratified. May their happiness be great even in this present world."

No. (3).—Obverse.

Locality.—Within the inscription cave attached to the Sudaungbye pagoda.

Date.—661 Sakkarâj (1299 A.D.).

Founder.—Queen Pwa Saw.*

Substance of inscription.—Building of religious edifices and dedication of slaves and land thereto.

On Saturday, the 3rd waning of Tabodwè 661 Sakkarâj, corresponding with the year of the Religion 1843, Queen Pwa Saw, being desirous of escaping the miseries of *samsaro* and attaining Nirvâna, built a beautiful bejewelled pagoda surrounded by a brick wall at Thitmati. She also had a copy of the Tripitaka prepared and placed it in a large monastery ornamented with rare paintings. Attached to the monastery was a *sîmâ*, and the various buildings were dedicated in the presence of the king, and high festivities were held. The paddy-fields on Kaunggamu island were offered for the

* Chief Queen of Narathihapade and his son Kyawzwa. It was only in the reign of her grandson Sawnit that she was known by this name; she was previously called Queen Asaw.

upkeep of the monastery. They measure 330 *pès* and contain 2,320 palm trees, 105 *môn* trees, and 95 mango trees. The slaves offered with these lands were Bônma Chittaya and sons Nga Yan, Nga Naung; Nga Yaung and brothers Nga Yauk Lwè, Nga Pi Tha; Nga Pauk Sin; Yaza Petkyan and son Nga Min Ngè; Nga Lôn Zin and son Nga Naung Kin; Bônmade; Bônmakyan; Bônmasi; Nga Naung Gan and brother Nga Hlun; total 15. For the making of the rice-offerings, the upkeep of the religious edifices and the maintenance of the monks throughout the period of the Religion, the following lands and slaves were dedicated, namely, Mawyigyo land and slaves; Salin land and slaves; and the slaves from Pagan consisting of the weavers and other Indians. The Magyigyo land was originally obtained by Pwa Saw's elder sister from the king, and on her death it passed on to Pwa Saw. The paddy-fields included in the land are: 170 *pès* at Ngakywè tank; 300 *pès* at Nga Shan tank; 100 at Opyiwa tank; 224 at Ywatha tank; 170 at Paukkôngyi; 130 at Paukkônngè; 237 at Yehlutkyi; 63 at Yehlut-tôn; 35 at Yehlutngè; 30 at Kyauktaing; 1,754 at Kanhein; 50 at Kônzwa tank; 30 at Ngabôk tank; total 3,293 *pès* of *mayin* paddy-land and 500 *pès* of *kaukkyi* paddy-land; grand total 3,793 *pès*. These should yield 12,000 baskets of *mayin* paddy and each *pè* of *kaukkyi* paddy-land should produce one basket of rice and 50 of sessamum yielding 20 measures of oil. Besides the fields mentioned there are several sessamum and *jowar* plantations. The revenue payable per *pè* is one pot of curry and one viss of oil and the total revenue should be 100 viss of oil and 100 pieces of cloth. The total number of *pès* of cultivated land is 7,563 and the slaves attached to the land are: Nga Pyi Mè and brother Nga Pa Lat; herdsman Nga Yaung and brother Nga Twe; Nga Chan; Theingo and son Nga Kan Ti, grandsons Nga Thaukkya and Nga Tha Ya; Nga Ko Ya and sons Nga Kin Maung; Nga Thu Hla; Nga Paung and son Nga Mein; Nga Yaung and sons Nga Shan Zôn, Nga Wa; Nga Nyo and brothers Nga Tha Ya and Nga Aung Myin; Nga Pyi and sons Nga Thet Si, Nga Kin Ba; Nga Pyi's brother Nga We; Nga La and brother Nga Makaung; Nga Taung We and son Nga Nauk Saung; . . . . Nga Lôn; Nga Palè and son Nga Lat; Nga Hmyo;

Reverse.

O Palè; Maung Ma and daughters O Kin, O Dôn; O Zwa; O Pôn and daughters O Myin, O Sin; O Let Ti and daughters O Pyi, O Tun, granddaughter O Thaya; O Chit Pôn; O Chit Hla and daughter Myet Hnatha, granddaughters O Chit Yauk, O Kaung

Sin; O Hla Ngè; Mi Kin and daughters O Paung Paw, O Tha; Wun Thaya; O Than Pa and daughter O Lôn, granddaughter O Pyit Sin; O Wa and daughter O Myo; Ma Kyaung Gya; O Kin Mi; O Mun Ywe; Nga Taing Bin; Ngu Min Gyi; Nga Chan; Nga Chit Kin; Nga Min Se; Nga Pyu; Pônnatte; Nga Pauk; Nga Hla Gyi; Nga Aung Zin Gaing; Nga Chan; Nga Thanda; Nga Pa; Nga Ywa Bu; Nga Pan Zin; Nga Pôn; Nga Swe; Nga Pôn Byu; Nga Pôn Mè; Nga Ma Ôk; Nga Yaman Dwe; Nga Ok Sôn; Nga Twe; Satapa; Nga Pyi Ngè; Nga Nathi; Nga Kya Ban; Nga Pyi Ngè's infant son; Nga Myit; Nga Pyi Gyi; Nga Yauk Pyi; Nga Sôn; Nga Myin; O Wun Tha; O Chit Pôn; O Lat; O Paung Wa; O Chit Kin; O Kaung Ngè; Nga Pyi Myi; Nga Aung Myin; Nga Thu Sin; Nga Nyo; Chin The; Yut Pyauk; Pôn Mathu; Thanpawa; Nga Hli; Pyet Manaing; Ma Seinda; Kaung Gin Kye; Nga Aung Zin; Nga Aung Myin; Nga Wun Byi; Nga Than Ba; Nga Shwe; Nga Naung Ngè; Nga Sein; Nga Kwin; Nga Pauk Sin; Nga Maung Yin; Nga Mywa; Nga Hlun; Nga Twe; total 111 male and 36 female slaves from Magyigyo; the Tabo field of 100 *pès* at Salin, together with the following slaves, namely, Nga Taung and son Nga Lat, and the Indian weavers Nga Nattaw; Nga Pyi Hla; Nga Tangu; Nga Lat; Nga Wa Gaung; Nga Kin Pyi; Nga Kin Lat; Nga Kin Pa; Nga Pa Ngè; Nga Pyi Ngè; Nga Yauk; Nga Wa Gyi; Nga Thauk Kya; Nga Talwe; Nga Thanbawa; Nga Nathi; Nga Manaing; Nga Sat; Nga U; Nga Sin Gyi; Nga Than Bawa; Nga Yauk; Nga Naung Ngè; Nga Kada; Nga Wa; Nga Twe; Nga Mun; Nga Wagôn; Nga Kin Hla; Nga Tôn; Nga Pa Twe; Nga Naing; Nga Aung; Nga Twe; total 34 males; O Thôk; Amaya; O Kyi; O Palè; O Kye; O Pwa; O Kyun; O Yin; O Pyi Zôn; O Nyè; O Kin Byi; total 11 females; also weavers Nga Shan; Nga Pôn; Nga San; Nga Kin Bye; Amin Ngè Myi; Nga Than Ba; Nga Hla Bye; Nga Pin Dè; Nga Sein; Nga Hla Bye; Amin Ngèbyu; Nga Myit; Nga Sôn; Nga Shwe; Nga Hla Yan; Nga Pyi Mun; Nga Kin Byu; Nga Kè; Nga Lat; Nga Wa; Nga U Pi; Nga Tin; Nga Lôn Nyi; total 23 males; O Pu; O Kyi; O Mi Ngè; O Kaung; O Hmo; O Pyi; O Pye; O Pôn; O Chit; O Pôn; Mi Pè; Mi Nyo; O Tôn; O Mya; O Che; U Pi; O Nyè; O Pyo and infant sister; O Pôn Ngè; O Thu Yein; total 21 females; Nga Than Ba; Nga Pôn; Nga Chit Ya; Nga Yauk; Nga Pan The; Nga Chit; Nga Ewe; total 7 males; the descendants of Nga Pauk Thin, an Arakanese, namely, O Shwe; Yadana; O Pyi; Ma Mya Bu; total 4; also Nga Pagan's daughter; O Kuni; Yapan; Amula; Tetmana; Ma Tôkta; Nga Kin Pa; total 7 curry-sellers; Kalabè; Kalalat; O Nyo; O Kywin; O Pyu; O Mun; Yaukpôn; O Tabo; Dewi; Nga Si: total

10 rice-sellers; O . . . . O Twe: total 4 meat-sellers; O Kaung; Chit Mwè She; Thana She: total 3 *pan*-sellers; Kokti; Kawati; Timuri; Dewa; Môkkati; Kawari; Nga Nila; Nga Lat; Ma San; Akandôn; O Kaung; Nga Pa; . . . . Nga Tôn; Nga Panaung's brother . . . . (last line).

No. (4).—Obverse.

Locality.—Within the inscription cave attached to the Sudaungbye pagoda.

Date.—740 Sakkarâj (1378 A.D.).

Founder.—Queen Pwa Saw's sister.

Substance of inscription.—Dedication of slaves and lands to monastery.

"On Saturday, the full-moon of Wagaung 663 Sakkarâj, the king, during an illness, dedicated to the royal monastery the Kaunggamu land, measuring 100 *pès* and 17 slaves; and the Tanlaing land at Sagu, 100 *pès*. These lands were originally granted by the king to my elder sister Mibaya Saw,* and on her death and my succession to her position they were transferred to my possession. The other lands and slaves dedicated at the same time were—Yedeingyi land at Taungdwin 100 *pès*; Linlè land 100 *pès* and 30 slaves; Watachaung land 150 *pès* and 50 slaves; Puyônbwet land 50 *pès* and 3 slaves; Ingungwet land 10 *pès*. The slaves from Pagan were —Nga Hnan; Nga San; Nga Lat; Nga Tu; Nga Sin Kyè; Nga Sin; Nga Pa U; Nga Kin Maung; Nga Mit; O Pu; Pattathi; O Twe; O Yauk Pôn; O Pyi Zôn; O Nyè U; Amaya; O Kandu. These slaves originally belonged to my sister Pwa Saw. The slaves purchased by me were—Nga Aung; Nga Kaung Be; Mingu; Fakir; Kaung Zwa; Wun Bye; Nga Yaman; Nga Pan; O Sat and husband Wun Bye; Nga Sein; Nga Tha Ya; Nga Tônda; O Lôn; O Chan; Kitu; Mathaya; O Yun; Heinkwa; Kaungthawsit; Kanya; Minpuya; Thanduthi; Ôksawli; Mipuyangè; Tharawa; Kalazu; O Sizein Pa; washerman Nga Ngè; Nga Naung Gyi; Nga Yaung Ngè; Nga Lôn; Nga Aung; Nga Than Ba; and Nga Kyin Ya. The slaves inherited by me from my elder sister were—Nga Shan; Nga Tôn; Nga Lat; Nga Mun U; Nga Hla Mun; Nga Yan; Nga Thaga; Nga Kyan; Nga Thu Byit; Nga Chit Twe; Nga Pyi Wa; Nga Chit Kyi; Nga Pôn; Nga Yôn; Nga Pa Gin; Ma Seinda; Nga Kè; Nga Pya Zwè; Nga Pyi Hla; total 19. The slaves purchased from O Pôn, a maid of honour, were—Nga Lôn; O Sin Kyè; Nga Chit U; Nga Chit U; Nga Pôn Za; Yaman Nyo; Nga

* The historians are silent as to this sister of Queen Asaw or Pwa Saw. She is evidently one of the queens of Narathihapade.

Pangè; Nga U; Nga Thu Zôn. The following slaves were purchased from others, namely, cartman Nga Kan Zi and wife O Wa, sons Nga Pu and Nga Pôn Lut; O Chit Pè; Thanle and wife Suntika, son Nga Pyi; O Taik; Nga Saik; Nga Yauk U, a Shan; Nga Hnaung; Ma Padônma; O Lat; Ma Kyaung Gya; O Tin Ma; O Kyi; Nga Sin; Nga Palè; Nga Lun Zan; Nga Pyit. The slaves presented to me by Thattaya's daughter were—Nga Panthe's wife O Wa; O Kandu; and O Nyè U. The remaining purchased slaves were—Nga Taya; O Palè; and Nga Kin Hla. The slaves presented to me by the Hngetpyittaung *pôngyi* were Nga Kukè; Nga Pôktaya; Nga Mun; Nga Hla; O Kandu; O Saik; Nga Lat; Nga Chan; Nga Mye Lu. I further dedicated 500 palm trees at Meikkun together with slave O Saung; also 3,000 palm trees at Thaman together with slaves Nga Hmeikkun and son, Nga Yauk Sôn and son Nga Shan Zôn.

"On Friday, the 1st waxing of Tazaungmôn 740 Sakkarâj, on the completion of their monastery, Nga Hla Shin and wife applied to the monks of my monastery for permission to offer them 50 ticals of silver so that it may be utilized together with the produce of my lands for making the daily rice and other offerings. The monks held a meeting at the *simâ* and after due deliberation among themselves and consultation with the learned ministers, replied that it was unlawful for them to accept this money, and recommended that a field called Kaingsein be offered instead . . . . (last line)."

Reverse.

"I further dedicate 104 palm trees looked after by Nga Kôn Zaung, 50 by Nga Pa Ba, 199 by Nga Pa Nyo, 104 by Nga Tha Din, 100 by Nga Sa Gyi, 50 by Nga Pyi Zôn, 10 by Nga Pa Za, together with toddy-tappers Nga Kôn Zaung, Than Ba Wa, San Pu Ka, Nga U Me, Nga Pa, Nga U, Nga Pyu, Nga Lôn Ma, Nga Chit Mun, Nga Tha Din, Nga Pu, Nga Pa Nyo, Nga Chit La, Nga Sa Gyi, Nga Pôn, Nga Chan, Nga Pyi Zôn, Nga Kyi, and Nga Ngè; also the following slaves, namely, Nga Than, Nga Chin, Nga Si Zein, Nga Naka, Nga Pa Zin, Nga Ti Ka, Nga Hla Bu, O Kè, O Sein, O Nyè U, O Kaung, O Chan Tha, O Hla Wun, Nga Yan, Nga Pyi Gyi, Nga Mun, O Yin Mo, O Kin, O Swe, O Saung Gwe, O Sat, O Kyaung Thi, O Hmyo, O Lôn, O Thadin, O Kyaung Zaung, Nga Tet Pyi, Nga Nyan, Nga Aung Naing, Nga Nat Saw, Nga Pwin, Indian Mingu, Fakir Kingu, Yaukkaman, Nga Kin Byi, Nga Pyit, Nga Pin Hla, Nga Pyi Hla, Nga Kôn, Nga Taba, Nga Pyu, Thanbaya, Myet Shu Ya, Mi Nyo, O Nyè U, O Kala, Nga

Pyi, Nga Chit Lun, Nga U Hla, O Sin Kyè, O Taung U, O Taing, O Myit U, Nga Pônna, O Kaung Yan, O Chan, O Tôn, O Chit Kin; also 136 other palm trees and 58 *môn* trees. The total number of *pès* of *mayin* paddy-land is 3,393, *kaukkyi* paddy-land 930, sessamum and *jowar* land 3,750; grand total 8,073 *pès*. The total number of slaves is 325. These are dedicated for the service of the monastery and the monks. Out of the produce of the lands one basket of rice per day shall be set apart for the rice-offerings at the pagoda, three handfuls a day for the library, one handful a day for the standing image, and one for the sitting image. Let a light be burnt at each of the four sides of my daughter's cave. Let the remainder of the usufruct be utilized for the maintenance of the monks, and let two pieces of cloth per Sabbath be offered them throughout the 48 Sabbath days in the year. Let 200 *pès* of paddy-land be specially set apart for the maintenance of the presiding monk, consisting of 50 *pès* of *mayin* and 50 of *kaukkyi* at Magyigyo, 50 *pès* of *kaukkyi* at Kaunggamu, and 50 of *mayin* at Salindabo. Let the weavers supply the presiding monk with a suit of yellow robes in Wazo, another in Wagaung, and another in Thadingyut; and let each of the monks who are in charge of the monastery obtain daily a *pyi* of rice, and two of paddy for the purchase of curry. For the remaining 108 monks let a daily offering be made to each of one handful of rice and one *pyi* of paddy for the purchase of curry and let each receive a suit of yellow robes at the beginning of Lent. Let the balance of the produce be utilized for the upkeep of the monastery and the maintenance of the menials attached to it."

"May every one from the king downwards, including the *nats* and every being inhabiting every region and universe, obtain a share of my merit. May those who in future support my offering share its merit equally with me. If a slave or a field of paddy-land offered by me be destroyed by any of my descendants . . . . (two lines)."

No. (5).

Locality.—Within the walls of Sudaungbye pagoda.

Date.—663 Sakkarâj (1301 A.D.).

Founder.—Min Chan Tha.

Substance of inscription.—Dedication of slaves and lands to pagoda.

On Saturday, the full moon of Wagaung 663 Sakkarâj, Queen Pwa Saw, during an illness of the king, dedicated* 3,000 palm trees

* This is intended to counteract the evil influence of the devils or witches who had caused the illness: a mixture of the indigenous beliefs with Buddhism.

at Pyun . . . . slaves. The boundaries of the palm-grove are: *north-east*, Bilu . . . . Thanbogôn, Magyinigôn, *south*, ... Pettawgun main stream; *west*, base of the hill, ... Ywazo, Thanattwin, Twinthamya, Aungyaung stream; Tinbaukaing, ..., Minganngè, Thetkègyin, Pyayaung.

Being desirous of supplementing these offerings, Min Chan Tha, a personal attendant of Queen Sawkônma,* applied for permission to dedicate a piece of land to the Shwezigôn pagoda. The application was made in the presence of Queen Pwa Saw's Royal Mentor Taingda Thingayaza and it was granted by the king . . . . (last line).

No. (6).

Locality.—Within the inscription cave attached to the Sudaungbye pagoda.

Date.—691 Sakkarâj (1329 A.D.).

Founder.—Monk Myingôndaing.

Substance of inscription.—Dedication of land.

ON Thursday, the 10th waning of Tabodwè 691 Sakkarâj, the king† asked monk Myingôndaing to place his Pâli manuscripts in a cave. The request was acceded to and in return the king offered 300 *pès* of State paddy-land to the monk by a royal order which was read out in the Tamaka monastery by Minister Thirimingalabiyit. The officials who demarcated the land were Nga Pyi Thin, Nga Pôn Biyit Thin, and Thaman. The monk, in his turn, dedicated this land to the pagoda built by him.

No. (7).

Locality.—Within the walls of the Thitsawadi pagoda.

Date.—696 Sakkarâj (1334 A.D.).

Founder.—Saw Mun Nit.

Substance of inscription.—Dedication of slaves to cave.

ON Thursday, the 3rd waxing of Thadingyut 696 Sakkarâj, Saw Mun Nit‡ dedicated the following slaves to the cave built by his grandmother Queen Pwa Saw, namely, Pè Sa U, Nga Pyi, Nga Yan Aung, O Chit Kè, O Chit Tôn, Thamôktasa, O Ngè Mun, Thuseikta, Mulèu, Withaka, O Kemata, O Nyo, Kusôktaya, O Twe, O Pègu, O Hlingè, O Tala, O Kinpè, O Ngè, O . . . . . . , O Myi

* Wife of King Kyawzwa.

† Uzana of Pinya.

‡ The last of the 55 Kings of Pagan, who was raised to the throne by Uzana of Pinya in 1327 A.D. He died after a reign of 43 years.

Pôn, O Kyi, O Yauk Pôn, Thumeikta, O Lat, Legamyi, O Yawun, O Tabaung, O . . . . . Kaung, O Hlwa, Thôndari, O . . . . . ., Taungyi, Tina, ..., Kanya, Nga Mi Laung, ..., Marapu, Kingu, ..., Nga Chit U, Nga Mya, ..., Thalinmya, Nga Yaku and wife, O Pa . . . . Li, Nga Kin Hla, Ngan San Ba, ..., San Bu, Thanamakyan, Nga Yan, Nga Wa, ..., Hla Gyi, Nga Lat . . . . Nga Twe, Nga Sin, ..., Nga Aung, ..., Nga Hla U, Nga U Hla, ..., Nga Chit, Nga Chan U, Nga Chet Su, ..., Nga Kyi, Nga Sin, Hemawata, ..., Nga Naing Gan, U Yaung and wife, ..., O Pôn, Kupiyayein and wife, Nga Pan Yan, ..., Nga Yauk U, Nga Li Ngè, Nga San and wife, ... (last line).

INSCRIPTIONS OF PAGAN.

XIII.—Found at Chaukpala.

No. (1).

Locality.—Within the large inscription cave.

Date.—632 Sakkarâj (1270 A.D.).

Founder.—King Narathihapade.*

Substance of inscription.—Re-dedication of slaves and lands originally dedicated by King Narapatisithu.

On . . . . waxing of Kasôn 550 Sakkarâj, King Narapatisithu dedicated to the image erected by a certain monk the following lands and slaves, namely, Pateik land 80 *pès* and slaves; Letyatheinga and . . . .; Myaiktanma 180 *pès* and slave Ôktapakyôn; Dipeshin land 500 *pès* and slaves Pônmatho, Tanpatatha, ..., Ôktarabarit; and 1,000 palm trees at Kenin and slaves Ein Gwe, Ein Lin, Ein Shan, Ein Zôn, Ein Ne Ein, Ein Chan Tha, Ein Kin, and U Pi. This dedication was made by a royal order in the presence of Minister Ôktama Parit and wife Ein Ngè.

On Thursday, the 9th waxing of Wazo 632 Sakkarâj, the king commanded that the abovementioned lands and slaves and palm trees be re-dedicated. The persons present at the time were the ministers and . . . . Nga Kan Tu, Nga U

* More commonly known as Tayôkpyemin [*vide* note to inscription No. (1) *ante*, found on the south of Pagan].

Lôn, Nga Yauk, ..., Nga Aung Din, ... (three lines).

NO. (2).

Locality.—Within the large inscription cave.

Substance of inscription.—Dedication of land.

. . . . . . land is dedicated to . . . . . It is demarcated with boundary pillars at the four corners.

" May my descendants and all future generations including kings, nobles, and monks, obtain a share of my merit. May those who support my offering share its merit equally with me. If they be kings, may they be powerful and able to promote the interests of the people. On the other hand, may those who destroy the same be liable to every form of punishment; may they suffer as charred pillars in the eight principal and 128 lesser hells. May they live miserable lives as men and when they die may the punishments herein mentioned befall them . . . . (last line).

NOS. (3) AND (4).

[THESE inscriptions are within the porch of a pagoda about 500 feet south-east of the inscription cave. They are so obliterated that even the number of lines on them cannot be counted.]

PINYA INSCRIPTIONS.

I.—Found at Pinya-Myohaung.

No. (1).

Locality.—On the north side of the Shwezigôn pagodà.

Founder.—Min Sawkè.

Substance of inscription.—Repairing a monastery.

MIN SAWKÈ, thugyi of Amyin,* and grandson of the most glorious King Thihathu, promoter of the Religion, disperser of an army of 120,000 soldiers led by Kan Min,† and possessor of several white elephants, begged of the king‡ at Kyunu to permit him to repair the queen's monastery, in order that the monks might be able to continue residing comfortably therein. Permission was accordingly granted by the king.

No. (2).—OBVERSE.

Locality.—Within the northernmost cave.

Date.—702 Sakkaràj (1340 A.D.).

Founder.—King Uzana.

Substance of inscription.—Building of cave and dedication of lands thereto.

ON Sunday, the full-moon of Wazo 702 Sakkaràj, King Uzana built a large cave at Einnein and covered it with plates of silver weighing altogether 64,000 *ticals;* and in order that the Religion might last 5,000 years, dedicated the following lands to the cave, namely, 110 *pès* of *mayin* and 275 *pès* of vegetable garden-land at Awahaung-Kyizaung; . . . *pès* of *mayin* and 200 of garden-lands at Setkya; 20 *pès* of *mayin* lands at Kainggyi; 75 *pès* at . . . .; 55 *pès* of *mayin*, 60 of *kaukkyi* and 300 of garden-land at Ngapagyi village; total 1,300 *pès*. Besides these the following lands were dedicated, namely, ... *pès* at Kamyu; total 200 *pès;* . . . . . (seven lines).

---

* This Prince subsequently became King Minkyizwasawke. He was created thugyi of Amyin while serving under Tayapya, King of Sagaing.

† Kublai Khan, the Chinese invader.

‡ Tayapya of Sagaing.

REVERSE.

Date.—729 Sakkarâj (1363 A.D.).
Founder.—Minister Mahapetteik.
Substance of inscription.—Building of cave-pagoda and dedication of slaves and lands thereto.

"I adore the Buddha!"

ON Tuesday, the 6th waning of Tagu 721 Sakkarâj, Minister Mahapetteik enshrined the remains of King Kyawzwa* in a cave-pagoda and placed an image at each of the four sides, each image being in charge of a family of slaves. Paddy-lands were also dedicated to these images for their upkeep. If any heretic attempted to destroy them they and their slaves and houses would be wholly destroyed. The paddy-lands were—Ôkkyin-Tanauktin land, 50 *pès;* Lezwetsan, 4 *pès;* Kathityasè, 4 *pès;* . . . . Einkè-laung, 5½ *pès;* Ngabyitkyi, 5 *pès;* Ngayat, 5 *pès;* Palè, 5 *pès;* Kyangan, 1¼ *pès;* Ngayu, 2 *pès;* . . . . . Sein, 5 *pès;* Ngakyet-tun, 4½ *pès.* "May those who destroy these lands. . . . ."

On Saturday, the 1st waxing of Tawthalin 729 Sakkarâj, the following slaves and lands were dedicated, namely, Linpade and family, Yanthit and family, ... and family, Yanaungbya and family; . . . *pès* at Myaungzôn: Minhla land, 10 *pès;* Tayônyin land, 2½ *pès;* Kyangan land at Minhla, 5 *pès;* 7 *pès* at Sathat called . . . .; 2 *pès* at Nga Hlauk Thin village. These 27¾ *pès* of paddy-land were dedicated in order that the daily rice-offerings may be made out of their produce. The lands dedicated to the "Law" were—Shabin land, 5 *pès;* Myôngin land, 5 *pès;* Seiksu land, 4 *pès;* . . . land, 1 *pè;* Indwet land, 1 *pè;* Lèdawtaung, 5 *pès;* Myagè land, 3 *pès;* total 24 *pès.*

"May those who destroy this offering in future live short and "miserable lives. May they never behold any of the coming Bud-"dhas. May they fall into *avîci.* On the other hand, may those "who support the same share its merit equally with me."

NO. (3).

Locality.—On the east side of the Shwezigôn pagoda.
Date.—727 Sakkarâj (1361 A.D.).
Founder.—Head page of King Thadominbya.
Substance of inscription.—Dedication of lands to Shwezigôn pagoda.

ON Wednesday, the . . . . Wazo 727 Sakkarâj, Nga Shwe Ket, head page, and his wife dedicated 10 *pès* of

* This is Kyawzwangè or Kyawzwa II.

paddy-land to the Shwezigôn pagoda. The land was granted by the king while sojourning in the temporary palace at Ava. It is situated in Kanbyu district.

"Let the produce of half of the land be utilized for the rice-offerings, and let that of the other half be given to Nga Ne Dwet and wife, the keepers of the land. May those who support my offering have a share of its merit. On the other hand, may those who destroy it live short lives. May they and their relatives, to the extent of seven generations, be ruined, and may they all suffer in hell. By virtue of this offering may I attain Buddhahood . . . .
. . . .
. . . .
. . . ."

The abovementioned offering was made by the head page Nga Shwe Ket and his wife in order that the Religion might last 5,000 years.

No. (4).

Locality.—On the east side of the Shwezigôn pagoda.
Date.—729 Sakkarâj (1363 A.D.).
Founder.—Thadominbya.
Substance of inscription.—Dedication of land.

In the year 729 Sakkarâj, the king dedicated 800 out of 1,000 *pès* of State land at Amyin. demarcated on the *south-east* by a *ma-u* tree and a pillar, *west* by the river, *south-west* by a *sit* tree and a pillar, *north-east* by the Thapan stream. The pillars were set up by Nga Kwe. A small village was founded near the land. The witnesses to the dedication were . . . .

No. (5).

Locality.—On the southern side of the Shwezigôn pagoda.
Date.—737 Sakkarâj (1375 A.D.).
Founder.—Asawmyatswa.
Substance of inscription.—Building of religious edifices.

"I adore the Law and the Monkhood!"

On Saturday, the 7th waning of Tazaungmôn 737 Sakkarâj, when Asawmyatswa,* ruler of Kayein, Kamaung, Paunglaung, and Tayo, received the Governorship of Toungoo from the hands of the Governor of Taungdwin,† he and his wife jointly performed the following acts with a view to attain Buddhahood, namely, enlarged the two pagodas situated on the Di stream *east* of Toun-

* Known in history as Asawmyatswa-Nawyata.
† Thihapade.

goo so that each attained a diameter of 40 cubits. A number of bricks containing gold and silver dust were used on that occasion. Likewise gold and silver dust formed half the ingredients of the plaster made for stucco-work. A *pyi* of precious stones was enshrined in the pagodas, and gold and silver flowers and a ruby ring were offered to it . . . . . A . . . . was carved and enshrined and a ball of gold was placed on each *ti* . . . . A three-tiered *tazaung* with overlapping roofs was next built over the pagodas to protect them, and a garden with a tank and flowering shrubs was cultivated near them . . . . When everything was completed the Governor's wife cut off all the hair from her head and, twisting it into a torch, lighted it at the shrine.

When the pagoda at Mataw village was dedicated, the following offerings were made, namely, an elephant, hundreds of ticals of silver, a number of villages, thousands of baskets of paddy, *padèsa* trees* of gold and silver, and heaps of betel-nut and chillies. Ten monasteries at east Mataw and ten at west Mataw were also built. The presiding monks of these monasteries were supplied with food and raiment and the offerings made at the Mataw pagoda were innumerable. These offerings were made continuously notwithstanding the fact that there was scarcity in the land at the time and rice was selling at only 5 *pyis* per tical of silver. A new monastery was built and the number of bowls of rice offered daily to the monasteries was 200. Besides this the immigrants who flocked into Toungoo consequent on the downfall of Sagaing and Pinya,† were sheltered and fed. Moreover, a tical of gold was contributed towards the Myinthidin pagoda.‡ When the Governor of Pagan despatched a *ti* for a pagoda in Ceylon, a ruby ring was placed on the *ti* of a small gold pagoda containing a sacred tooth; and the emissaries were given 40 ticals of silver for their passage. The other meritorious deeds performed in Toungoo were: seven three-storied monasteries, two gilt *simâs*, five smaller monasteries . . . . (five lines).

No. (6).

Locality.—Eastern side of the Shwezigôn pagoda.

Date.—747 Sakkarâj (1358 A.D.).

Founder.—Ein Kin Hla Kè.

Substance of inscription.—Building of monastery and chapel and dedication thereto of lands and palm trees.

---

* Made somewhat after the fashion of Christmas trees.

† These towns were captured by Zalôn, *Sawbwa* of Mohnyin, in 1364 A.D. from Narathu.

‡ Now known as Shwemyindin.

"I adore the Buddha!"

THE monastery and chapel built by Ein Kin Hla Kè on the western side of the Shwezigôn pagoda at Pinya in order that she might safely cross the sea of *samsaro* was completed in Wazo 747 Sakkarāj. A piece of land purchased for 100 ticals of silver was attached to the buildings for their upkeep. It was purchased from the thugyi and his son out of their Indwin land. Ein Kin Hla Kè's mother also dedicated 105 palm trees, raising the total number dedicated to 333. At the time of the dedication, the headman of the village and other helpers were granted a reward consisting of 5 ticals of silver, three cows, one goat, as well as food and clothing. The witnesses to the dedication were— . . . . ; Sizein Thugyi; Einchit Sanpa; Min Yè; . . . .

"May those who support my offering share its merit with me. Whosoever destroys it, may he and his relatives live short and miserable lives. May I, by virtue of this offering, attain Nirvâna. I offer 20 ticals of silver, 50 baskets of paddy, and five mats to the monks in King Narathu's* monastery. May those who destroy this offering never have the opportunity of beholding any of the coming Buddhas. May they become charred pillars in hell."

On the death of the founder . . . . (five lines).

No. (7).

Locality.—Within a cave north-east of the Shwezigôn pagoda.

Founder.—Sinbyuyin (1763—1766 A.D.).

Substance of inscription.—Dedication of lands to Shwezigôn pagoda.

"Reverence to the Blessed, Holy and Enlightened One!"

THIS inscription is founded by command of His Majesty King Sinbyuyin in order that the Religion might last 5,000 years, and in order that the meritorious deed performed by his ancestor King Thihathu might last for all time, namely, the Shwezigôn pagoda, which encloses a shrine made of six slabs of emerald obtained through supernatural power exercised by the *theras* and king of *nats*, together with a number of sacred relics, gold and silver flowers, and precious gems, and placed at Pinya, a short distance east of Ava, the seat of learning and centre of the Religion promulgated by Gautama Buddha, who, having acquired every virtue and vanquished every foe, attained Buddhahood beneath the golden banyan tree which germ-

---

* Mentioned in the inscriptions as the king who was carried away captive to Maw territory by Zalôn, Chief of Mohnyin.

inated simultaneously with his final birth. The boundaries of the land dedicated to the pagoda by the king are *north*, a line running from . . . . gate round the base of Nwalè hill; then along the *thalweg* of the river; thence starting from Sabyu . . . . southwards to Kyatkya and Kalayewin canal; thence . . . . —wards to . . . . tank. The villagers of Inywa were also dedicated to the pagoda to look after it throughout the 5,000 years of the Religion.

"By virtue of this meritorious deed, may I in the present existence enjoy perfect immunity from every evil and every danger; may I be victorious over my enemies from the eight quarters of the earth; may I have every happiness; may I enjoy long life and be the possessor of everything desirable, including good ministers and servants; may I throughout *samsaro* be free from every form of misery. If I be born again as a plebeian, may I become a rich banker able to supply the wants of everybody; if a king, may I become the king of kings; if a *nat*, may I become the king of *nats*, having the opportunity of acquiring every virtue. May I, throughout *samsaro*, be the possessor of beauty, power, health, amiableness, wisdom, and every other desirable thing; and in my ultimate existence may I be in the position to guide my fellow beings to Nirvâna. . . . . May my father, mother, elder brother, ...

PINYA INSCRIPTIONS.

II.—Found on the south of Pinya.

No. (1).

Locality.—On the eastern side of the Bônsan monastery ruins, south of Shwezigôn.

Date.—749 Sakkarâj (1387 A.D.).

Founder.—Queen Kamyimi.

Substance of inscription.—Dedication of paddy-lands to monastery.

"I adore the Buddha!"

On Thursday, the 6th waning of Pyatho 731 Sakkarâj, King Tayapya directed the head of the Buddhist clergy to dedicate to the monastery the pieces of land indicated by his royal mother, namely, the Tanbingauk village lands and 100 *pès* of State paddy-land; Tiyazabôntha village lands and 100 *pès* of State paddy-land; *west*, Taungpi field, 30 *pès*; *east*, Kangwe field, 10 *pès*; west,

Taungpi palm-grove, containing 100 full-grown and 400 young trees; Sigyi village lands and 10 *pès* of paddy-land; Kannet village lands and 10 *pès* of paddy-land; Kaing village lands and 10 *pès* of paddy-land; Neki garden-land *south* of Sabaso, and 30 *pès* of paddy-land. These lands are dedicated for the upkeep of the monastery and the maintenance of the monks.

On Wednesday, the 10th waxing of Pyatho 749 Sakkarâj, Queen Kamyimi, consort of Tayapya, made a present of 1,000 ticals of silver to the king and obtained permission to dedicate the following lands to the monastery, namely, the Linzin village lands in Myittha district, together with 100 *pès* of State paddy-land. Out of the revenue of 1,000 baskets obtained from these lands, 600 are for the presiding monk and 400 for the upkeep of the monastery.

No. (2).

Locality.—Near the Myinbahu pagoda.

Date.—737 Sakkarâj (1375 A.D.).

Founder.—King of Toungoo.*

Substance of inscription.—Building of monastery and dedication of lands thereto.

On Thursday, the 2nd waxing of Tabaung 737 Sakkarâj, the King of Toungoo, realizing that in the present dispensation of the Lord of the three superior beings, it is very difficult to be born as a man, and being moved by fervent piety and a desire to promote the cause of the Religion throughout its period of 5,000 years, built a large brick monastery and dedicated thereto the following lands which he obtained as a gift from Tayapya, King of Ava, in return for a present of a pair of young elephants, namely, Ngamungè land, 5 *pès*; Ngalinban, 5 *pès*; Einbôngyaung, 83 *pès*; Nyanmè, 5 *pès*; Ngakunbin, 1½ *pès*; Einbaukkyi, 3 *pès*; Ngakanbaing, 2½ *pès*; Nyeinya, 5 *pès*; Ngataka, 5 *pès*; Ngakun, 5 *pès*; Einzaungbo, 5 *pès*; Ngapa, 5 *pès*; Ngapwin, 4½ *pès*; Nganaunggaung, 5 *pès*; Ngasadaung, 5 *pès*; Ngatè, 5 *pès*; Ngasanbyi, 5 *pès*; Ngachimo, 1 *pè*; north Paungli, 4 *pès*; Ngapayin, 5 *pès*; Einlaung, 5 *pès*; Eingyit, 5 *pès*; Einyôn, 5 *pès*; total 100 *pès*. Of these, 60 *pès* are for the upkeep of the monastery and 40 for the maintenance of the presiding monk.

"May those who support this offering have all their wishes fulfilled. On the other hand, may those who destroy the same fall headlong into hell and remain there for a period of years equal in number to that of the atoms in the 100 *pès* of land."

---

* Pyanchigyi [*see* note under inscription No. (36) *ante*, found at Ledaunggan, Pagan].

No. (3).—Obverse.

Locality.—At the Taungdaw pagoda, about 2 miles south of Pinya.

Date.—1187 Sakkarâj (1825 A.D.).

Founder.—King Bagyidaw.

Substance of inscription.—Prohibition of hunting and trapping round about Tayingye hill and founding a village of game-keepers.

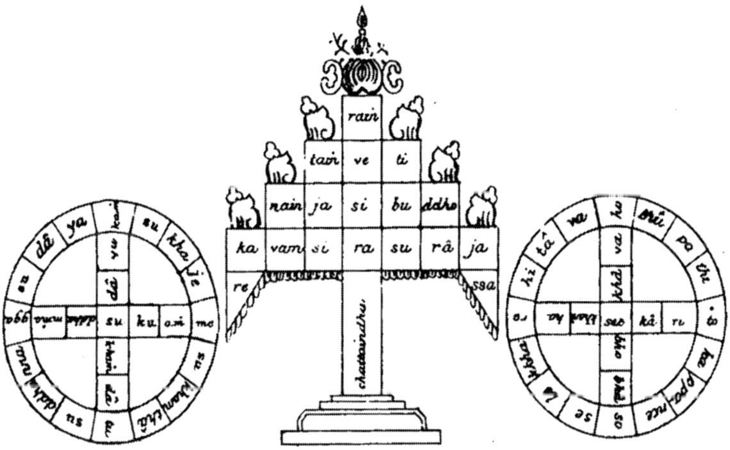

"Reverence to the Blessed, Holy and Enlightened One! I adore the Buddha, who during his existence as a horse saved mankind from the ravages of the ogres. I adore his law and monkhood also, and I proceed to inscribe the command of His Majesty the founder

* (*Centre*) Chattaṁdharasurâjassa Chattaṁdhara sivam kare rasi buddho rasi janaṁ siveti sivetaṁ veraṁ.

(*Right circle*) Sukarito subhobhâso sukhaṁ karo sukhâvaho thûpo thito kappañceso selekkharo hitâvaho.

(*Left circle*) Suddhammaggasudâyukaṁ sukujaṁ me sukhaṁ dâtu suddhannagga-sudâyakaṁ sukhaje me sukhaṁ thâtu.

Translation.

As the white umbrella confers peace on the ruler whom it covers, so the excellent Buddha, who possesses the Arbattapala white umbrella, propitiates the enemies of all sentient beings and brings them peace.

May this beautiful and beneficent pagoda, and this inscription, being erected in the interests of *nats* and men, last to the end of the world.

May the Buddha who is the giver of the law pertaining to Nirvâna confer on me the bliss of Nirvâna. May the Buddha who is the provider of that excellent food, namely, the law, confer happiness on me who desires it.

of the (4th) city of Ava prohibiting the killing of game and fish. His Majesty, who is a great-grandson of Alompra, the eminent king of kings, and a direct descendant of the founders of Sagaing, Ava, and Amarapura; who is the builder of the Thetkyathiha image, which is 10 cubits high, the Shinbyu pagoda, which is 81½ cubits in height and 120 cubits in diameter at the base, and the Mahawizayayanthi pagoda, which is 114 cubits high; and who is entitled the Sîritribhavanâdityadhipatipavarapaṇḍitamahâdhammarâjâdhirâjâ, being with his royal family as highly pious as Asoka, invited a number of learned monks to the capital and employed them to promote the cause of the Religion. It happened that one of these eminent monks, known by the name of Ngagôn *Sadaw*, took up his residence near an ancient pagoda on Tayingye hill.

*

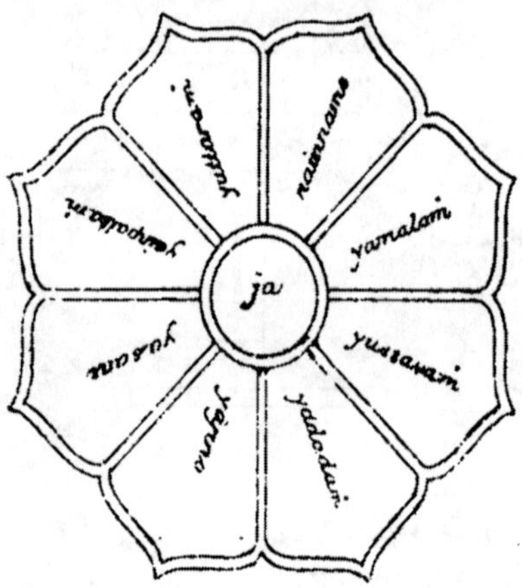

This monk and pagoda soon became the objects of adoration of the people, and the king, recollecting that in ages gone by, when the embryo Buddha was a horse, he managed to save life at a certain place, bethought himself to follow that excellent example by prohibiting the hunting and trapping of birds and beasts within certain circumscribed limits, and so leave behind him a good example for his descendants. Accordingly His Majesty prohibits the

---

* Jayamalaṁ jayussavaṁ jayadadaṁ jayâjino jayasane jayaṁpattaṁ jayuttaraṁ janaṁ name.

Translation.

"I adore the Buddha, who has overcome the impurities of *kilesâ*, who has celebrated his victory, who confers victory, who overcomes every opposition, who attained the throne of victory after having conquered the five *mâras*, and whose victories are excellent."

taking of life within the following limits, namely, *east*, the Panlaung river; *south*, Mingan village; *west*, the king's highway; and *north*, a masonry tank. These limits were demarcated by boundary pillars, and Minister Minhla Mindin Kyawthu was deputed to found a village in the neighbourhood. This village flourished and was known far and wide as Bemè* village.

"For this act of preservation of life, may I, throughout every existence, be free from all danger, and ultimately reach Nirvâna, the haven of rest and peace. Having attained Buddhahood, may I be able to convey both *nats* and men to the other shore, namely, Nirvâna. My meritorious deed was accomplished in the month of Wagaung of the 6th year of my reign, which commenced from 1181 Sakkarâj. May my great-grandfather Alompra, my three grandfathers, the founders of Sagaing, Ava, and Amarapura, my parents and other kinsmen as well as my nobles and subjects and all sentient beings obtain a share of my merit. May they all joyfully approve of my offering and soon attain Nirvâna, where existence and rebirths cease."

This inscription was made and erected by command of His Majesty the founder of the fourth city of Ava by the Royal Herald Shwedaungthirikyawdin *alias* Kyawdinzeyanawyata.

PINYA INSCRIPTIONS.

III.—Found on the north of Pinya.

No. (1).

Locality.—Within the Yagyi group of monasteries, about 1,000 feet west of Tada-u village.

Date.—721 Sakkarâj (1359 A.D.).

Founder.—Sattalingathu.

Substance of inscription.—Building of monastery and pagodas and dedication thereto of paddy-land.

"I adore the Buddha!"

SATTALINGATHU, a distinguished general of King Kyawzwa,† son of King Ngazishin, entitled Sîritribhavanâdityapavaradhammarâjâthihathu, being a highly pious man, built a pagoda at Heinsaw, a monastery and three golden images at Pinya, and at his request he was permitted to dedicate to the same 30 *pès* to-

* Literally "without danger."

† More commonly known as Kyawzwangè of Pinya.

gether with a pony and trappings which was originally presented to the king.

On Saturday, the 6th waxing of Tabodwè 721 Sakkarâj, the following lands were further dedicated in order that the Religion might last 5,000 years, namely, Nga Za's land, 5 *pès*; land west of Nga Za's, 5 *pès*; Lèpein land, 1½ *pès*; Pyeinbyein land, 1 *pè*; Lègauk, 1 *pè*; Thamanngôk, 3 *pès*; northern Put land, 3 *pès*; southern Put land, 1½ *pès*; Nga Pyu's land, 2 *pès*; Myaungtaungbet land, 1 *pè*; field near Lègauk, 1 *pè*; Saw land, 1 *pè*; Ko land, 2 *pès*; Ngamwengè, 1 *pè*; field adjacent to Kaleinyinzeik, 1½ *pès*; Yelôn south 8 *pès* and north 12 *pès*. Five villages of slaves were also dedicated at the same time. The witnesses to the dedication were Nga Pwin Thin, Pônmathaman, headman of Sindè village, Nga Hle Thi, Tetgathu, and Nga Wa Gyi Mye.

" May those who support my offering share its merit equally with me. On the other hand, may those who destroy the same be far beyond the saving influence of all future Buddhas, and may they be burnt in *avîci*."

No. (2).—Obverse.

Locality.—Within the Yagyi group of monasteries.

Date.—731 Sakkarâj (1369 A.D.).

Founder.—King Minkyizwasawkè.

Substance of inscription.—Building of a pagoda and monastery and dedication thereto of slaves and lands.

" I adore the Buddha!"

When the Burmese Empire was disintegrated by internal strife and the interests of the Religion were injuriously affected, the King of *nats* looked about him for one who might be able to retrieve the fortunes of the dynasty, and found a fitting agent in the Governor of Yamèthin, a grandson of the illustrious King Thihathu. Accordingly, the celestial mandate favoured the governor's arms and the governor became the consolidator of the Empire under the title of Siritribhavanâdityapavaradhammarâjâ.* The king was noted for his great piety, and even when he was still Governor of Talôkmyo built a cave and monastery and dedicated paddy-lands to the same. While at Yamèthin he built a monastery and dedicated thereto several pieces of land. When he ascended the throne he re-dedicated the religious lands offered by the ancient kings.

* Minkyizwasawkè [*vide* note *ante* under inscription No. (18) found at the Shwezigôn pagoda].

On Monday, the 5th waning Tazaungmôn 730 Sakkarâj, the king, in conjunction with the queen, the granddaughter of the Governor of Sagaing, built a very beautiful monastery at Pinyangè and rewarded the carpenters and masons handsomely.

On Monday, the full-moon of Wazo 731 Sakkarâj, the monastery was formally dedicated and made over to the monks; and in order that the Religion might last 5,000 years, the king offered the following lands after pouring out the water of dedication from a golden lota, namely, the Nyaungzauk village lands including Pônmathu's land, 5 *pès*; O Twe Kyi's, 5 *pès*; Nga Che O's, 5 *pès*; O Kyan Thin's, 5 *pès*; Meinuwin field, 5 *pès*; Yedwin field, 5 *pès*; field opposite Nga Set Thin's monastery, 5 *pès*; Saunggyaung field, 5 *pès*; Sachi Ngè's land, 5 *pès*; Nga Myin's, 5 *pès*; Nga Wè's, 5 *pès*; Taungônhmauk field, 5 *pès*; Nga Let Thi's land, 5 *pès*; Salè field, 5 *pès*; Nga San Bu's land, 5 *pès*; maize plantation, 5 *pès*; field south of Nga Set Thin's monastery, 5 *pès*; *ya* land, 5 *pès*; O Thun's land, 5 *pès*; Apyaukthi's land, 5 *pès*; Nga Myin's fishery land, 3 *pès*; Nga Pyun's land, $5\frac{3}{4}$ *pès*; Nga She Thin's, 3 *pès*; O Kaung's, 3 *pès*; Ywagya field, 5 *pès*; Nga Myin U's land, 5 *pès*; Zayatyin field, 5 *pès*; Tanyônshe field, 5 *pès*; Nga Maung's land, 5 *pès*; Mibaya's, 5 *pès*; Nga Ka's, 5 *pès*; Uyin field, 5 *pès*; field at the back of Magyi village, 5 *pès*; Salèo field, 5 *pès*; O Lu's land, 5 *pès*; Manaw Yaza's, 5 *pès*; field behind palm grove, 5 *pès*; Ywazongè field, 5 *pès*; Kathityin field, 5 *pès*; O Lwe's land, 5 *pès*; Nga Mya's, 5 *pès*; Panlin field, 5 *pès*; O Thadi's land, 5 *pès*; O Thaya's, 5 *pès*; Nga Taung Bo's, 5 *pès*; Nga Pan's, 5 *pès*; O Thu's, 5 *pès*; Paukpin field, 5 *pès*; Nga Lônla's land, 5 *pès*; Ywaungauk field, 5 *pès*; Chanpi field, 5 *pès*; Yataung field, 5 *pès*; Nga Hnôk's land, 5 *pès*; Nga Ôk's fishery land, 5 *pès*; O Tayin's land, 5 *pès*; O Sun's, 5 *pès*; Nga Sin Daing's, 5 *pès*; Nga Laung's, 5 *pès*; O Pwa's, 5 *pès*; O Pôk's, 5 *pès*; Kyadaw land, 53 *pès*; Nga La Tha's land, 5 *pès*; Nga Paw's, 5 *pès*; Sandawda field, $2\frac{1}{3}$ *pès*; Talaingo field, 10 *pès*; total, 327 *pès*: also the Ôngyithin tract consisting of the Myaungbin field, 5 *pès*; Aung Bu's land, 5 *pès*; Nga Mo Gyo's, 5 *pès*; Nga Paung Gyo's, 5 *pès*; Nga Mu Yo's, 5 *pès*; Nga Mwa Bo's, 5 *pès*; Wetpo field, 5 *pès*; Sithi field, $4\frac{1}{2}$ *pès*; Lanbu field, 5 *pès*; O Tin Ma's land, 5 *pès*; Pinti Ma Ngè's land, 5 *pès*; Ywaya field, 5 *pès*; Kyuyin field, 5 *pès*; O Chit No's land, 5 *pès*; Thindeingyi field, 5 *pès*; O Thu Po's land, 5 *pès*; Nga Pya Thi's, 5 *pès*; Nga U Byaung's, 5 *pès*; Muhnanbaung field, 5 *pès*; Chanma field, 5 *pès*; Nga Myinthe field, 5 *pès*; Sadaing field, 5 *pès*; Kyetthungyin field, 5 *pès*; Nga Mwè Gyi's land, 5 *pès*; Myauksithi field, 4 *pès*; Seikthan-Sinbauk field, 5 *pès*; Ywashe field, 8 *pès*; total, 137 *pès*; also the Pyuywagyi village land, consisting of Taga-Ônyin field, 5 *pès*; Ywathwe field, 5 *pès*; Nga Kauk Pôn's land, 5 *pès*; Teinmanaing field, 5 *pès*; Zayatyin field, 5 *pès*; Nga Shan Gaung's land, 5 *pès*; field west of monastery, 5 *pès*; field south of monastery, 5 *pès*; O Myin Pa's land; Kathityin field, 5 *pès*; Yèdalin field, 5 *pès*; Nga Si Thin's land, 5 *pès*; Nga Po Zin's land, 5 *pès*; Nga Yauk Thin's land, 5 *pès*; Chattaya's, 5 *pès*; Nga Lan's, 5 *pès*; Nga Ye Dwin's, 5 *pès*; O Taung We's, 5 *pès*; Nga Pyu Thwè's, 5 *pès*; Pan Yin's, 5 *pès*; Nga Mè's, 5 *pès*; field behind village, 4 *pès*; total, 109 *pès*; also . . . . . . village lands consisting of Nga Taung Bo's land, 5 *pès*; Alègyaung field, 5 *pès*; Kyinhna field, 5 *pès*; Seiksubaung field, 5 *pès*; Ywagyet field, 5 *pès*; total, 25 *pès*; also the Tabahein tract, consisting of Nga Yin Ma's land, 5 *pès*; Galan field, 5 *pès*; . . . . ; Tahnauktaung field, 5 *pès*; Nga Yin Thin's land, 5 *pès*; Kayin field, 5 *pès* . . . .

On Monday, the . . . . 755 Sakkarâj, Salinthu's wife made a present of 25 ticals of gold and 50 of silver to the king, and in return obtained permission to dedicate to her husband's monastery the following State lands, namely, Thansho field of 1 *pè* situated in front of Ngakèbin village, 1 *pè* of garden-land near the same, also Kyangangyi field 1 *pè*, Sinmibyan field 1 *pè*, Thayetyin field 1 *pè*; total, 5 *pès*.

REVERSE.

The following lands were also dedicated by the king to his pagoda and monastery: Tabahein paddy lands, consisting of Yinma, 5 *pès*; Kalan, 5 *pès*; Lèbi, 5 *pès*; field behind Hetshit monastery, 1 *pè*; Tahnauktaung, 5 *pès*; Nga Yin Thin's land, 5 *pès*; Kayin's land, 5 *pès*; Nga Pyi Gyi's, 5 *pès*; O Chit Mi's, 5 *pès*; Paganthi's, 5 *pès*; Ye Myet's, 5 *pès*; Than Yin's, 5 *pès*; Nga Mo Gyo's, 5 *pès*; Ye U's, 5 *pès*; Nga Pauk Kyi's, 5 *pès*; Kantaunglaung field, 5 *pès*; Hetshit-Kyaunggyi field, 5 *pès*; Nga Ingapa's field, 5 *pès*; total, 90 *pès*; also the palm groves at Ôngyi village, namely, Ywèmi, Naka, Udaungngè, Ngakwa, Tanbingyi, Tabahein, Ngwegun, Kandungè, Kyakat, Nasingyi, Matet, Sadaungngè, Pyunwagyi, Pyunwangè, Kyaban, Koya, Sachidi, Thanbyinmwè, Tazo, Potobyu and Pona, which altogether contain over 2,000 palm trees: also the Ngwegun paddy-fields, consisting of O Pu Hnôk's, 5 *pès*; Tahnaungyin field, 5 *pès*; Nga Sit Ko's field, 5 *pès*; Cheingwin field, 5 *pès*; Ye-u field, 5 *pès*; Kyangan field, 5 *pès*; Taungbyet field, 10 *pès*; total, 40 *pès*: also the Taunggwin fields, consisting of O Mè's, 5 *pès*; Nga Yaung's, 5 *pès*; O Yaung's, 5 *pès*; O Kin Ngè's, 5 *pès*; Nga Wun's, 5 *pès*; Thuyin's, 5 *pès*; Yè Byu's, 5 *pès*; Nga Pyi Wa's, 5 *pès*; Nga Mo Gyo's, 5 *pès*;

Kathityin field, 5 *pès;* Nga Ku Ma's, 5 *pès;* Neyagin field, 3 *pès;* total, 63 *pès:* also the whole of the Ongyi-Awunthin lands, consisting of . . . . *pès:* also the Myingabet fields, consisting of Thôn Bè's, 5 *pès;* Thein Daung's, 5 *pès;* Nga Yan Maung Ngè's son's, 5 *pès;* O Pathin Ngè's, 5 *pès;* A Pwa's, 5 *pès;* Paukpin field, 5 *pès;* Lèzabe field, 5 *pès;* O Pa U's father's field, 5 *pès;* Wet Yu's, 5 *pès;* Laikkabauk field, 5 *pès;* Lègauk field, 5 *pès;* Nga Twe Ngè's, 5 *pès;* Zayatyin field, 5 *pès;* Selaung field, 5 *pès;* Thipônyin field, 5 *pès;* O Pôk's, 5 *pès;* Nga Kyat's, 5 *pès;* Nga Se Daik's, 5 *pès;* Sôndalin field, 5 *pès;* Udaungbo field, 5 *pès;* Pyaunggingyi field, 15 *pès;* Nga Wet's, 5 *pès;* Nga Mi Yaung's, 5 *pès;* Lègauk field, 5 *pès;* Chibyet field, 5 *pès;* Nga Ye Byit's land, 5 *pès;* Nga Nanda's, 5 *pès;* Pyinmayin land, 5 *pès;* Theindaung field, 5 *pès;* Lègauk field, 5 *pès;* Kwèya-Nanwin field, 5 *pès;* Yandathu's land, 5 *pès;* Tahnaungyin field, 5 *pès;* Nga Shan Thi's land, 5 *pès;* Mi Be's, 5 *pès;* Monk Thitpasa's, 5 *pès;* Yandaba's, 3½ *pès;* Nga Tanzeik's, 5 *pès;* Lègauk field, 5½ *pès;* Nga Chi O's land, 5 *pès;* Nga Pyin's, 5 *pès;* In field, 5 *pès;* Magyibindaing field, 5 *pès;* Chinhmauk-Lègauk field, 5 *pès;* O Chit Swa's father's land, 5 *pès;* Nga Chit Hla's father's land, 5 *pès;* Nga Thi Zôk's land, 5 *pès;* Thônthit field, 5 *pès;* Nga Taba Ngè's land, 5 *pès;* Nga Shan Thin's field, 5 *pès;* Inauk field, 5 *pès;* Nga Sè Thin's land, 5 *pès;* Nga Mi Gyaung's, 5 *pès;* Letpanbinbya field, 5 *pès;* Kyauksauk field, 5 *pès;* Lèwun field, 5 *pès;* Lègauk field, 3½ *pès;* Nga Mya's land, 13½ *pès.* The boundaries of the monastery land are: east, ... (last line).

No. (3).

Locality.—Within the Yagyi group of monasteries.

Date.—774 Sakkarâj (1412 A.D.).

Founder.—Archbishop and Royal Preceptor to Minkyizwasawkè.

Substance of inscription.—Presentation of monastery.

ON Thursday, the full-moon of Kasôn 774 Sakkarâj, the king's* monastery was completed. It was then presented to the learned, illustrious and highly pious monk,† the Archbishop and Royal Preceptor of Tayapya,‡ who bore the title of Sîritribhavanâdityapavarapaṇḍitadhammarâjâ.

---

* Mingaunggyi of Ava.

† This monk is mentioned in the histories as a learned Arakanese divine, who, having been Minkyizwasawkè's teacher in youth, was sent for to the capital when the king ascended the throne.

‡ More commonly known as Minkyizwasawkè.

No. (4).—Obverse.

Locality.—Within the Yagyi group of monasteries.

Date.—793 Sakkarâj (1431 A.D.).

Founder.—King Mohnyin Mindaya's grandfather.

Substance of inscription.—Building of monastery and dedication thereto of paddy lands.

"Reverence to the Blessed, Holy and Enlightened One!"

On Thursday, the 5th waxing Nayôn 793 Sakkarâj, the king's grandfather, the minister, presented the king with a beautiful light grey pony and trappings and asked a boon in the presence of Sintha Pyanchi, the king's son-in-law; Einpyitsaya, Letmataung thugyi; Thuthut thugyi, Atwinthin thugyi, and other courtiers. His Majesty was pleased to grant the lands asked for after pouring out the water of dedication with the prayer that he might obtain a share of his grandfather's merit. The lands thus obtained measure 50 *pès* and include . . . . . . and 5 *pès* of Kayan Thaing's land. The western boundary of the tract of land was demarcated by five stone pillars. The northern boundary, which runs along the bank of the Shunbauk stream, was marked by five other such pillars. Along the north-eastern boundary were placed four stone pillars and a *galôn* (garuda bird) statue. On the south-west the tract adjoins the Sindè and Einnein religious lands, and on the south-eastern side were placed a stone pillar and a statue of a lion. The tract was demarcated by Minister Athandaw Mahaw and he was rewarded with four brass trays, four pieces of loin-cloth, a roan pony, a piece of turban cloth,

Reverse.

and a bed sheet. The headman of the . . . . . . village was rewarded with a piece of black cloth, another of white cloth, a piece of turban cloth, a brass tray, and a bed sheet; the villagers with a piece of turban cloth; the headmen of Inlein village, Dangmeyit village and Ywanè village with a piece of turban cloth each; Kya Thaing with a piece of turban cloth, a tray, and a bed sheet; and Kyauk Pyôk . . . . with a tray and a bed sheet. A large shed was then erected at Myaukpadôn, several bullocks and large game were killed, and after spreading a sumptuous feast, including large quantities of liquor, rice and condiments, the *nats* were invoked, and several water-pots were simultaneously broken.

"The tract of land thus obtained I dedicate to my monastery for the maintenance of the monks residing therein and in order that the Religion might last 5,000 years. May those who support my offering, from the King, Queens and Ministers downwards, enjoy a share of my merit. On the other hand, may those who destroy the same always find themselves in poverty and want, and be, together with their families, as miserable as the *petas*; and when they die, may they become charred pillars in hell, beyond the saving influence of all future Buddhas."

No. (5).

Locality.—Within the Yagyi group of monasteries.

Date.—873 Sakkarâj (1511 A.D.).

Founders.—Archbishops of Tada-u and Pinya and other monks.

Substance of inscription.—Building of a *simâ*.

On the full-moon day of Tabaung 873 Sakkarâj a number of monks, headed by the Archbishops of Tada-u and Pinya, purchased a piece of land, with toddy and cocoanut palm trees thereon, within the Ôngyi *Kyaungtaga's* monastery land for 28 viss of gold, and built a *simâ* there with the prayer that every sentient being, from the highest heaven to *avîci*, the lowest hell, might obtain a share of the merit.

No. (6).—Obverse.

Locality.—Within the Nanyagyi group of monasteries.

Date.—1243 Sakkarâj (1881 A.D.).

Founder.—Myotha Wundauk.*

Substance of inscription.—Building of a *simâ*.

"May there be victory! May the influence of the Buddha be as glorious and lasting as the glory of the sun and moon in the firmament. May this institution of charity serve as a support to the cause of the Buddha!"

Having, during a period extending over an innumerable number of *kalpas*, acquired the millions of virtues which accompanied him continuously like the four kinds of armies,† the embryo Buddha was born as Siddhatta, being the 334569th direct descendant from the royal line of Mahâ Samata, the first king of this fortunate ‡ world. This incomparable embryo Buddha spurned the celestial arms tendered by the *nats* as he would a pool of spittle, and having renounced the world, followed the eight sublime paths and attained Nirvâna. Just before this attainment, however, the Buddha having administered the law to the host of disciples numbering over 24 *asankheyyas*, beginning with Koṇḍañña and ending with Subadda, was moved by his infinite charity to provide for those who would come within the five dispensations of his Religion, which he prophesied would extend

* A history of the services rendered by this official is given in the inscription itself.

† Infantry, cavalry, elephanteers, charioteers.

‡ So-called because five Buddhas instead of one, which is said to be the rule, are destined to appear in this *kalpa*.

for a period of 5,000 years. Accordingly the Religion flourished in fourteen kingdoms* including Tagaung, Prome, Pagan, Ava, Shwebo and Mandalay, the last being founded by the convener of the fifth great Buddhist synod and His Majesty's illustrious father. The Religion continues to flourish because His Majesty takes an active interest in its support, having himself successfully passed three examinations in Buddhist religious lore before his accession to the throne. During this auspicious reign, therefore, the Myotha Wundauk, who passed the Patamabyan Pâli examinations at the age of ten, who subsequently joined the service of the king and acquired varied and extensive knowledge of Pâli and Burmese literature, of science and arts and of politics; who served as a clerk under the Kyiwun in Pagan Min's reign; as a Nakan, a Myowun, a Hlutdaw chief clerk, a Sitkè, Burmese Judge in the British Residency Court, Civil Judge and Wundauk in Mindôn's reign; and as Patanago Myoza Wundauk in Thebaw's reign, realized the impermanency of all things temporal, and wishing to escape the miseries of *samsaro*, repaired the ancient Shinbin Shwepônnyun pagoda standing on a piece of land called Neikbanseik-u within the Nanyagyi group of monasteries south of Tada-u village, Ava, and having obtained from the king an unconditional grant of a portion of the pagoda land measuring a *ta* of seven cubits square, † and conformed to the other requirements necessary to secure the validity of the consecration, performed the usual ceremonies with the assistance of five titled *Sadaws* and 49 other monks, and built a *simâ* thereon with the prayer that the cause of the Religion might be promoted . . . .

REVERSE.

His Majesty being well acquainted with the proper modes of desecrating and consecrating a *simâ*, directed the manner in which the ceremony relating to the present *simâ* should be performed by the monks, and the *kamavâcâ* was accordingly read correctly with proper intonation and articulation. As soon as the ceremony was completed, therefore, thousands of clouds ascended from all quarters and soon filled the whole firmament. There were then a storm and an earthquake and the crowds assembled acclaimed their approbation to the echo. The meritorious deed was thus approved of by the guardian *nats* of the Religion, and a command of the Buddha was by this means perpetuated.

---

* Ceylon, Thatôn, Prome, Pagan, Ava, Pegu, Pinya, Myebôntha, Thettha-Padaung, Shwebôntha, Mandalay, Tagaung, Kaungtôn, Ngasaunggyan.

† There is evidently a mistake here. The square would be too narrow for the large number of monks herein mentioned to move about and perform the ceremony in. According to the *Vinayâlankâyaṭikâ* a *simâ* should be large enough to accommodate 21 monks, but should not exceed three *yojanas* in extent.

This inscription is recorded in order that the monkhood might know that the *simâ* has been carefully constructed and consecrated in strict accordance with the scriptures, with a view that it might serve to promote the cause of the Religion of the excellent Buddha. May there be victory!

The total value of the offerings made by the Myotha Wundauk between the ages of 17 and 55 is Rs. 51,445. These he made in order to attain Nirvâna, realizing that the cessation of existence is bliss . . . .

The number of *simâs* consecrated by him is . . . .

INSCRIPTIONS FOUND AT AVA.

NO. (1).—OBVERSE.

Locality.—About half a mile west of Tada-u village.

Date.—760 Sakkarâj (1398 A.D.).

Founder.—Minkyizwasawkè and Queen Shinsawgyi.

Substance of inscription.—Building of monastery and dedication of lands thereto.

"I adore the Buddha!"

WHILE the Burmese Empire was on the decline owing to civil wars, and the interests of the Religion were injuriously affected, the King of *devâs* looked about him for some champion likely to be able to retrieve its fortunes, and he lighted upon the Governor of Yamèthin, a grandson of the famous King Thihathu who invaded China. Accordingly the King of *nats* favoured the governor's arms, and the governor was thus enabled to overcome every opponent and consolidate the Burmese Empire. This king is now known as Minkyizwasawkè, entitled Sîritribhavanâdityapavaradhammarâjâ. He married his cousin Shin Saw Gyi, daughter of Athincha, Governor of Sagaing, and this queen is known far and wide as Mibaya Saw. When their daughter Princess Saw Myat Kè died, the king and queen, wishing to have her escape the miseries of *samsaro* and attain the bliss of Nirvâna, built a beautifully gilt monastery at a place called Thinban, which was previously so intended by the princess herself. The monastery was formally consecrated on Wednesday, the 12th waxing Wazo 760 Sakkarâj, and the following lands were attached to it for the maintenance of the monks residing therein throughout the 5,000 years of the Religion, namely, the whole of the Einpakadinthin paddy-lands situated between Kyauktalôn and Inganet, and bounded on the east by Inganet; on the north-west by Chaungbit stream, Nga Chit Thin's tank, Ngasha hill and Ngalônma stream; west by Kanningè tank up to the borders of Aungtabyi land; south by the Opagandaw stream up to the palm tree near Nga Kyan Thin's tank; west by a watershed up to the Kushan channel; and west by the Shwepyithin island. Besides the above, their majesties offered the betel-vine garden south-east of King Anawrata's *simâ* on Myaunghla land. The garden is bounded on the east by Nga Mwe Hauk's land, south and west by the river, and north by two banyan trees.

"May those who destroy our offering never have the opportunity of beholding any of the Buddhas of the coming ages. May they become charred pillars in hell. Even if they are ever reborn as human beings, may they become *petas*. On the other hand, may those who support our offering have a share of our merit. May they become kings of *nats*, and, while existing as human beings, may they become wealthy citizens and happy kings. On the advent of Metteyya Buddha may they become *rahans* and attain the bliss of Nirvâna."

On Thursday, the 5th waxing Nayôn 754 Sakkarâj, Shinbôn Ngè obtained permission from the king to make the following offerings, namely, 20 *pès* of land south of . . . . . village in the . . . . district, 7½ *pès* south-east of Kanpulu in the Myothitngè township,

REVERSE.

a gold drinking-bowl used by her deceased husband, and a . . . .; 300 pieces of cloth for the . . . . .; . . . . for the monks; 100 pieces of cloth towards the repairing of the summit of the Governor of Taungdwin's pagoda; 50 *pès* of paddy-land to the monastery built by her parents; an elephant towards the repairing of their . . . .; 50 *pès* of paddy land and three slaves to her own monastery at . . . . .; 50 *pès* more to the monks residing therein; 37 fowls, 200 baskets of paddy, and . . . . to the famine-stricken, as well as other provisions to the families of those who fell with her husband in battle; also . . . . (14 lines).

NO. (2).

Locality.—Near the western wall of the Tihlaingshin pagoda.

Date.—872 Sakkarâj (1510 A.D.).

Founder.—Narapati.*

Substance of inscription.—Building of the palace.

[THIS inscription contains the architectural details of the palace of Ava, but it is in such a fragmentary state of preservation that no connected translation of it can be made.]

---

* Narapati was the second son of Mingaung II of Ava. Before his accession to the throne he was called Prince Minswe, and when he had completed the building of the palace, which took him a year, he was styled the Shwenangyawyin, or Lord of the exquisite golden palace.

No. (3).—Obverse.

Locality.—On the site of Modi monastery, south of Ava.

Date.—1140 Sakkarâj (1778 A.D.).

Founder.—King Singu Min.

Substance of inscription.—Building of five-tiered monastery with out-buildings, tank and bridge, and dedication thereto of lands and slaves.

"May the Religion of the Buddha overcome every obstacle!"

As the birth of a scion of the Saka family of kings is always made apparent a thousand years before the event, so the advent of the mighty Alompra in 1113 Sakkarâj was foretold a century previously. Alompra, His Majesty's grandfather, was as able to defend and promote the cause of the Religion as the illustrious Emperor Asoka; was an ardent devotee of the Buddha who possessed the 16 kinds of divine wisdom and overcame the five kinds of passion; was, like the famous Emperor Sudassana, suzerain of the 16 provinces of Sunâparanta, Tampadîpa, Jayavaḍḍhana, Sîrikhettarâma, Ramañña, Ayuddaya, Lavaraṭṭha, Haribhuñja, Khemâvara, Mahânagara, Kaṁboja, Mahiṁsaka, Moriya, Zein (Cinaraṭṭha), Âḷavî, and Manipûra; was replete with every kingly attribute; was the founder of a dynasty of mighty kings; was the builder of Shwebo with its fort, palace, moat, belfry, tank and pagoda; and was the ruler of a vast empire. When King Sinbyuyin ascended the throne of his illustrious father, he lost no time in building the Kandwin pagoda, Mahabôntha monastery, Pada pagoda, and Shwezettawya rest-house. He removed his capital from Pinya to Sagaing and thence to Ava like Asoka, who removed from Uccenî to Pâtaliputra, and like the embryo Buddha, who removed from Devadaha to Kaliya and thence to Kappîlavastu. Ava is situated at the junction of five rivers, namely, the Irrawaddy, Metkaya, Sanma, Panlaung and Myitngè, and the building of the city and palace was commenced in 1126 Sakkarâj. The city measured 1,320 *tas* in perimeter. The palace was 120 *thandaungs* high and was surrounded by 40 beautiful out-buildings. When the Chinese army of over four hundred thousand men made their ill-advised invasion, His Majesty defeated them in a short time and seized all their arms and ammunition. The king subsequently enlarged the capital, so that it measured 2,444 *tas* in perimeter, and built four large and beautiful monasteries each having four storeys and each surrounded by 40 smaller monasteries. He next placed a *ti* on the Shwezigôn pagoda, wherein his eminent ancestor Anawrata enshrined the frontal bone of Gautama Buddha, and another on the pagoda* wherein eight hairs of Gautama Buddha were enshrined by

* The Shwedagôn in Rangoon.

the brothers Taphussa and Bhallika of Pôkkharavatl. The old *ti* of the latter pagoda was taken away by the *devas** in order that His Majesty might have an opportunity of acquiring merit, and the new bejewelled *ti* was plated with 88$\frac{4}{5}$ viss of gold, being double the weight of His Majesty. The ceremony of putting on the *ti* was performed in the presence of the Royal Family, the Ministers and a large army and navy. King Sinbyuyin was furthermore the builder of the Neikbanseik-u pagoda,† enshrining several relics of Gautama Buddha, and of the Nyandawmyina pagoda on Bôndaung hill; and his dominion was so vast that tribute in the shape of spices reached him even from the distant island of Malayu ‡ in fleets of ships. He was also the possessor of white elephants, and gold, silver, emerald and amber mines. Such was the royal parent of His Majesty the present king, who succeeded to the abovementioned vast heritage in the year 2320 of the Religion, corresponding with the year 1138 Sakkarâj (1776 A.D.), in fulfilment of the prophecy of the *devas* and *rishis* made on the occasion of the building of the great Shwezigôn pagoda. Shortly after the coronation ceremonies the king, with a view to promote the cause of the Religion, had the three *pitakas* transcribed in gold on richly gilt palm leaves; but not satisfied with this meritorious deed, he thought himself to surpass the good works of his eminent ancestors by founding some religious institution, which they had never done, either at Prome, Pegu, Toungoo, Pagan, Pinya, Ava or Sagaing. Accordingly His Majesty built a very large and most beautiful golden monastery after the model of the famous *jetavaṁ* in Sâvatthi, deserving the praise of even the king of *devas*. The length of the building is 125$\frac{1}{4}$ cubits, breadth 89$\frac{1}{2}$ cubits, and height 100 cubits. It is adorned with statues, glass beadings and inlaid and stucco work, and has 32 staircases. It is five-storeyed and resembles the palace of the king of *devas*. A library similar to the monastery in architectural style was built near it and a beautiful tank was also dug. The main monastery is surrounded by 12 smaller three-storeyed monasteries decorated on the same grand scale. The whole is surrounded by a double wall 250 *tas* in perimeter, and there is a beautiful bridge attached to the tank which can be traversed by 40 men marching abreast.

On Friday, the 1st waning of Tabaung 1139 Sakkarâj, His Majesty, in emulation of the King of Sâvatthi, who had the opportunity of ministering to the Buddha and his disciples, held charitable festivals at seven places simultaneously and offered 100 articles of monastic use to each of 2,500 monks.

---

* It came down during an earthquake.

† At Pinya.

‡ Off the coast of Arakan: probably the *Malaiur* of Marco Polo.

On Sunday, the 9th waxing of the following month, His Majesty personally demarcated the ground-plan of the monastery buildings and upturned the first sod with a golden hoe the same afternoon. The carpenters and masons and other workmen employed were regularly paid their wages out of the royal coffers, and the buildings were successfully completed within 12 months. The main monastery appears like a golden mountain which had risen out of the earth at the bidding of the king of *devas*, and it is situated at an adequate distance from the palace. His Majesty then commanded preparations to be made for offering the monastery formally to the Archbishop,* who is highly pious and learned both in ecclesiastical as well as secular literature, and who has been a distinguished monk for the last 50 years. In addition to the 2,500 monks invited from the 16 provinces of Sunaparanta, Tampadîpa, &c., 1,070 monks from the capital were fed and supplied with yellow robes and other necessaries amidst high festivals, which were held from the 10th waxing of Tabaung till the full-moon day, when the Royal Family witnessed the festivals in state. The royal procession was headed by the queen dowager surrounded by her numerous attendants; then came the princes, the king's sister and her attendants, and lastly the chief queen

Reverse.

and six lesser queens with attendants and musicians. Puppet shows and other entertainments were held all round the monasteries, and there was a grand parade of infantry and cavalry including a company of elephanteers, the animals being adorned with rich trappings studded with jewels. The princes and princesses of the royal household, as well as the ministers, the wealthy merchants and their families, all richly dressed, were also present in large numbers. On the 2nd waning of the month the king himself attended the festivities in state. The royal carriage was drawn by eight white horses richly caparisoned, and His Majesty was sheltered under eight white umbrellas. The array of royal attendants and appurtenances was so glorious that the splendour checked, as it were, the penetrating rays of even the sun. The royal progress was through the Kyawbôn gate and the Mogaung gate, over the Hanthawaddy bridge, and along the eastern main road to the festive pavilion. His Majesty was surrounded by all the ministers

---

* This is the Atula *Sayadaw*, who was *Thathanabaing* in the reigns of Sinbyuyin, Singu Min, and Maung Maung. Shortly after Bodawpaya's accession to the throne, the *Sayadaw* happened to express an opinion that monks might, without infringing the Vinaya or Code of Monastic Discipline, go about without strictly adhering to the rule regarding the adjustment of the upper robe, and he was therefore replaced by the Maungdaung *Sayadaw*.

and tributary chiefs, and the assembly of over 2,500 monks were offered 100 articles of monastic use each. Some of the ministers were appointed to supervise the various dramatic performances and sports and fireworks. When the auspicious moment arrived, His Majesty consecrated the monasteries by pouring out water in the presence of the Royal Family and the vast attendant assemblage of monks and laymen belonging to all classes of society, and formally offered them to the Archbishop, entitled the Tipitakalankarasami-mahâdhammarâjâdhirâjâguru, on the morning of the full-moon of Tabaung 1140 Sakkarâj. Moreover, in order that the Religion might continue to flourish during its period of 5,000 years, the king dedicated to the monasteries 29 families of slaves and two pieces of land called Myinmye and Myinzilat. To those who were employed in the building of the monasteries and the supervision of the festivities the king granted many rewards in the shape of towns, villages, titles, wearing apparel, money, paddy and rice, and alms were freely distributed among over a thousand mendicants. His Majesty performed these meritorious deeds with the prayer that he might ultimately attain Buddhahood; that in the meantime should he be born again as a man, he might become the king of kings; if as a *devâ*, the king of *devâs*; and that all his kinsmen, his ministers and subjects, as well as every being inhabiting the three *lokas*, might obtain a share of his merit. The following are the names of the slaves. Yaka, Thada Thuka, Thada Pônnya, Mi Ngan Bye, Mi Leik Pyi, Tagun Mi Bye, Nga Mun Ni, Nga Tagun Pa . . . . Hawkkun Pye, Nga E and wife . . . . wife Mi Ngaik Sun Pye, Nga Pyi Dat, Mi San Yauk, Yin Bye, Nga Kundi and wife Mi . . . Nat, Nga Law Baw, Nga Pa Ngan and wife Mi Ngan Bye, Mi Leik San, Mi Pa Ngan, Mi Paw Pani, ... and wife Mi Lila Pati, Nga Poya Nandaw and wife Mi To Nu, daughter . . . . (7 lines).

No. (4).—Obverse.

Locality.—Zegyi quarter, Ava.

Date.—1140 Sakkarâj (1778 A.D.).

Founders.—Minister Maha Nawyata and wife.

Substance of inscription.—Repairing of pagoda built by Alompra and building of images, rest-houses, libraries, and other religious edifices.

"Reverence to the Blessed, Holy and Enlightened One! May the Religion overcome every obstacle."

The Buddha has founded the great city of Nirvâna in the land of diligence and equanimity, intending it as a refuge for the vast number of sentient beings of this auspicious *kalpa* wherein five

Buddhas are destined to appear, and has laid out eight sublime paths leading to the same. Round the city he has planted trees of the four species of *Iddhipada*, in order that those who are deserving may partake of the fruit thereof. He has thus effected the happiness of four *asankheyyas* and 600 million beings, and provided for the welfare of those that remain by ordaining that his Religion shall last 5,000 years and shall flourish in various countries. The 16 provinces of Sunaparanta, Tampadîpa, &c., enjoy this privilege, and the Religion has continued to flourish from the time of Alompra, Naungdawgyi, and Sinbyuyin up to the present glorious reign. His Majesty is replete with every kingly virtue and his accession to the throne was foretold by *devas*. Being a highly pious monarch, His Majesty regilt the Shwezigôn, Mahamyatmani and Lawkatharapu pagodas and built new monasteries and rest-houses near them. He also built the five-tiered monastery and out-buildings at Aungmyesanlut and ornamented them with rich decorations in gold and colours. His Majesty was the founder of several other religious institutions and was instrumental in encouraging several members of the Royal Family, the Ministers, and others to follow his excellent example for the good of the Religion. When the above mentioned great monastery was offered to the *Thathanabaing* on Monday the full-moon of Tabaung 1140 Sakkarâj, His Majesty presented 160,000 articles of monastic use to 2,000 monks; and on the same occasion had the Lawkamanaung pagoda repaired by Minister Mahanawyata.* His Majesty further induced the Minister to erect a wall round the pagoda, to dig a tank and build a library near it. The Minister and his wife being replete with the seven kinds of lawful riches, founded these institutions with hearty good-will, and on Friday the 6th waxing of Tabodwè 1140 Sakkarâj enshrined the following in a nine-roomed vault: namely, several caskets of sacred relics, 723 statuettes illustrating the life of Gautama from the time of his attainment of Buddhahood till he reached Nirvâna, 28 statues of different Buddhas, 80 statuettes of Gautama's disciples, several statues of kings, *devas* and *brahmas*, miniature golden umbrellas, flags and banners and jewellery. Over this vault was built an octagonal pagoda 46½ cubits in diameter (at the base) and 75½ cubits high. It is surrounded with eight statues of lions, one at each corner. On the eastern face a large rest-house was built. Round the whole a brick wall having a linear measurement of 368 cubits was erected

REVERSE.

with four gates and porchways, and ornamented with 12 large statues of lions. Other religious institutions were also founded,

* The histories do not mention the fact that this minister was an *Atwinwun* under Singu Min.

namely, a circular library 10 cubits in diameter and a tank 13 by 8 by 15 *tas*, enclosed by a wall 15 by 30 *tas*. On the day fixed for dedicating these religious works several articles of monastic use were kept ready to be offered to a number of monks. Two thousand and one hundred packets of gold-leaf were used in gilding the various edifices. When everything was ready, the king was approached with the request that he might be graciously pleased to perform the necessary rites of dedication. Accordingly, on Monday the 3rd waning of Tabaung 1141 Sakkarâj, the king appeared in state, and being the founder of several religious institutions himself, gladly performed the agreeable duty. On the same day the king formally consecrated the monastery and pagoda erected by the Ministers Yakaingwun and Mahadantaikwun, and after witnessing the various festivals held on the occasion, returned to the palace in the cool of the evening. Subsequently the king built the Lawkamanaung pagoda, adorned with several statues, images, and paintings; presented the eminent monk Palaing *Sadaw* with an image fashioned out of a piece of sandalwood; placed a new brass image in the Bônzantulut monastery; presented the monk Atula *Sadaw** with a sandalwood image and a box containing 1,000 *angâs* of palm-leaf manuscripts; placed a brass pagoda weighing 1,000 viss, gold and silver caskets containing sacred relics, and a number of small images in the Umin *Sadaw's* monastery; built a flag-staff at the Shwedagôn pagoda, Rangoon; built a row of rest-houses on the north side of the Shwezigôn pagoda, Pagan; erected monasteries at Ngatha-aw, Thawtapan quarter, Sagaing, Thudatthana quarter in the capital, and founded several other religious institutions with the prayer that His Majesty and Royal consort might ultimately reach Nirvâna; that they might in the meanwhile enjoy immunity from every danger and obtain every happiness either as human beings or as *devâs*; that their descendants and other relatives and friends, as well as those who assisted in the founding of these institutions, might obtain the same blessings; that their merit might be shared by their parents, grand-parents, teachers and mentors, by the King and the Royal Family, by the nobles and their families, by the guardian *nats* of the Religion, the universe, the city, the palace, the umbrella, the trees, the earth and the sky, and by every sentient being inhabiting every universe; but that those who destroy or cause damage to these institutions might encounter every evil and abide in distress always.

The lands dedicated to these institutions in order that the necessary offerings and repairs might be made to them are: the whole of the Pagadin village lands, bounded on the east by the Tabè lands

* The *Thathanabaing* or Archbishop (*vide* note under previous inscription).

between Nga Chit Thin's tank adjoining the Thinganet stream and Nga Wa Thin's tank situated on the west bank of Ngalônba stream; on the south by the watershed between Einpakadin stream and the lower end of Nga Kyan Thin's tank; west by the said watershed up to Kushan channel in front of Kanhla village; and north by the Shwepyiyin island. The slaves dedicated consisted of four families of Manipuris and Chins. Their names are Nga Sandaraw, Mi Sanpa, Nga Pôk Saw, Nga Mauk Pa, Nga Chin O, Mi Nyein Gyan, Nga Pein Gyaw, Mi Taw Nu, Nga Pyu, Mi Nyo and infant son, total 11.

No. (5).

Locality.—Outside the southern gate of Ava.

Date.—1184 Sakkarâj (1822 A.D.).

Founder.—Salin Mintha.*

Substance of inscription.—Building of Mahazeyapata bridge.

"THE Buddha has struck the drum of righteousness and has thus made known its voice; he has also administered the food of law. May he always keep me in the way of the law!"

The excellent Buddha Gautama, the wise leader of *nats* and men through the sea of *samsaro,* ordained that those who were not fortunate enough to benefit by his personal teaching should, after his demise, enjoy the same privileges by the propagation of his Religion at certain favoured places. Accordingly the Religion flourished successively at Prome, Pagan, Myinzaing, Pinya, Sagaing, Shwebo, Amarapura and Ava. When His Majesty the present King of Ava (Bagyidaw) ascended the throne of his ancestors the illustrious Alompra and Naungdawgyi, in company with the Chief Queen Sîripavaratilokamahârâjindâratanâdevî and attended by the princes, princesses and nobles, the glory of the pageant was as that of the full moon.

The founder of the bridge, namely, the Prince entitled Sîrisumahâdhammarâjâ, is His Majesty's brother-in-law, being the brother of Queen Nyanannyunbya,† daughter of Thihakyawzwa, son of Thakinmun, daughter of Balathaman, son of Tuyinpyitsi, son of Thirinandayet, son of Thayesithu, son of Athinkaya, son of Sadukamani, son of Sawmindut, daughter of the king who visited Prome,‡ son of the founder of Tupayôn pagoda,§ son of Mohnyin

* Maung O, brother of Bagyidaw's Chief Queen Mè Nu, on whom, by the influence of his sister, was conferred the honorary rank and appanage of a prince. He was a native of Palangôn village, Ye-u district.

† Mè Nu, grandmother of *ex*-Queen Supayalat.

‡ Mahathihathuya.

§ Narapati.

Mindaya, son of Narapatisithu, great grandson of Anawrata, whose glory was like that of the morning star. The Prince and his wife the Princess Sìrisumangalâratanâdevî and two daughters, performed this meritorious deed in order that they might escape the miseries of the whirlpool of *samsaro*, and in emulation of others who had for the same object founded various institutions. The bridge is situated on the south of the capital. Its length is 500 *tas*, and it is so broad that four carriages can traverse it abreast. Along it and on both sides are built resting-places. At the southern end of the bridge are two leogryphs and at the northern end is built a large hostel for the convenience of wayfarers. The whole work was completed on Friday evening the 6th waxing of Tabodwè 1184 Sakkarâj, corresponding with the era of the Religion 2366, at a total expenditure of 1,000 viss of silver. It was not for love of praise and worldly fame that the prince erected this grand bridge named Mahâjeyapatha, but simply to acquire merit towards the attainment of Nirvâna.

This inscription is erected in order to perpetuate the fact that the Salin Prince and Princess, with their two daughters, built the grand bridge at Ava in order to increase the glory of the capital, and in order that they themselves might acquire merit day and night thereby.

NO. (6).—OBVERSE.

Locality.—About 300 feet west of the Thetkyathiha pagoda.

Date.—1192 Sakkarâj (1830 A.D.).

Founder.—King Bagyidaw.

Substance of inscription.—Building of monastery and re-dedication of pagoda slaves.

"THE excellent Buddha, who has achieved a splendid victory over desire, realizing that great benefit would accrue to many in Burma if he wended his way thither, visited our country on several occasions. I adore this Buddha, who is replete with excellent wisdom, who is ever promoting the welfare of others, and who is endowed with prophetic vision. In other words, the Buddha, whose feet are each marked on the soles with 108 emblems, visited Burma and preached the law for seven whole days in the Sandagu chapel. When about to depart he left two impressions of his feet, one on the summit of the Thitsabanda hill* and the other on the bank of the Nanpada stream.† From that time up to the present the

* The present Shwezettaw pagoda hill at Sagu in the Minbu district. Thitsabanda is said to have been an ascetic who was the first disciple of Gautama in Burma.

† This stream is now known as Mangyaung. The classical appellation is after that of a fabulous dragon.

Religion has flourished in Burma without abatement. I adore the Buddha, who is deserving of all adoration, whose glory is six-fold, who is conversant with the Law."

When the Buddha Dîpankarâ, who had attained Buddhahood after having acquired the necessary amount of merit during a period extending over 16 *asankheyyas* and 100,000 *kalpas*, was propagating the law leading to Nirvâna to vast assemblies of men, *devâs* and *brahmâs*, our embryo Buddha was a *rishi* known as Sumedâ. He was then so far advanced in merit that he obtained a prophecy from Dîpankarâ to the effect that he would himself attain Buddhahood four *asankheyyas* and 100,000 *kalpas* subsequently. During this period our embryo Buddha acquired virtues as numerous as the atoms composing the earth, and ultimately becoming a Buddha, administered the law with the assistance of his chief disciples, Sâriputtarâ, Moggalâna, Mahakassápa and others, exercising every form of wisdom, vigilance and foresight. The Buddha has thus led multitudes of sentient beings to the blissful city of Nirvâna. He attained Buddhahood at the age of 35 and propagated the law unceasingly for 45 years in every land. When he was sojourning in the Sandagu chapel, he imprinted a foot on the Thitsabanda hill and another on the bank of the Nanpada stream. These two places have thus acquired particular sanctity and they are situated within the Empire of His most glorious Majesty the founder of the fourth city and palace of Ava; a direct royal descendant of the founders of the dynasties of Prome, Pagan, Myinzaing, Shwebo, Ava, Sagaing and Amarapura; the ruler of an Empire as vast and glorious as those of Mahathamada, Kusa and Nemi, and as powerful as Kapilavastu. His Majesty is virtuous, powerful and wise, and was accordingly appointed heir apparent to the throne at the youthful age of ten.

OBVERSE—SECOND STONE.

Soon after the demise of Bodawpaya, on the full-moon day of Nayôn 1181, His Majesty ascended the throne and lost no time in emulating the example of Asoka by having the old pagodas and monasteries renovated, and infusing new energy into ecclesiastical matters. His Majesty next removed the capital from Amarapura to Ava, a distance of 4,000 *tas*. The coronation ceremonies, however, took place just before this removal, and when they were completed His Majesty assumed the glorious title of Sîritribhavanâdityâdhipatipavarapaṇḍitamahâdhammarâjâdhirâjâ. Though enjoying every advantage attendant on such an exalted position, His Majesty realizes, as one whose virtues are almost ripe for the attainment of Nirvâna, that those who are in *samsaro* are like the foolish ravens which congregate on an elephant's carcase floating about in mid-ocean, and are so blinded by the five kinds of worldly desires that they never even dream of the law affecting their future welfare; that we therefore should strive by good works to gain merit; and those who are rich in worldly goods should be lavish in their offerings and so strive to cultivate charity. Moreover, His Majesty recollects the sayings of the Buddha to the effect that by virtue of his good deeds he had in his career enjoyed 36 existences as king of the *devâs*, 100 as Çakravatin, and innumerable existences as emperor and king, and that offerings made in the form of monasteries are the most meritorious. Accordingly, not satisfied with having built a large number of magnificent pagodas, His Majesty emulated the example of Parakkamabâhu, King of Ceylon, built a grand monastery on the south-west corner of the city and completed it on Wednesday the 10th waning Thadingyut 1185 Sakkarâj, corresponding with the year of the Religion 2367, at a cost of 1,200 viss of silver. The monastery is three-tiered, and the number of posts is altogether 210. There are two offering platforms in front, ornamented with glass mosaic work, and close by are figures of an elephant, a lion and a *nat* striking a drum with the foot. The porches are ornamented with figures of *brahmâs* and *devâs* and in the front room is placed an image of the Buddha covered with four white umbrellas. There are many other figures at the doors, porches and archways, and several rich carvings. The spire is equally rich in ornaments and is 53 cubits high. It vies with the abode of the king of *devâs* in appearance. The main building has 26 doors and six ornamented staircases. The number of bundles of gold-leaf used in the building is 25,000. His Majesty personally superintended the construction and was assisted by a Wundauk and two clerks. There are also out-houses and the whole is enclosed by a wall having a perimeter of 120 *tas*. When completed His Majesty named the monastery as Maha-Aungmyebôntha and held various festivals, shows, theatricals, sports and other entertainments in celebration of the occasion, the entertainments consisting of fire-works, living pictures, legerdemain, acrobatic feats, boxing, dramatic performances, marionettes, and Burmese, Talaing, Siamese, Shan, Indian, Chinese and Thibetan music. The lavish offerings made were on the scale of the ancient kings Vessantarâ and Kosala, and the monastery was formally dedicated to the monkhood headed by the Archbishop Munindâbhivamsadhammasenâpatimahâdhammarâjâdhirâjâguru,* together with various offerings befitting monks. On Sunday the 13th waning Tabaung 1190 Sakkarâj, corresponding

* Salin *Sayadaw*.

with the year of the Religion 2372, His Majesty performed this meritorious deed with the prayer that he might attain Buddhahood after having passed through *samsaro* doing good in every existence, and that his ancestors and parents might obtain a share of his merit.

REVERSE.

His Majesty has thus made due provision for his future welfare, treating high and low alike in making his lavish offerings. The immense crowds of people witnessing the festivals, consisting of nobles of every rank and grade, merchants and traders and people of various nationalities were presented with articles of clothing, money, cattle, food-stuffs and medicinal drugs, and numbers of convicts were liberated as an act of grace. The officials who assisted in superintending the construction of the monastery were granted promotion departmentally, and the architects received titles and decorations in addition to their emoluments. This inscription is erected simultaneously with that relating to the Mahathetkyayanthi pagoda. It is erected by the learned Minister Mahathinkaya in order that it may be known that His Majesty built this golden monastery after he had built and repaired the Mahawizayayanthi and several other pagodas, monasteries, caves and rest-houses. The slaves dedicated to the Maha-Aungmyebôntha monastery are the following descendants of those who were originally dedicated to the Pôkpayôn monastery by King Thadominbya, and transferred to the Yadanabôngyaw monastery by King Bodawpaya, founder of Amarapura, the head slaves being Nga Ôn and Nga Aung Tha: Nga Ôn, Mi Kaw Yan, Nga Kyi, Mi Kè, Nga Hnaw, Nga Sein Bu, Mi Min E, Nga Tha Be, Mi Min Le, Nga Kala, Nga Aung Tha, Mi E, Nga Myat Sein, Mi U, Mi Min Baw, Mi Yin, Nga Myat E, Nga Kyan Baw, Nga Myat Shin, Mi Min Bo, Nga Lôn, Nga Tha Do, Mi Hla Tha, Nga Nyo, Nga Myat Kyaw, Mi Hle, Mi Wa, Nga Waing, Nga Shwe Kya, Nga Ni, Mi Wa, Nga In, Mi Gaung Bôn, Nga San Tha, Mi Kaung Hla, Nga Pe, Mi Taung, Nga Tha Zan, Nga Hmôn, Nga Kywet, Mi Baing, Nga Shwe Byaw, Mi Payit, Nga Shwe I, Mi Baw, Mi Hla Tha, Nga Shwe Ket, Nga San Gaung, Mi Nyein, Mi Ya Tha, Nga Kathè, Mi Kè, Nga Baw U, Mi Ya, Nga San Tha, Nga Maung, Mi Dwa, Nga Ywè, Nga Shwe Be, Nga Pein, Nga Waing, Mi Myat Pu, Nga Kaing, Mi Hla, Mi Bôk, Nga Kaing, Mi Yauk, Mi Gôn, Nga Tha Min, Mi Ba Lôk, Mi Se, Nga Aw, Nga Nyun, Nga Paw I, Mi Sa, Mi Hla Nyo, Nga Si, Mi Nan Yan, Nga Shwin, Nga Lu Maung, Nga Mya San, Mi Ke, Nga Shwe Ye, Nga Wa, Mi Bye, Mi Kathè, Nga U, Nga Baw, Mi Hla Wun, Nga Myat Kaung, Mi Zan Bi, Nga Bun, Nga Wet, Mi Mi, Nga Tha Lwin, Mi Win, Mi Talaing, Nga Nyo Min,

Mi Hnin Bauk, Nga Shwe Nu, Nga Tha Byu, Mi Min, Mi San Ya, Nga Pin, Nga Shwe Hmôn, Mi San Dun, Nga Shwe Yan, Nga Tun Hla, Mi Kya, Mi Hnin Bauk, Nga Kwe, Mi Sein, Nga Pauk, Nga Aing, Mi Kyaung, Nga Pein, Mi Min Nu, Mi Pan Bu, Nga Kya Daw, Nga In, Mi Kathè, Nga Myat Nu, Mi Min U, Nga Lwin, Mi Min Zan, Mi Baw, Mi Gaing, Nga Shwe U, Mi Gaung, Nga Sein, Nga Myat Tun Aung, Mi Bein, Nga Pa, Mi Pe Za, Mi Tôk, Nga E, Mi Kwe, Mi Min Nu, Mi Myat Pu, Nga Pya, Mi E, Nga In, Mi Be, Nga Kyi, Mi Wa, Nga Kywè, Mi Waing, Mi Yin, Mi Nyein, Mi Hnaung, Nga Myat Tun, Mi Twe, Nga Ywe, Nga I, Nga Sein, Nga Tha Hnyin, Mi Pyu, Mi Hnin, Nga Kyaw Gaing, Mi Min Gauk, Nga Ywè, Mi Kadu, Nga Pya, Mi Bôk Sôn, Nga Tôk Kyi, Mi Min Aung, Nga Chan Zan, Nga I, Mi E, Nga Pu, Mi Thwin, Nga Nan Thu, Mi Tin, Nga Pôn, Nga Sa, Mi Min Hla, Nga Nwè, Nga Hle, Mi Min Ya, Nga Hnin, Nga Taung Bo, Nga Waing, Mi Zan, Mi Min, Nga Myat Paw, Mi Hnin, Mi Wa, Nga Shwe Daik, Nga Myat Hmwe, Mi Wa, Mi Lun Myat, Mi Hla Ya, Nga Hmaing, Nga Kyaw Yun, Nga Myat Tôk, Mi Paw, Mi Hnyin, Mi Kè, Nga Shwe U, Nga Sein Bin, Mi Min E, Nga Tun Nyo, Mi Shwe Thwin, Nga Si, Mi Baing, Nga Wa, Min U, Nga Shwe U, Nga San Thu, Mi Bè, Mi Hla Tha, Mi Nan Ôk, Nga Hmôn, Mi Nan Thu, Nga Myat Pu, Mi Hla Bè, Nga Nu, Mi Bwe, Mi Hle, Mi Ein Dun, Nga Kwè, Mi Nyein Ya, Nga Ni, Nga Tha Hmwe, Mi Sa, Nga Tha I, Nga Myat Pu, Mi Hnin Ngôn, Mi Aing, Nga Shwe Pu, Mi Nyein Gaung, Nga Tha Wun, Mi O, Nga Pyu, Nga Myat Tun, Mi Thi, Nga Nyein, Mi Bye, Nga Tha Zan, Nga Shwe Thi, Nga Kya, Mi Hla U, Nga Aw, Nga Shwe Ya, Mi Min Ye, Mi Sein, Mi Gyôk, Nga Kin, Nga Ko, Mi Lun Bye, Mi Naw, Nga Chaw, Mi Ngè, Nga Po, Nga Lu, Mi Hnin Bin, Nga Chan Mya, Nga Myat Thu, Nga Thet, Nga Ya Taw, Mi Mi, Nga Yauk, Mi Chan Tha, Nga Aung Ya, Nga Hmôn, Mi Bayet, Nga Sôn, Mi Thu, Nga Kyaw We, Mi Pyu, Nga Paw, Nga Tun Zan, Mi Ywè, Nga So Bôn, Nga Kut Ta, Mi Nyet Twa, Nga Pyaw, Nga Pyu Win, Mi Tin, Mi Baing Byu, Mi Hnin, Nga Ya Taw, Nga Myat Wa, Mi Min Byaw, Mi Min Ôk, Nga Myat Ye, Mi Min Ya, Nga Tha In, Mi Lun Ya, Nga Hle, Mi Ywè, Nga Tun Zan, Nga Kyaw Tha, Nga Hlaw, Mi Nan Tha, Mi Sa Hle, Nga Shwe Kya, Nga Tha Byu, Nga Myat Twa, Mi Min Nyo, Nga Pauk Twe, Nga Chan Thu, Mi Ke, Mi Si, Nga Ko, Nga Tha Do, Mi Ke, Mi Mein, Nga Po, Mi Sa U, Mi Kyi, Nga Min, Mi Ngè, Nga Hnin Gyi, Mi Min Aung, Nga Tha Ya, Nga Hmôn, Mi Galôn, Nga Tin, Nga Shwe Bo, Nga Aung Gya, Mi Min Aung, Nga Tha U, Nga Tin, Mi Nu, Nga Myat Pu, Mi Cho, Nga Kala, Nga Myat Sein, Nga Tha Min, Nga Kin, Mi Min Dwe, Nga Kyaw Ni, Mi Min Tha, Mi Hla Gyaw, Nga Nyo Mya, Mi Ywè, Nga Pyu Win,

Mi Kadu, Nga Lauk, Mi Nyein Ya, Nga Shwe Ba, Mi Bwe, Nga Kan Ya, Nga Si, Nga Mo, Mi Ngwe U, Mi Min Wa, Nga Pa, Mi Kywin, Nga Tha Hnin, Nga Paw Daung, Nga Paw Hlaing, Nga U, Mi Pyu, Mi Ḥla Aung, Nga Ngè, Mi Min Byu, Mi Ka, Mi Kaya, Mi Pè, Nga Pwa, Mi Mein Kale, Nga Ko, Nga Shwin, Nga Tin, Mi Hla Byu, Nga Myat Win, Nga Tu Te, Mi Thwè, Nga Nan O, Mi Ye, Nga Kwe Bin, Nga Te Naung, Nga Myat Waing, Mi Tôk, Mi Nyein, Mi Ya, Nga Kan Be, Nga Pan, Mi Tha Byu, Nga Shwe Gyaw, Mi Shwin, Nga Shwe Tu, Nga Ka, Nga Maung, Mi Min U, Nga Shwe Aung, Nga Hnin, Mi Nyein Gaung, Nga Shwe Tun, Mi Win Nyo, Mi Myet Shu, Nga Ye, Nga Yin, Mi Inma, Nga Be, Mi Twe, Mi San Dun, Nga Saing, Mi Min Ya, Mi Min U, Nga Ya Taw, Mi Hmat Nyo, Nga Thi, Nga Pye, Mi Kathè, Mi Hla Gôn, Mi Hmat San, Nga Kywet, Mi Hnè, Nga Shwe Yi, Mi Waing, Nga Po, Mi Aung Lit, Nga Hmo, Mi Myitta, Nga Te Te, Mi Sein, Nga Aung Mya, Mi San Nyet, Mi Hmo Thè, Nga Shwe Hmaw, Nga Shwe Nu, Nga Lu Bôn, Nga Pyu Dôk, Mi Min Ya, Nga Lu Bein, Mi Min Tha, Nga Myat Shwè, Nga Baw, Nga Shwè, Mi Hnin Ngôn and infant, Mi Bôk Sôn, Mi Hmat Taw, Nga Paw, Mi Hla U, Nga Tha Ywè, Mi Thè Gya, Nga Kan Be, Mi Mein Kale, Nga Nu, Mi Kè, Mi Min Ya, Mi Myo Ya, Mi Hmo U, Mi Min U, Nga Kôn, Nga Kyu, Mi Kye, Nga E Baw, Mi Mi, Mi Hmwe Nyet, Nga Ngè, Nga Mya Yi, Nga Myat Paw, Mi Ngwe U, Nga Ywè, Mi San Tha, Nga Pe, Nga Shwe To, Nga Shwe Hmè, Nga Hmo, Mi Min Kye, Nga Pyu, Mi Min U, Nga Chein, Nga Lwin, Mi Mi, Nga Shwè, Nga Pyo, Mi Naw, Mi Wun, Mi Hmo U, Mi Myo Ya, Nga Tôk Kyi, Mi Tu Za, Nga Pyan, Mi San Bôn, Nga Tha Shwin, Mi I, Mi Naw Za, Mi Min Wa, Nga Tha Baw, Nga Kyaung, Nga Tha U, Nga Ywè, Mi Twa, Nga Tha Byu, Mi, Hnin E, Nga Ka, Mi Hla Bu, Nga Yan Gin, Nga Kyaw Gaung, Mi San, Nga Nyo, Mi Chin, Nga Pe, Nga Kyaw Gè, Mi So, Nga Kyi, Nga Pu, Mi Myo, Nga Myat Shun, Mi Wathu, Nga Myat, Mi Sa, Mi Win U, Nga Tha Be, Nga Pwe, Mi U, Nga Kywè, Mi Saung, Nga Hmôn, Mi Hla Ye, Nga Tun Nyo, Mi Mo, Nga Shwe Hnyin, Nga Kan, Mi Min Gya, Nga Shwe Gè, Mi Bôk, Nga Shwe Mo, Nga Shwe Yut, Nga Nyo Thu, Mi Mi, Mi Mya Yi, Nga Shwe Yi, Mi Min Dun, Nga Shwe Thi, Nga Ya Taw, Mi Cho, Mi Tha Gaung, Mi Ôn Ma, Nga Shwe Nu, Nga Yauk, Mi Pe Zôn, Nga Maung, Nga Tha Hnin, Mi U, Nga Shwe Yan, Mi Yin, Mi Sein Za, Mi Lein Ma, Nga Tha Hnin, Nga Tha Gè, Mi Kye, Nga Shwe Bya, Mi Net, Nga Shwe Saing, Nga Si Bin, Mi Min Hla, Mi Hnin, Nga Tha Lu, Mi Hnin Bauk, Nga Myat Twe, Nga Saing, Nga Shwe To, Nga Shwe Yo, Mi Baing, Nga Kyaw O, Nga Shwe Maung, Mi Hla Ye, Nga Pè, Mi Balôn, Mi Kathè, Nga Yan Nin, Mi Hla Ywe, Nga Cho E, Mi Pè, Nga Tha Be, Mi Mi, Nga Shwe To, Mi

Min Ya, Nga So, Mi Mi, Nga Tha Lu, Mi Min Tha, Nga Shwe Dôk, Nga Taung Bo, Nga Tha In, Mi Min Ya, Mi Po, Mi Shun, Nga Kyaung, Mi Nan Tha, Nga Kyi, Mi Nan Hmwe, Nga Tha Baik, Mi Min U, Nga Kya Ban, Mi Myat Pyu, Nga Myat Twe, Nga Shwe Gè, Mi Po, Mi Pè U, Nga Shwe Bin, Mi Min Ôk, Nga San Ya, Nga Kwè, Mi Manga, Nga Nyo Hla, Mi Min Bu, Nga Shwe Ywet, Nga Shwe Gan, Mi Naw Za, Nga Cho E, Mi Min U, Nga Tha Ya, Nga Tôk Kyi, Mi Taw, Nga Pyan, Mi Hnin Byu, Nga San, Mi Hnin Bauk, Nga Shwe To, Mi Min Hla, Mi Ywet, Nga Po Zi, Mi Ne Tha, Nga Po, Mi Kyi, Nga Shwe U, Mi Min Hmôn, Nga Pe, Nga Shwe Nyein, Nga Hmaing, Mi Yi Ywè, Nga Win, Mi Lôn Bôn, Nga Myat Tha, Nga Nyo Win, Mi Hnin, Nga E, Mi Kyaung, Nga Shwe Maung, Nga Tha Dôk, Mi In, Mi Thwè, Nga Hmôn, Mi Mè, Nga Pyi, Nga Sein, Mi Hla Saw, Nga Shwe Yi, Nga Chein, Nga At, Mi Kathè, Nga Kyôk, Mi Paw Thu, Nga Sein Bin, Mi Min Nu, Nga Tôk, Nga Sein U, Mi Min Bu, Mi Pye Ya, Nga Te Ni, Nga Aung Ban, Nga Hmwe, Mi Min Byu, Nga Shwe Tu, Nga Su, Mi Hle, Nga Tin, Mi Ko, Nga Shwe Daik, Mi Ye, Nga Yan Myo, Nga Hmôn, Nga Nyo, Mi Thè U, Nga San Ya, Mi Lun, Mi Kye, Nga Nyo Shun, Nga Pein, Mi Zalat, Mein Kale, Nga Ye, Nga Saw, Nga So Bôn, Mi Ywè, Nga San Baw, Nga Lauk, Mi Myo Tha, Nga Tha Win, Mi Win Tha, Mi Hnin Wa, Nga Shun, Mi Tun Hla, Nga Shan, Mi Hmôn, Mi Mi, Nga Yan Min, Mi Kywè, Nga Tha Ye, Nga Kya Ye, Mi San Daw, Mi Mi, Mi Baw U, Mi Paw La, Nga Kaing, Mi Mi, Nga Waing, Nga Tha Nyun, Mi Bwe Dôk, Mi Pyu, Mi Nyet Sa, Mi Ngwe U, Nga Mo, Nga Nan Gyaung, Mi Hnin Tha, Nga Pe, Nga Chan Zan, Nga Hmaing, Mi Kaung Bôn, Nga Tha Daw, Nga Tha Yaw, Mi Nyein Tha, Nga Tha Ywè, Nga Pu, Mi Bu Aung, Nga Paw I, Mi Mi, Mi Hle, Mi Pu Lôn, Nga U, Nga Kan, Mi Ngwe, Nga Tha I, Mi Min Nu, Mi Mi, Nga Win, Mi Mein Ma, Nga Shwe Ye, Mi Kin, Nga Kala, Mi San, Nga Waing, Mi Wè, Mi Hla Ye, Nga Shwe Nu, Nga Shwin, Mi Taw, Mi Naw Twe, Nga Baw, Mi Kyaung, Nga Win, Mi Hnin We, Nga Kyaw, Mi Lun Ya, Mi Si, Nga Kyaw Yi, Mi Mi, Mi Min Tha, Nga Ôk, Mi Lun, Nga Chan Bin, Nga Kya In, Nga Shwe U, Mi Ye, Nga Hmaw, Nga Pauk, Nga Chan Ya, Mi Mi, Nga Ma, Mi Zalat, Mi Naw, Mi Min Byu, Nga Maung Gale, Nga Pya, Mi Min Wa, Nga Pe Tu, Mi Bwe, Nga Pyu, Mi Aung, Mi Hnin Nyo, Nga Tôk Kyi, Nga Myat Pu, Nga Ni, Nga Hmo, Nga Ko, Nga Chit Tha, Mi Min I, Mi Nu, Nga Shwè, Mi Kwe, Nga Kala, Nga Tha U, Mi Kè, Nga Tha Hnyin, Mi Shan Ma, Mi Ban, Nga Hmaing, Nga Lun, Mi Hla Ngôn, Paw Dun, Mi Min Bôn, Nga Paw Aung, Nga Sein Bin, Nga Nyun, Mi Ein Saung, Nga Kywet, Mi Ngwe U, Nga Hnin, Mi Kyi Bôn, Nga Pa, Mi Ngwe, Nga San Ywe, Mi Lauk, Nga Pu, Nga Thin, Nga Pye, Mi Si, Nga

Chan, Mi Shan Ma, Nga Myat Pu, Nga E Baw, Nga Thi, Mi Gauk Te, Nga Nyo Mya, Mi Pan Bu, Nga Shwe Ka, Mi Bada, Nga Pe, Mi Baik, Mi Kwe Ma, Nga Taw, Mi Ein Tha, Nga Pè, Mi Mi and infant, Mi Ein Tha, Nga U, Nga Waing, Mi Win Bôn; Nga Hmaing, Mi Min Nu, Nga Myat Pu, Mi E Tha, Nga Lwin, Mi Nan Ko, Nga Nat Pe, Me U Gyi, Mi Mi, Nga Tha Shun, Mi Hla Hmwe, Nga Paw Wa, Mi Min Gè, Mi Te, Nga Kan Be, Nga Hmaing, Mi Hmwe, Mi Cho, Nga Maung, Nga Shun, Mi Ngôn, Nga Wet, Mi Min Nu, Nga Wet, Mi Min I, Nga So, Mi Nan, Nga Shwe Ko, Mi Myet Cha, Nga Tha Kè, Mi Kyi, Nga Hle, Mi Mi, Nga Ye, Mi Myat Hmwe, Nga Thu, Mi Ngwe U, Nga Shwe Ya, Mi Tha E, Nga Kyaung, Nga Yan Gin, Mi Mi, Nga Saw, Mi No, Nga Kè, Mi So, Nga Shwe Ye, Nga Aung Mya, Nga Tôk Kyi, Nga Tha Hla, Nga Tha Wa, Nga Tha Lu, Nga Cho E, Mi Win Nyo, Nga O, Mi Min Bauk, Nga Tha Be, Nga Ye, Nga Tha Dwe, Mi Min Thu, Nga Kyaw Gaung, Mi Palu, Mi Lè, Nga Ta, Mi Tun E, Nga Shwe Pu, Mi Min, Mi Hmwe, Nga Tha Zôn, Mi Ke, Nga Lu Nyo, Mi Min Yan, Mi Twe Tha, Nga Kyaw, Mi Lôn Bôn, Nga Shwe Bin, Mi Min Le, Nga Myat Kè, Mi Mi, Nga Twa, Nga Tet, Mi Myo Hla, Mi Ngè, Nga Kyaw Shun, Mi Sein Gwe, Nga Pyo Tha, Mi Hnin Byu, Mi Win U, Nga Shwe Lan, Nga Pôk, Nga Kyaw Dun, Mi Tha Ywè, Mi Nyein U, Nga Aung Ban, Mi Sè, Nga Shwe Ban, Mi Yôn, Nga Shwe I, Mi Min Thu, Mi Kya U, Nga Tet, Nga Hmwe Byaw, Mi Tun Hla, Nga Po, Mi Mi, Mi Hla Dun, Nga Tha Za, Mi Ko, Nga Tha Hla, Mi Mi, Mi Min Ya, Nga Aung Dun, Mi Min Ye, Nga Myat San, Mi Baing, Nga Ôn Bin, Nga Ôn Gaing, Min Ya, Nga Paw Aung, Nga Pu, Mi Tha Yauk, Nga To, Nga Ko, Mi Hla Ywè, Mi Lun Ya, Nga Shwe Tha, Mi Pu Leik, Mi Kye, Nga Shwe Hmwe, Nga Shwe Hle, Nga Pu, Mi Bya, Mi Sein, Mi Min Ye, Nga Ôn, Mi San Ywe, Nga U, Nga Bye, Mi Gôn, Nga San, Nga Lwin, Mi Kè, Mi Ngè, Nga Tha Hla, Mi Bayet, Nga Shwe Tha, Mi Hnin Wa, Mi Pè, Mi Ke, Nga Tha Hnyin, Nga Shwe Yo, ...
Nga Pwe, Nga Tôk Kyi, Mi Kathè, Mi Net, Nga Shwe Yi, Mi Nin Ye, Nga Po, Mi Hla Byu, Nga Gwe, Mi Min Bu, Nga Myin, Mi Pato, Nga In, Mi Min Hmôn, Nga Tet Tu, Mi Mi, Nga Shwe, Mi Pyu, Nga Shwe Pu, Nga Shwe San, Mi Ein Bôn, Nga Pu, Mi E Tha, Mi Be, Nga Nyun, Nga Kya Gaing, Mi Kyu, Nga Kya Ywet, Nga Myat E, Mi Nyein Ya, Mi Kywin, Nga Hmo, Mi Win Bôn, Nga Tha Myo, Mi Pu, Mi Hnin Bin, Nga Talôk, Nga Tha Be, Mi Hnin Byu, Nga Naw, Mi Min Byu, Nga Tha Hla, Nga Kywe, Mi Min U, Nga Tha Nyein, Mi Min Tha, Mi Kyi, Nga Tha Pu, Nga Tha Be, Mi Ywe, Mi Tin, Nga Pyu, Mi Win, Nga Chan Ya, Mi In, Nga Kyaw Tha, Nga Yun, Nga Shan Byu, Mi Myo

Ya, Mi Cho, Nga Pe, Mi San Tha, Nga Wa, Nga Tha Shun, Mi Waing, Mi Lôn Tha, Nga Shwe Bin, Nga Ywe, Mi Ywet, Mi Kun, Nga U, Nga Yauk, Mi Bein, Nga Nyo Gè, Nga Yan Gin, Mi Mi, Nga Shwe Yin, Mi Be, Nga Saung, Nga Kin, Mi Min Bôn, Nga Taw, Mi Kwe, Mi Mi, Nga Chaw Thu, Nga Cho Tha, Mi Hnin U, Nga Shwe Yan, Mi Min Bauk, Nga Myat Kaung, Mi Sa, Nga Hmaing, Mi Bôk Sôn, Nga Pe, Nga Pye, Mi Bayet, Mi Hla Zan, Mi Min I, Mi Hnin Be, Nga Kyi, Mi Hnin Dun, Nga Shwe Kya, Mi Yit, Mi Pè, Nga Hmaing, Mi E, Nga Kywet, Mi Pu, Nga Shwe Eik, Nga Ya Mè, Mi Min Thu, Nga Sein Dun, Mi Gôn, Nga Kaing, Nga Shwe Bin, Mi Wa, Nga Myat U, Nga Tha Shun, Mi Hla Yin, Mi Hnin Bauk, Nga Yauk, Nga Te Zaw, Mi Sein, Nga Pa, Mi Hnin U, Nga Shwe Hla, Mi Dwe Byu, Nga Kyi, Nga Waing, Mi Min Yaung, Nga Tun Wa, Nga Myat No, Mi Min Bôn, Nga Paw I, Mi Hnin Dan, Nga Shwe O, Nga Shwe Min, Nga Pauk, Mi In Nyo, Mi U Gya, Nga Chin Hlaw, Nga Shwe Tha, Mi O, Mi Taw, Mi Bôk, Nga Kan Hmwe, Mi Bye, Nga Tha Za, Mi Waing, Nga Tôk, Nga Tun Tha, Mi Nyein Ya, Mi Min Baw, Mi Pyaw U, Mi Sa U, Mi Galôn, Nga Kan Tha, Aung Dun, Mi Mi, Nga Po, Mi Byaung, Nga Tha Ya, Mi Myat Pyu, Mi Hnin Bauk, Mi Pu, Nga Pè, Mi Pyo, Nga Baw, Nga Pyaw, Mi Hla Ywè, Nga We, Mi Lauk, Nga Hmôn, Nga Myat Aung, Mi Yin Nu, Nga Yauk, Mi Naw, Nga Win, Nga Pè, Nga So, Nga Myat Tôk, Mi Dwe, ...Nga Kya In, Mi Min Yan, Nga Tha Hla, Nga Aung Thu, Mi Taw Ku, Mi Min Wa, Nga San Ba, Mi Hla U, Nga Ni Ta, Mi Tha Yit, Nga Myet, Kya Bin, Nga Sin, Mi Gwè, Mi Pu, Nga Waing, Nga Nyat Shwin, Mi Myat . . . . ., Nga Myat Cho, Mi Chin Ma, Nga Paw, Nga Pe, Mi Hnin Bwin, Mi Kathe, Nga Tet, Nga Ywe, Mi Min Hla, Nga Tu, Nga U, Mi Mi, Nga Shwe Sein, Mi Thaing, Mi Byaw, Mi Shu, Nga Shwe Baw, Mi Min, Mi Wa Bauk, Nga Tôk Pyu, Mi Ôn, Nga Cho E, Mi Min Thu, Nga Shwe O, Mi Min Byu, Nga Shwe Yi, Nga Shwe Daik, Nga Shwe So, Nga Myat Ya, Mi Ngwe U, Mi Ya Thi, Nga Tha Tin, Nga U, Nga Tet.

No. (7).—Obverse.

Locality.—North-west of Lawkamanaung pagoda.

Date.—1208 Sakkaràj (1846 A.D.).

Founder.—Kolôndaga* and wife.

Substance of inscription.—Erection of images, *simâ*, monastery, rest-house, bridge, and library.

---

* So called because he was the donor of the nine boxes of manuscripts mentioned in the inscription.

"May there be victory!"

HIS MAJESTY* the founder of the third city of Amarapura and a supporter of the wonderful Religion, who is as eminent as Asoka and other ancient kings, was graciously pleased to grant a piece of *visumgâma* land, 4 *tas* square, within the precincts of the Lawkamanaung pagoda at Ava, to Nemyothihakyawgaung, the royal umbrella-bearer. This official presented the land to his uncle and aunt, the Kolôndaga and wife, and the latter petitioned the *Thathanabaing* and 33 other learned monks to consecrate a *simâ* on the same. Accordingly the land was cleared of jungle growth, levelled, and otherwise prepared in accordance with law. It was then subdivided into 72 allotments, each 4 cubits 2 *maiks* long by 2 cubits 1 *maik* wide, marked with gold, silver, and sandalwood pegs. Next, having placed a number of monks round about the land to prevent other monks from trespassing on it, the chapter of 34 monks, headed by the *Thathanabaing*, stationed themselves on the said allotments, 7 each on four plots and 6 on one at a time, and thus traversed the whole number of plots. On the first plot three of the monks intoned the *kamavâcâ*, so that any *simâ* which might have existed on the same site might be desecrated. This was repeated on all the other plots also. Trenches were then dug all round the land and filled with water, and at a distance of 2 cubits and 1 *maik* from these trenches towards the centre the boundaries of the *visumgâma* land were marked. The *Thathanabaing*, surrounded by the subordinate monks, next proceeded along the boundaries of the proposed *simâ* with a *kamavâcâ* in his hands, and on approaching the eastern trench asked: "Puratthimâya disâya kiṁ nimittaṁ?" The monk in charge of the trench answered, "Udakaṁ bhante," and the *Thathanabaing* proclaimed: "Etaṁ udakaṁ nimittaṁ." Similar questions, answers and proclamations were made also at the south-eastern, southern, south-western, western, north-western, northern, and north-eastern points of the site, and for a second time at the first points already proclaimed. This ceremony was repeated in turn by the Modi *Sayadaw*, Thayettaw *Sayadaw*, Tawya *Sayadaw*, and Thitsein *Sayadaw*. After the boundaries had thus been proclaimed five times, the *kamavâcâ* connected with the consecration of a *samâna-samvâsa simâ* was intoned by the *Thathanabaing*, the Tawya *Sayadaw* and the Taiktaw *Sayadaw*, and subsequently the *kamavâcâ* for the consecration of an *avippavâsa simâ* was intoned. This latter ceremony was repeated for the second time by the Modi *Sayadaw*, Weyansanhlut *Sayadaw*, and Nyaungbintha *Sayadaw*; for the third time by the Thayettaw and Thitsein *Sayadaws* and monk Paññasîha; for the fourth time by the Taungbaing *Sayadaw*, *Gaingdauk* Sîri and monk Sîri; for the fifth time by the Myedu, Mèdi and Kinôk *Sayadaws*; for the

* Pagan Min.

sixth time by the Pye and Inleywa *Sayadaws* and monk Sîlâcâra; and for the seventh time by monks Sîla, Sumana and Yasa. Thus the chapter of 34 monks, headed by the *Thathanabaing*, avoided consecrating a *simâ* falling under the category of the eleven kinds of invalid *simâs*, namely, those that are too small, too large, not properly demarcated, those having the shadows of hills and trees as boundaries, those having no boundaries at all, those that were consecrated from without, those in rivers and streams, those on the seas and oceans, those on lakes, those adjoining others, and those overlapping others. This *simâ*, measuring 28 cubits square, was therefore consecrated in the orthodox manner on the morning of Tuesday the 6th waning Tagu 1208 Sakkarâj, corresponding with the year of the Religion 2390. The extraordinary events connected with the present *simâ* are the non-fading of the flowers and sprigs used at the ceremonial of consecration, the non-evaporation of the water in the trenches marking the boundaries, and the hearing of celestial music on the completion of the ceremonial.

The *Thathanabaing* and subordinate monks who officiated at the consecration were offered suits of robes and other articles of monastic use by the Kolôndaga and family, and the *simâ* was in their presence dedicated to the monkhood for the performance of their rites and ceremonies. The same family erected a large gilt image 6 cubits and 1 *maik* high near the Lawkamanaung pagoda, together with a monastery and rest-houses. To monk Sîlâcâra they dedicated a monastery and four rest-houses beyond the northern porch of the Lawkamanaung pagoda. The other meritorous deeds performed by them are the erection of 5 glass pagodas, 9 images, 9 libraries containing 700 *angâs* of manuscripts and 9 cones of offerings in connection with the Yadanamyitzu pagoda, Amarapura, a bridge and a rest-house in behalf of a neighbour, 3 festivals connected with the installation of novices for the monkhood, and a brick rest-house and image erected near the present *simâ*.

"By virtue of the meritorious acts enumerated above, may we ultimately reach Nirvâna. In the meantime may we in every existence enjoy immunity from every form of misery and danger and be able to dispense charity with a lavish hand and thus acquire the ten kinds of virtue. May those who have assisted us in our acts also attain Nirvâna, and to that end may they become virtuous men and *devâs*. May our parents and ancestors, as well as the king and all sentient beings inhabiting the 31 regions, enjoy a share of our merit."

No. (8).—Obverse.

Locality.—Within the Mawgun group of monasteries south of Ava.

Date.—1208 Sakkarâj (1846 A.D.).

Founders.—Maung Pe and wife Shin I.

Substance of inscription.—Building of monastery and *simâ.*

"Reverence to the Blessed, Holy and Enlightened One!"

OUR incomparable Buddha attained supreme wisdom exactly four *asankheyyas* and 100,000 *kalpas* after obtaining a prophecy from the Buddha Dîpankarâ that he would then attain Buddhahood. Our Buddha then administered the law to the inhabitants of the three *lôkas* and admonished them to follow strictly in his path. His Religion flourished to such an extent that it reached even the kingdom of ancient Prome founded by Duttabaung and has continued to flourish down to the present reign of His Majesty the royal descendant of the founders of Amarapura, Sagaing and Ava. Soon after the accession of His Majesty to the throne of his illustrious father, Maung Pe and his wife Shin Min I, in emulation of His Majesty and with a view to provide for their welfare in their future existences by furthering the cause of the Religion in accordance with the Law, built a large three-storied monastery, furnished it and dedicated it to the monkhood.

REVERSE.

This beautifully and wonderfully built monastery was then formally handed over to monk Jinârâma. Not satisfied with having performed this meritorious act, *Kyaungtaga* Maung Pe and his spouse decided to erect a *simâ* on the *visumgâma* land attached to the Mawgun monasteries, and having had a plot measuring 32 *tas* in perimeter marked out and cleared, requested a number of eminent monks to consecrate a *simâ* thereon. It was accordingly done on the 2nd waning of Tagu 1208 Sakkarâj. The said charitable couple have therefore, in addition to a large monastery on which a considerable sum of money was expended, built a *simâ* after the model of the great Kalyani *simâ** of King Râmâdhipati, and under the direction of the *Thathanabaing* and his titled *Sadaws*. The ceremonial was completed on Saturday the 2nd waning of Tagu 1208 Sakkarâj.

"By virtue of these meritorious deeds, may we be instrumental in saving *nats* and men from the sea of *samsaro* by means of the vessel of the law. Let the king of *nats* bear witness to our dedication of this monastery to the eminent monk Jinârâma. May His Majesty the King, our parents, ancestors and relatives, and every being inhabiting the three *lokas*, have a share of our merit and acclaim their approval."

NO. (9).—FIRST STONE.

Locality.—Within the Yethapan group of monasteries east of the Mingalazedi pagoda.

---

* Situated near Pegu. The inscriptions attached to it have been edited and translated with notes by Mr. Taw Sein Ko.

Date.—1245 Sakkarâj (1883 A.D.).

Founder.—Sadaiktagama, her family and others.

Substance of inscription.—Building of pagoda or cave enclosing remains of monk U Pyinnya Zawta, and repairing of old well.

DATPAUNGMYINZU PAGODA INSCRIPTION.

"Reverence to the Blessed, Holy and Enlightened One!"

THE highly adorable Buddha, having expounded the laws of nature for the benefit of all sentient beings, passed away to Nirvâna at Kusinnârum. May the present pagoda, enshrining some of his sacred relics, last throughout the whole period of the Religion. Although the Buddha has passed away to Nirvâna, yet his Religion still continues to flourish owing to the pious efforts of the convener * of the fifth great synod. It was in the reign of that eminent king that the illustrious monk U Pyinnya Zawta lived and held ecclesiastical sway over a group of monasteries called Yethapan, situated on the east of Tada-u village in the Ava district. The monk departed this life at the age of 62 and in the 43rd year of his monastic career, being unable, like even the Buddha himself, to rise above the province of the law of natural mortality. He was attended on by the best medical practitioners, but, in spite of their unremitted efforts, he passed away into a new existence on the morning of Wednesday the 7th waxing Tabodwè 1243 Sakkarâj and was deeply mourned by a large number of pupils and adherents. The usual funeral rites and ceremonies were duly performed under the guidance of his three chief disciples, Shin Nyana, Shin Zagara, and Shin Nyaneinda

SECOND STONE.

on the 2nd waxing of Hnaung-Tagu of the same year, and the remains were interred in a brick cave on the 2nd waning of the same month. The coffin was surrounded with four white and eight golden umbrellas. When these ceremonies were completed, Shin Zagara proposed and the two other chief disciples Shin Nyana and Shin Nyaneinda agreed to have a pagoda built over the cave. They accordingly raised subscriptions and immediately commenced to build. When the first relic chamber was completed, they placed in it seven silver images of Buddha in different attitudes, surrounded by over 120 images of *rahantâs*. When the second chamber was completed they placed in it 28 images representing the 28 Buddhas, an image of the *rishi* Sumedhâ receiving his prophecy from Dîpankarâ, another of Prince Siddhatta Kumâra renouncing the world, another of Gautama Buddha represented as delivering a sermon and fashioned out of a piece of the true Bodhi tree under which he at-

* King Mindôn.

tained Buddhahood, and over 500 smaller images in gold, silver, brass and copper. The remaining portion of the pagoda was completed in about nine months, and a *ti* measuring 7½ cubits high, with the proper complement of bells, was then put on. The expenditure incurred for the whole work amounted to Rs. 650. The pagoda measures altogether 38 cubits in height and is named Datpaung-myinzu. This inscription is erected by the Sadaiktagama, her sons Maung Shwe Kun, Maung Tha Dun, Maung Po San, and her daughter Ma Ma, in order that the pagoda might not be tampered with, but that it might last throughout the period of the Religion. These pious people also repaired the old well on the south side of the monasteries on Sunday the 10th waning Hnaung-Tagu 1244, and completed the work on Thursday the 6th waning Kasôn 1245 at a cost of Rs. 138. The well then measured 2½ cubits in diameter and 22½ cubits in depth.

"May we, by virtue of these meritorious deeds, be free from all kinds of evil in our future existences, be replete with everything that is good, and be rewarded ultimately with the bliss of Buddhahood. May our parents, ancestors and teachers, as well as every being inhabiting the earth, the sea, and the heavens, share our merit equally with us!"

G. B. C. P. O.—No. 6919, B. S., 24-7-99—254.